Wo
Re
a
in I

G000081043

John Bowker's interest in the interaction between religions began when he was doing National Service in West Africa nearly thirty years ago. Since then he has also extended his interests to include an attempt to understand the continuing roles of religion in an increasingly scientific and technological world, and is vice-president of the Institute of Religion in an Age of Science. He began his teaching career at Corpus Christi College, Cambridge, and is now Professor of Religious Studies at the University of Lancaster, and author of several other books, including *Problems of Suffering in Religions of the World*, *The Religious Imagination and the Sense of God*, *Jesus and the Pharisees*, and a book for children, *Uncle Bolpenny Tries Things Out*.

WORLDS OF FAITH

RELIGIOUS BELIEF AND PRACTICE IN BRITAIN TODAY

JOHN BOWKER

ARIEL BOOKS
BRITISH BROADCASTING CORPORATION

© John Bowker 1983

First published 1983

Published by the British Broadcasting Corporation
35 Marylebone High Street London W1M 4AA

Typeset by Phoenix Photosetting, Chatham
Printed in England by Mackays of Chatham Ltd, Kent

Set in 10/11 point Linotron Ehrhardt

ISBN 0 563 20197 5

Contents

Introduction

The idea for the programmes on which this book is based was first suggested by David Craig, a BBC producer, in the summer of 1981. The basic proposal was to look at the practice of religion in Britain today. It soon became obvious that nothing so vast could possibly be done. We therefore decided to take six historically long-standing religions which have taken root in this country, in order to find out what they mean to the people who belong to them, and how those people work out the meaning of their faith in life today. It also seemed to me to be essential to draw out and illustrate the fact that *none* of the six religions (Judaism, Christianity, Hinduism, Islam, Buddhism, Sikhism) is uniform or simple: there are arguments and divisions in each of them, and it seemed to me important that these too should be reflected.

Since we were hoping to learn how people live and think about their faith in the ordinary circumstances of life, we did not talk to any trained experts – rabbis, clergy, imams, theologians, etc. Also, we decided deliberately to talk to those who have persisted and gone on in their respective religions. We did meet some who have lost or abandoned their faith, but our main purpose was to understand why people adhere to their commitment, and what it means to them. It is, of course, equally interesting and important to know why people change or give up their religious allegiance; but that really requires a separate inquiry.

As it was, we had more on our hands than we could cope with! We interviewed people in the winter of 1981/2: few interviews were less than an hour; the longest was more than five hours. The youngest person we interviewed (*not* for five hours!) was seven years old; the oldest was eighty-eight. There was an outline plan of ground to be covered, but no set list of questions, since we were anxious to allow people to say what *they* wanted to say about the meaning and practice of their faith.

As a result of the interviews, we were left with about 300 hours of tape, which I listened to and indexed, and then organised into subject areas. From these, the programmes themselves emerged fairly naturally. It was an absurd way to make the series (as we were frequently told) in view of the amount of work it involved; but it did mean that the programmes and the book faithfully reflect what the people themselves wanted to say about their faith, not what I might have wanted to say or impose on them. In the book, I have also been able to include very much more of what they said than was possible in the series, even in twelve thirty-minute programmes.

I had no idea, when I set out, that it was going to be such an enormous and time-consuming task. One person more than any other took the strain of successive crises and moments of defeat, and that was Margaret, my wife: to her, my deeply grateful thanks; as also to David Craig, the producer of the programmes: without his encouragement and inspiration they would not have been attempted; without his constant professional skill, they would not have been made.

Equally, without the commitment of Michael Lawton doing the preliminary research, and of both his and Hugh Faupel's planning and editorial work, the project would have come to an early halt.

To Eleanor Nicholls we all owe particular thanks for professional advice on recently arrived religions (especially Sikhism), and for undertaking the interviews where I (as a man) could not do them. I am grateful also to Paul Morris, who decoded several Yiddish dialects which to my untutored ear were unintelligible!

Wendy Maugham, Mari Pickin and Celia Thompson undertook the task of finding, in the 300 hours of taped interviews, the extracts we needed, and then also of typing draft scripts from very complicated material. The series owes a lot to their skill and patience; as it does also to a large number of BBC engineers and to the tolerance of the Religious Broadcasting Department at Manchester, the life of which was often considerably disrupted.

Finally, I would like to thank the then Controller of Radio 4, Miss Monica Sims, for agreeing to the series and for her constant encouragement; David Winter (Head of Religious Broadcasting Radio) for steering the series through its final stages of preparation; Anne Dalton for converting incoherent pages into a typescript; and Sheila Ableman, as editor, for converting a typescript into a book. Above all, my thanks – and our thanks – go to the many people who allowed us to visit them in their homes, and who shared their experience so willingly with us. It is their words and their lives which have created this book.

I

The Life I Live: The Religions in Britain

I suppose this book (and the series of programmes on which it is based) first began to take shape some time in 1954. I was a young National Serviceman in Nigeria, and I remember very well the afternoon when I was sent out to the local market place to sort out a riot – not a race riot, but a religious riot. I was absolutely terrified. The trouble had begun because some people, who belonged to two different religions, were fighting over a donkey. Why, I haven't the slightest idea; and I don't think we ever found out. But while I stood there, trying to reason with them, they literally pulled the donkey apart, limb from limb.

It was at that moment, standing there and looking at the anger and hatred in those faces, that I set out on a journey which has brought me to the beginning of these programmes. Much of my time since then has been spent trying to understand what it is about religion which makes religious people so angry and passionate. Think how easily those passions and emotions explode into violence: bombs in Hyde Park and Ballykelly and many other parts of Northern Ireland; the destruction of Beirut; the whole conflict over Israel/ Palestine in the Near East; the bitter divisions between black and white in the apartheid system of South Africa; Cyprus; India and Pakistan; Poland; the Philippines; Iran; Afghanistan. The list is almost endless. Even while we were making the first programme, Sikhs were rioting in India, and in Northern Nigeria 450 people were killed in religious riots.

No one's going to say that the troubles in Ireland, or the system of apartheid in South Africa, or any of those other issues, are caused by religion alone. But equally, there's no doubt either that religion has had a tremendous part to play in all those conflicts. And it still does. The emotions of religion are extremely powerful, as we saw during the Pope's recent visit to this country; and they can be very easily, and very dangerously, manipulated. The vast Nazi rallies were by no means devoid of religious input and symbolism – to say the least.

The power of religion to do great damage is surely enough to make it clear why, for the peace of this country, let alone of the world, we need to understand religions much more clearly than we do. But of course there's much more to be said about religions than that. Religious believers don't spend *all* their time pulling donkeys to pieces, burning heretics, and fighting holy wars. In other words, there is another side to the coin. Religious belief has always been the very deepest resource of human hope and courage and happiness, the inspiration of some of our greatest and most enduring creativity. And this remains as much so now, in the present, as it ever was in the past, in art, in music, in poetry, in spiritual exploration. So what are these religions? And why do they matter so much to those who belong to them?

Keeping Faith

Basically, religions are the consequence of people coming to the deepest and furthest sense of what they are – of what their lives are meant to be – of discovering that they add up to something more than the mere accident of being born. Religions are journeys. They are journeys of exploration and of discovery. They touch truth in ways that cannot be arrived at by any other route. That's why religions matter so much to those who belong to them. That's why, when we listened to more than a hundred people in making these programmes, every single one of them agreed that they'd never give up their faith (or even the outward signs of their faith, like a turban for a Sikh): if they come under pressure to do so, they'd rather die than give up. Mrs Qureshi, a Muslim who lives in Coventry, spoke for many when she said:

> I will never give up my faith. If I can't go to mosque, that's something different. I don't have to go to mosque to pray to God. I can sit inside the house and pray. Whatever happens, if the worst comes to the worst my faith cannot be snatched from me. That's a part of my body, that's something attached to my heart that only dies when I die.

'The blood of the martyrs is the seed of the Church.' And that's true not simply of Christianity. Mr Douber Klein is a Hasidic Jew (which means that he is scrupulously careful in keeping Jewish Law). He put it this way:

> Maybe if a person dies because they won't transgress one of the Commandments, maybe this is a way of educating the rest

of the Jewish people, in a way you could not achieve with fifty years more life spent in teaching people how to live as a Jew.

He too made exactly the same point as Mrs Qureshi did, that for him and for all Jews there are some things which they could never abandon: they would rather die first:

There are three Commandments which a person must not transgress even under penalty of death. First of all, to murder somebody else. Secondly, immoral sexual relationships. And third, idolatry. Under no circumstances could one do any of those three – under whatever pressure. Maybe it's being arrogant – it's difficult to know what one would do in the circumstances – but I cannot see another man telling me to do something against the will of God, and me doing it because he's got a gun on my head, or something like that.

Mind you, his wife came in at that point, and emphasised that you don't have to die for *everything*; and that if necessary you would have to move to another country:

According to the Law, you're not allowed to sacrifice your life for a little thing, like shaving your beard. You can't sacrifice your life for that law, because without your beard you can still do the Commandments of God. But if you are killed for that, you can't do them. So if something like that was not allowed, I suppose the simplest thing would be to move to another country – if that was possible.

Harbans Singh Sagoo is a Sikh who used to be an air traffic controller in East Africa. He made exactly the same point: under pressure, you die – or you move. A Sikh is not allowed to cut his hair, so he wears the familiar turban to keep his hair tidy. Consequently, the turban becomes a vivid mark of faith, as he said: 'There's no way I'll give up my turban, that's for sure. I'd rather die or get out, but I'd maintain my turban and my faith.' Many others said the same: if their faith came under pressure, they would, if it were possible, move – as the Quran actually commands a Muslim to do. Mr Khan is a lecturer in law at a Polytechnic in the Midlands, so he is sensitive to what the Quran (the Holy Book of the Muslims) legally allows or commands:

The fundamentals are given in the Holy Quran. And Islam has given us the commands, you do certain things, and you don't do certain other things. Now if those are made impossible, then the only way is exit. You leave that country, and

> the Holy Quran says so: if you find that one place in this earth has become difficult for you to live in, this earth is very big, so you move from that place.

That view – that one should move rather than abandon one's faith – was reinforced by another Muslim who said: 'Nobody in the world can stop anybody's religion. But if they do, if we really want to stick to our religion, we would rather leave the country, and go to our own country and carry on with our religion.' That emphasis – on moving, rather than giving up your faith – is hardly surprising when you realise how many of the people we talked to have had to do exactly that: they are already refugees who've had to move: Buddhists from Tibet and Vietnam; Hindus and Sikhs from Uganda; Muslims from India; Jews and Christians from Hitler's Europe. The storm tides of suffering have carried into this country a constant succession of those who have lost virtually everything – everything except their lives and their faith.

Faith and Faiths in Britain

'The life I live in this body, I live by faith.' That's what Paul wrote to the Christians in Galatia long ago. But living now in the United Kingdom, we could easily rewrite that sentence in the plural. The lives we live, we live by faiths. Faiths in the plural because there are now more different religions per square yard in Britain than even in a traditionally religious country like India. We can't deal with all the religions in this book. What we've done is take six, Hindus, Buddhists, Sikhs, Jews, Christians, Muslims. All those religions came originally from somewhere else, from overseas. Even Christianity had to arrive here once as a new religion. So what happens to these religions when they settle in this country? Can you be a Hindu, Muslim, Sikh, Buddhist, here – and now? Or must these religions change? Even religions which have been established in this country for many centuries – Christianity and Judaism – are facing momentous changes in the ways people live. What is happening to all these religions as their believers try to 'sing the Lord's Song in a strange land' – or in a strange new world? Does their faith change? Can it change? Should it change? Hindu life in an Indian village is one thing. Hindu life in Coventry or Leeds, is very different indeed. A whole lifestyle has to change when you can't drop into your local temple on the way home from work, as a Sikh, Gurbachan Singh

Sidhu told me: 'Normally,' he said, 'in India people would go to the temple almost every day, early in the morning, and sometimes in the evening. But here it's different, you know. People go to the temple on a Saturday or Sunday, if they have the time.'

I met Mrs Chauhan in Leeds, and she described the difference this makes:

> We have a temple everywhere in India, and in the morning you go to temple. But when we're living here, it's such a different way of life. We have to go to work in the morning, so we've got no time to go to the temple in the morning – and there aren't many temples here anyway. But in India, everybody goes to the temple: they get up in the morning and have a bath, and then they go to the temple and pray. And after that they go to work or schools, or whatever they do.

Take another obvious example: in India the cow is reverenced as the sacred mother. It really is a case of 'the sacred cow', because you can't have village religion without the cow as mother, the great symbol of birth and life. What that means in India is that a cow is allowed to wander freely and should be allowed to die a natural death. So there are religious reasons why the cow is important, but there are also believed to be reasons of diet and ecology, as a Hindu from Leeds explained to me.

> A cow's milk is a complete food. If you live on cow's milk throughout your life you won't find any deficiency in your physical nutrition. Also, in India, most of the mothers used to die at childbirth, and children were kept on cow's milk. And this is why we have got respect for the cow.

So the sacred cow really does matter. But even in the most Hindu parts of Leeds you won't expect to find them wandering around freely, even in a pedestrian precinct.

And there are other differences as well – the British weather for one. *Holi* is an important spring festival in India. It's been described as combining erotic games, comic operas, and folk dancing. That's not so easy to stage, without the Indian sun, as Mr Patel, who now lives in Coventry, explained:

> The most celebrated festival, which I have always liked, was *Holi*, but it's not celebrated in this country as much as one would like it. Because of the climatic conditions, people are not geared to enjoy the festival of *Holi*, with the colours and throwing of water and all that. And maybe people are feeling

> they are too sophisticated to play in that type of festival season – that's basically what it is.

So Indian festivals and prayers are clearly a lot less inhibited than Anglican Mattins. But then, what about the complaints from the neighbours? 'In this sort of environment,' said Mrs Chatterji, a Hindu teacher, 'it doesn't come out so nicely as it should in a tropical climate. There are quite a few rituals like blowing conch shells. We start with that in the evening and in the morning, which you wouldn't be allowed to do here.' I asked her why not. She answered:

> I don't know. We have never done it. I don't see any Hindu families doing it. And also we were brainwashed from the very beginning when we came here. People said, Oh, if you go to England, you don't do those things, probably – it won't be nice, your next door neighbours might think something else.

And indeed they do, as Mr Ladd, who also lives in Coventry, made clear: 'The birth of Lord Krishna is celebrated at midnight. So we have trouble from the people living around because of the noise. You know, we pray *loudly*.'

So noisy prayers and the English weather call in question traditional ways of doing things. But those are relatively small differences. What is far more disturbing is when the traditional patterns of life which take people from birth to death can no longer be followed or lived. In India, a man's life was traditionally divided into four stages, four *ashramas*: first, he's a student, then he gets married and has a family, next he retires into meditation, and then finally, even beyond that, renunciation, *sannyasin*; and that means giving up everything, except a cup for water, a bowl for begging food and a loincloth. And sometimes you don't even keep the loincloth. In Britain that just isn't possible, for obvious reasons. But even this can be adapted. Hindus find their own ways of interpreting those traditional four stages, even if they don't go the whole way to total renunciation and detachment, as a Hindu wife said of her husband:

> They more or less try to lead a very simple and humble life as they grow older, taking up the philosophy of *sannyasin* as such. I can see my husband now wearing a suit and everything, drinking and what not. But when he will achieve an older age, and my daughters are married, probably in his late seventies, he will accept the life of very simple living, which the *sannyasis* do.

Far more difficult to adapt are the outward and visible signs of the inward and spiritual commitment, those outward signs which show which religion you belong to – holy days and festivals, specific laws and commands and practices. We've already seen that Sikhs will not give up their uncut hair and their turbans. For Muslims and Jews there are requirements of diet, which are a matter of obligation. The Quran says to Muslims:

> Forbidden to you is carrion, blood, the flesh of pigs. Forbidden to you is what has been offered to anything other than God. Forbidden to you is the beast strangled, the beast gored, the beast beaten down in his tracks or partly taken by the beasts of prey.

That creates obvious difficulties for Muslims in this country, as Mr Khan, again with his lawyer's eye for detail, makes clear:

> The Muslims are not allowed to take pork or any part of pig in any form. Unfortunately pig is the favourite in this country, and it appears in all forms. That is to say, if I buy bread from the shops there is the lard in it, or if I go to the various restaurants, nothing is available about which I can be certain that it has been cooked in butter or margarine.

There are problems also of prayer. Muslims are commanded to pray at five separate times a day – commanded ultimately by God. But in England, much further north than Mecca, there are problems, as Mr Khan went on to say:

> In winter months the sun rises very late, and it is possible to offer the morning prayers at seven o'clock; and the other prayers will be offered say about one o'clock, three o'clock, four o'clock and six o'clock. So in the months of winter, that creates a problem, because the prayers which are at the times of one, three and four, they are usually in the time when I am at the office. And it is not very convenient to offer prayers in the office itself.

Even in summer, tea-breaks don't coincide with the hours of prayers, as Mrs Qureshi pointed out: 'In the office,' she said, 'I don't get facilities to go to pray five times a day, or make special prayers on Friday – as you know, the Muslim special day is Friday. Whereas if I was in Pakistan, I would be granted some time off to pray.'

Festivals and Holidays

But the single most important problem in moving to Britain lies in the difference between the public calendar and the many different calendars in each religion. Important religious festivals are no longer public holidays. If they were, we'd be on holiday every day of the year – which is exactly how one Hindu described India: 'There is a proverb in India, "In twelve months you have thirteen festivals". That means people enjoy festivals more than anything else. That's a part of life.'

So we can't keep all the religious festivals as holidays, as Holy Days. What that means is that the public life of these religions is in danger, because the festivals have to be moved to the nearest available weekend. And even then they can only be celebrated in a cut-down way. Mr Wickramaratne, originally from Sri Lanka, is President of the Sri Lankan Association of North London. Here he is describing the festival of *Vesak*, and talking about the problems of celebrating it in London:

> In Sri Lanka, with about seventy-five per cent of the people being Buddhists, *Vesak* is celebrated in a big way. On that occasion here in London, we all gather at the Buddhist temple, and there is quite a big function that goes on all day. The significance of *Vesak* itself is, of course, the birth of Lord Buddha, the attainment of Enlightenment, and also the *nibbana*, or passing away. All three are supposed to have happened on the same day. There are quite a number of *pereheras*, what we call *pereheras*, which are big processions with elephants, quite a number of elephants, in the parade. But also they build *pendals* all over the island where they depict the Buddha's life from the beginning to the end. And then, more than anything, of course, people spend most of the day in the temples, mainly doing meditation. And almost any house would welcome any poor person who comes to ask for a meal. He would never be refused. What we do *here* in the temple is that we carry on the tradition, because we all take food to the temple; and everyone, whoever comes there, is given free food. And then apart from that, of course, there's hundreds of people who do meditation, which is the main thing there, really; and then there are lectures that go on all day.

Sikhs and Hindus also have to shift their festivals. Mrs Kania is a Hindu, who told me how frustrating this can be:

> If Christmas Day happens to be on a Wednesday in this

country everything comes to a stop. If a Hindu festival happens to be on a Monday or a Wednesday or a Friday, everything in this country doesn't come to a stop. You would like to have time for your personal reasons, just as you would like to spend a Christmas Day at home. You would like to celebrate a big family day. But what you do here is, you try and cram as much as you can before you go to school in the morning, and you cram as much as you can when you come home in the evening.

Adaptation and Change

In that sort of way, religions do adapt as far as they can. But what they emphasise is that they must respect and keep the laws of the country they are living in. As Mr Abdul Rahman put it, 'Islam says, you know, that you must respect the law of the land. And you must respect your superiors.' So in practice these religions respect the laws of the land, even when it involves a conflict, as it may do in the particular case of marriage:

> Islam itself does not recognise any other form of marriage except the *nikah*, the Muslim marriage ceremony. But since we live in this land and we must obey the laws of the land, our marriage, to be recognised as a marriage, has to be registered. And so we go to the Registry.

But the conflict isn't always as clear cut as that. It may be more general, as a Tibetan Buddhist made apparent:

> The Western way of life and Buddhism I don't think mix terribly well together. We are far too materialistic – I am far too materialistic. I spend all my time at work, wondering how to get more money, and that does worry me, because I don't think you can live properly in the West and be a good Buddhist. That does worry me.

But not everyone is worried. Others see adventure and challenge in the Western influence on religion. They see it as a test of their own faith. That at least is how Gurbachan Singh Sidhu saw it:

> There are so many problems, and there are so many different pressures, that would tend to restrict the Sikh way of life. The society we are living in is a very permissive society you know. Whereas a Sikh is supposed to be very much above this sort of thing. And again society expects some sort of norms of be-

> haviour. For example, they would expect in this country that somebody wouldn't carry a sword; but we have to, because it's part of our life. Then the boys and girl friends: that's a tradition that is quite alien to Sikhism; and we wouldn't tolerate premarital or extramarital relations. But the thing is that when Sikhism came into existence, there were pressures all the same. And we had to steer clear of all these pressures. And we are supposed to live anywhere in this world.

So the point is, that while it may indeed be easier to practise a religion in one place rather than another, in the end faith can be lived anywhere. All sorts of prayers and practices can change, leaders and liturgies can disappear, but the fundamental faith goes on. It was an Orthodox Jew, strict in his own observance of the dietary laws, who made this distinction very clear, the distinction between what can and cannot be given up:

> I once had a discussion with a Jehovah's Witness, and he said to me, 'Well, if you were on a desert island and there was only pork around, would you eat it?' I said, 'I most certainly would, of course I would.' Of course I would, because I want to live. If that's the only thing I could eat, I would eat it. At least if I got off the desert island, I could always repent and ask for forgiveness.

So while circumstances may well challenge and change a religion, that central commitment of faith goes on. That's why for some people change in the basis of their religion is completely unthinkable – and especially for those religions which have a strong sense of law (revealed law) coming straight from God, like Judaism or Islam. An Orthodox Jew comments:

> When the Jewish people were gathered together at Mount Sinai, God revealed himself to them, and gave them the laws of the universe. These laws of the universe affect every aspect of life in every single part of the world. And, therefore, if in any way one neglects these laws, one is doing harm, not only to the Jewish world, but also to the entire universe.

As Mr Lakdawala, a teacher in a comprehensive school, told me:

> Islam is a simple religion and shouldn't be led away by customs so much. Sometimes we consider a few cultural things and customs as more important than the belief itself. So it's time to separate the grain from the chaff.

But it isn't only the Muslims who are worried by change. Religions *are* changing, and they're becoming more Westernised. But what's the point of assimilating, if it makes no difference to being accepted in this country? That was the point put to me very passionately by many people:

> I think as long as a community feels threatened, then it will try and align itself with its own kind. But there has got to come a time when that community assimilates itself with the community at large. And now, as you know, we've come to the point where we are getting first, second generation Indians, who are in fact British. They are the ones that are going to be assimilated and become part of this country. They are already, to all intents and purposes, but the community at large isn't accepting them readily. All the forces available at hand to the Government, the welfare workers, the race relations people, have got to channel things so there is a better understanding of each other's way of life, and a ready acceptance of each other's way of life.

Change, then, may be a threat. But it can equally be welcomed as a chance for growth or development. In Christianity, the Roman Catholic Church has changed almost beyond recognition since the Second Vatican Council in the 1960s. In spite of some of the reaction against it, not one of the Roman Catholics we listened to had anything but enthusiasm for what had happened:

> To me the most wonderful thing that ever happened in the Catholic Church was when they did away with the Latin. I loved the old ceremony of the Latin, I loved the theatrical performance, but I didn't really understand what was going on. All right, they had it in English on the other side, but the priest was three weeks ahead of me while I was reading it. The Eucharist now to me is tremendous; and going to Communion is the climax to it.

Another Roman Catholic, Christopher Gajewski, recognised the upset caused to an older generation. But even so he was glad that it had happened:

> I like this change, but a lot of the old people in the Church now, who've been brought up in the traditional way, are turning round and saying, 'Well, all these years the things I have done have been a total waste of time.' One old lady was in tears because she thought she'd wasted her life. She'd devoted

> her life to personal prayer and tried to be a good person without any contact with others. And she did feel upset and disheartened. But I need contact with other people, and I'm glad the changes have come.

Maybe a Sikh, Harbans Singh Sagoo, was wisest in summing up his attitude to all these changes:

> When your tradition changes, something that has been with you for ages and something that you have known through the experience of your parents, of yourself and your grandparents changes; a system that has worked and has been known as a good and a proven system: any changes to it, of course, can only be seen with a little bit of, what's the word, apathy – or regret. But only time will prove whether the change was for the better or for the worse.

Faith and Persecution

All these problems do create real difficulties for believers in keeping their faith. But they are relatively small, compared with the persecution of believers in many parts of the world. What happens when a religion comes under real pressure? What if the practice of a religion is actually forbidden by a hostile government? Each year a party of Muslims from Yorkshire visits a different Communist country, as part of their annual holiday. Mr Mohammed Ali, a guard on British Rail, told me what they found:

> Last year, we are the first ones ever to go to Czechoslovakia as a religious body – and a few people went to Albania, a few went to Yugoslavia and different countries; and they found that Albania is the most difficult country for the Muslims to live in. And the Muslims there have such a hard life. Young people are not supposed to go to mosque, and young people who go to mosque, their job is at stake. So they have a hard life. Older people only are allowed to go to mosque. So for a Muslim who believes truly (in part of Russia there is an underground), they carry on their work, regardless of oppression. Because belief is inside. What you do in prayer is just to perform those duties to God. So sincere belief in the Oneness of God, nobody can take away. The only tragedy, though, is that people born in that country, the new generation, without Islam and religious knowledge, they will be the

ones who lose the hold; otherwise, those who know about Islam, and are guided, and are blessed by God, they never go astray.

What they found, then, is that faith does hold fast, so long as people are immersed in what they believe. And that's true for everyone. The 'hanging on' to that faith is not in any way easy, as I heard from Twewang Topgyal, a Tibetan Buddhist who's now a teacher in London. A Buddhist is supposed to have compassion for all living creatures, even to the extent of not killing a mosquito, as we shall hear in a later programme. But what about compassion for the Chinese soldier who kills your father?

I left Tibet in 1959, when the Chinese occupied Tibet, and went to India along with my parents. My father was killed in the conflict with the Chinese in 1959. I had rather a difficult childhood. For instance, from the age of eight to thirteen, I was working in a road construction camp. And I think, you know, that that has contributed tremendously towards my understanding of people. I know what poverty means. I know what a refugee means. I know what losing a close member of a family means – in a conflict or something like that. Of course, I don't think anything bad about the Chinese soldier, or soldiers, who were involved in killing my father, or anything else like that.

But what he did admit was that his faith was tested: 'Yes, definitely it was. I mean there was a stage when I wasn't quite sure which way I was going to turn. Definitely, I can remember that quite clearly.' So how, in those very testing circumstances, was he able to keep his faith alive?

It was sheer hard work. And I think, you know, that in terms of religious practice, or of trying to be a better person, it is effort, and effort, and effort. I don't think there is any short-cut to that. I am now a school teacher, and sometimes I compare what I used to do at their age and what they are doing now. When I was thirteen, I couldn't read or write, and I started schooling when I was about fourteen: I used to get up at about four o'clock in the morning. But these days, the children don't even do half an hour's homework, you know.

So in the light of all that experience, what remains for him as the enduring meaning of Buddhism?

Basically, I think, it is compassion, not limited to human kind,

> but extended to all the living creatures. I think that is the essence, compassion. Without that, I think there is nothing else.

The faith and the hope endure, but the most enduring is love. That's what comes across in the stories of so many people who have arrived in this country as refugees, out of great suffering or persecution. If ever a century deserved to be called the century of the martyrs, it's this one. Never before have so many religions been so violently and savagely attacked. That's why those who really know what persecution means are so important, because they are usually the most vigilant in the defence of liberty and tolerance. Of all people, they are the most sensitive to the accents of oppression sounding through the rhetoric of political extremes. The persistence of faith under persecution is written deeply into memory, and so into the living of life. Here is a Jewish mother, Mrs Jacobs, in Manchester, describing her sense of privilege that her daughter married into a family of what are known as 'survivors':

> The first time that I saw our daughter's father-in-law wearing a short-sleeved shirt, it was the first time that I had ever seen somebody with a concentration camp number on his arm, and I was quite overwhelmed by it, because, I suppose, even in the most believing of persons, sometimes there's some kind of shadow of wonder – not of doubt, but of wonder – as to whether the facts about the camps are exactly as we've been told so many times by so many different people. And I think that seeing that number tattooed on Yehoshua's arm made me realise all sorts of things. Certainly that our daughter was a privileged girl to have married into such a remarkable and distinguished family.

Here is faith being written literally in flesh and blood. Human life and history are full of almost unimaginable violence and irrational, unreasonable hatred. It is part of the dark ambiguity of religion that it so often *initiates* the violence and hatred. Believers are the persecutors as well as the persecuted; they are the predators as well as the prey. And yet, as a Jew put it, the *point* of religion is constantly to meet this unreasonable hatred, with a correspondingly extravagant and unreasonable love.

> We have to correct this error by what is called the unreasonable love of one man for another. This means that one should love every man as himself.

So what are these religions? What do they basically believe? Why do these beliefs matter so much to those who hold them that they'd rather move or die than give them up? In this chapter we've taken a first brief look at some of the things that have happened to these religions as they've moved to this country, and as they've tried to make sense of the great changes which are occurring in the Western world. In later chapters we shall look at these issues in more detail. But first we need to establish what the main beliefs and practices of these religions are – what broadly and characteristically makes them what they are.

2
I Live by Faith: The Religions Described

In the first chapter, we saw something of what happens to these six religions (Hinduism, Buddhism, Sikhism, Judaism, Christianity, Islam) as they settle in this country, and as they try to work out the meaning and practice of their faith in an increasingly secular country. But what *are* these religions? What do those who belong to them identify as the most important beliefs and practices?

In this chapter we shall be seeing some answers to those questions – in very broad and general terms: in a single chapter, it's not possible to give a detailed description of six religions. In any case, many of the details will come out in the later chapters. But at this stage, what we need to establish are the main beliefs and ideas which give to each of these religions its distinctive character and style.

Hinduism

Mind you, if we begin with Hinduism, we're already in trouble. Hinduism is not a single, simple religion: it's a coalition of many different teachings and practices; it's a religion without a founder or a founding figure (such as Jesus or Muhammad), but it does have many teachers (gurus), many holy men and women, who have their own succession of disciples. The uniformity of Hinduism is much more in the way society is organised than it is in religious belief. In fact, that's the point that was made to me most often by Hindus, that Hinduism is *not* a religion! It's a *dharma*, to use their word: a way of life leading to the goal; and it's only one way among many. Dr Gokal, a consultant renologist at a Manchester hospital, explained this:

> Hinduism is a way of life, rather than a religion. And I think if you practise religion and base it along those lines, then all religions seem to blend into one. The principles of Hinduism

> are no different in reality from Christianity or Islam or Buddhism. The basis seems to be honesty, being unselfish, caring for others, and trying to bring about a betterment of mankind. If you can achieve that, then you are a good person. So the whole aim in life should be to attain oneness with the Almighty; and if you can achieve that oneness and unity, then the Hindu philosophy says that you don't have to come back to this earth time and time again: you achieve it, and that's it. You have achieved the utmost.

Already we have picked up two key points in Hinduism. The first is what the goal is: it is to achieve unity with the Almighty – or in the Hindu term, *Brahman*. Some Hindus regard *Brahman* as the personal God from whom all things are derived and to whom the divine within us can relate; others regard *Brahman* as beyond any idea or concept of God, being itself eternal, self-existent, impersonal, but still the origin and end of all things. Since the abiding, eternal reality is already within us, as *atman*, soul, the purpose of our life must be to realise what is already the case, namely, that you (what you really and essentially *are*) are *Brahman*. The goal of life is to realise – or bring into reality as a matter of fact – our union with *Brahman*.

The second key point is that it may take a long time to do that. Dr Gokal referred to the fact that when you have achieved that 'oneness and unity', you no longer have to return to this earth; but if you don't achieve it, then (as we shall see in Chapter 10 on death) you may have to be reborn millions of times. That's why Dr Gupta, a Hindu who has now returned to India, emphasised the importance of following the example of holy teachers *in practice* – thinking and arguing about it leads nowhere. Hinduism is a *practical* philosophy leading to enlightenment and union with the One:

> I was born in a family where my parents used to practise all the religious rituals; my father used to wake up early in the morning (we always preferred to wake up early in the morning), and he used to read an epic called *Ramayana*. So in my life I have been greatly influenced by *Ramayana* and the *Gita* [the *Gita* is part of another epic, the *Mahabharata*, and it is the holy book held in greatest reverence by most Hindus], and I've also come in contact with many saints and holy men – and I listened to them very carefully. So now I'm coming to the conclusion that if I want to search out all these things, then I'm going to spend my whole life without coming to any con-

> clusion. So it's better to follow what has been practised by others, and I believe that I *must* practise.

I asked him what the point of the practice is – where is it all leading? He answered:

> I believe that if I've done any good deeds in my life, then I'll be reborn as a human being. It has been said in Hinduism that there are 84,000, if I'm not wrong – or 840,000 – different kinds of living creatures on this earth, some in the water, some that can fly. And according to our deeds, we have to pass through these. This is a cycle. But there are some who do good deeds: they may bypass all this. Otherwise we have to go through the cycle. The main aim of this whole life, as I trust, and as it has been said in the *Bhagavad-Gita* and in all the religious books, is to attain Enlightenment; and if we can achieve that, we won't come back. So first of all, I must detach myself from all my possessions. Even though I have the possessions, if anybody wants this jacket, if I give it without any feeling that I am giving anything, then it means I'm totally detached from it. But if I'm giving it and I'm saying, 'Oh, I'm giving it', it still means I've not reached to that state. When I reach *that* state, then I've passed one stage; but then there are further stages, and then I must find my eternal Master, who can guide me; because without the Master, it's impossible to achieve Enlightenment. You can reach to a certain stage, but he is the only one who can guide you properly.
>
> So Hinduism is so simple – and so difficult. But those who are ignorant, and know only a few norms of the religion and their followings, well, someone has said, 'Truthfulness is the only Hinduism.' So if that person follows that, throughout his life, and is truthful, then I think he has at least achieved something – rather than a person who knows he must be honest, he must be truthful, he must be well-behaved, and he must not hurt anybody, while he is not practising. So the important point is, you *must* practise. So if you inspect the basics of any religion, they will come out the same. But the only necessity is, you must practise.

So Hinduism offers many different ways, leading through many different lives, to Enlightenment and union with *Brahman*; and to attain that union is *moksha* – release from our attachment to this world and to the constant succession of rebirth:

> *Moksha* emanates from the cycle of birth and death. I don't

> want to be born again. This is my last journey in the world, and I never want to come back. I'll be one with God, and I have that positive thinking that I am sure he would want me to be with him. He would never send me back now, because this world is full of miseries and so on. *I* am not miserable, but I don't want to come back to this world. There is far more happiness with him, and I hope I will attain that.

We shall hear much more about *moksha* and Hindu practices later on. At the moment, we need simply to recognise that Hinduism does not claim to be the *only* way leading to the goal; but it is *all*-embracing, as Mr Singh explained to me in Leeds:

> Hinduism is not a religion, in the same sense in which Christianity is a religion, Islam is a religion, and even Buddhism is a religion. Hinduism really doesn't mean the religion of a group of people: it's supposed to mean the religion of human beings. In human beings, there is the element of wonder at this universe – the creation, and the creator, and the self. Therefore, Hinduism deals with these fundamental things. The other things are just accessory to it, you see. They are involved with life, because life has got so many aspects. But this basic aspect, of this spiritualism, that is – well, you may say, it's Hinduism. But it's not confined to Hinduism, because it is also in Christianity, it is in Islam, it is in all other religions. But in Hinduism *this* is the *basic* thing. Therefore, the main point in Hinduism is about the self and the creator, how this universe has come into being, what is at the back of this, and how it is related to our own self. And the realisation of this unity of the soul with that force that has created all this universe, *this* is the main topic of religion, this is the main subject.

Buddhism

Buddhism began historically in the sixth century BC, as (in part) a protest against a prevailing tendency in Indian religion at that time to rely on sacrifices and rituals to ensure one's successful progress through life. The term 'Buddha' means 'Enlightened One'.

So the main point of departure for Buddhism is the Enlightenment of Gautama – his deep realisation of what are known as The Four Noble Truths: the truth that nothing (absolutely nothing) can escape the condition of transience, suffering and decay (no matter how long anything lasts, it will one day disappear); the truth of how this suffering (which in Pali is called *dukkha*) originates; the truth of how *dukkha* nevertheless can cease; and the truth of the path that leads to the ceasing of *dukkha* – the eight-runged ladder of Buddhist belief and action, which leads beyond the bondage of *dukkha*.

The Four Noble Truths and the Eightfold Path combine with the Five Precepts (five mainly ethical principles) to make the most basic summary of what Buddhism involves, as Dr Fernando explained to me. Dr Fernando is a dentist in North London who lived originally in Sri Lanka. Like the Hindus, he stressed that Buddhism is a practical path, and that the Buddha's purpose was simply to show us the *dharma* (in Pali, the *dhamma*), the path to follow which will lead the way out of our bondage to suffering and death:

> The Buddha was only a teacher. He showed us the Way. We call Buddhists, the observers of the *dhamma*. The *dhamma* is the doctrine. It's a practical philosophy – a philosophy that has to be practised. The Five Precepts are meant for the layman [as opposed to the *bhikkus*, the Buddhist monks]; but to understand this, we must first understand the Four Noble Truths. The Buddha enunciated four of them. The first is, that there is sorrow in the world, from the time of birth to the time of death; there *are* moments of happiness, but they are just gilded sorrow. Then the cause of this sorrow (it's really stress: you can use the word 'sorrow' for want of a better term, but I would use the word 'stress'), this stress is there from the time you are born. So the second truth is the cause of sorrow. Now, like a physician, the Buddha is diagnosing this so-called affliction. He knows *what* it is, but now he wants to know what the cause is. What causes sorrow? There must be a cause; and you can't attack the problem unless you know the cause. And the cause, according to him, is *tanha* – that is in Pali: for want of a better term you may call it 'craving', which includes all these emotions like hatred, anger, lust, envy, jealousy, quickness of temper. They are all included under *tanha*. In Buddhism the main thing is moderation, not to carry anything to excess.
>
> So up to this stage, people have described it as a very pessimistic view. But it's *not* a pessimistic view. Even if it is pessimistic at this stage, when you discuss the other two Truths, it becomes the most optimistic philosophy one could ever find;

> because now he discusses the *destruction* of the sorrow: for any energy to flow, there must be a motivating force; it is *tanha* which is this motivating force (in driving our lives), according to the Buddha. If you remove that force – that causative factor – then the energy must lose its momentum and come to a standstill. That is what we could understand as *nirvana*.

Of course, it's a question what exactly *nirvana*, the ultimate goal for Buddhists, is – and Dr Fernando had something to say about that. But before pursuing that question, I asked him to tell me what the Fourth Noble Truth is:

> The fourth is – and it's the most optimistic – how to destroy this so-called sorrow; and that is by establishing oneself on the Eightfold Path; and that is, right understanding, right thought, right speech, right action, right livelihood, right effort, right mindfulness and right concentration. The first one that I mentioned, right understanding, is the most important, because without the right understanding you will never observe the other seven. Now the right understanding leads us to the Five Precepts: because of this understanding, they are not *laws*. Through a right understanding, one says to oneself, I resolve – I make a resolution – not to take life, because the life is precious to the person who has it – maybe it's a little insect: to us he's an insect, like the Lilliputians who were almost insects to Gulliver, but Gulliver was himself an insect in another land. They're all relative terms, but life is still important: life was important to Gulliver when he was among the Lilliputians, and life was still important to him when he was in the land of the giants; but still it was the same Gulliver. So however mean, however small, the animal may seem, life to that animal is as important and precious as it is to us.
>
> The second precept is, I resolve not to take anything that does not belong to me. If you take two people: one may not steal because he fears the consequences of being caught in the act or of a prison sentence; the other will not steal even if the opportunity presents itself and he knows that he will never be caught – but he still will not steal, because he knows it doesn't rightly belong to him. Both people are not committing the act of stealing, but one is with a different motive: and here we come to the *motive*, which is very, very important – the *motive*.
>
> The third is, I resolve not to indulge in excessive sensual pleasure – not adultery: in excessive sensual pleasures – that is, the five senses – anything in excess. Even where sexual

> behaviour is concerned, indulging in excessive sexual pleasure with one's own wife is not conducive to mental culture.
>
> In the fourth one, I resolve not to tell lies, to deceive, to slander, to cause ill-will between two people by spreading rumours.
>
> The fifth is, I resolve not to indulge in intoxicants. Now if I've been asked to take a bit of whisky or brandy – a capful every night – I'm not taking a delight in it, but to me it is a medicine, and I do so. It is not an absolute prohibition: it's something I must be in control of.

So the key-point here is discipline and control; and it's leading, as Dr Fernando said, to the final goal of *nirvana*. But he couldn't say what *nirvana* is, because the Buddha couldn't talk about it either:

> He never discussed what *nirvana* was. He never told us what *nirvana* was, because he couldn't describe it. It is something that one can only experience, never describe. By what words can you describe the indescribable? He said, 'I can only show you the way. It is something that you must experience for yourself'; and by reasoning, you experience it. So he didn't say that *nirvana* is a state which does exist, neither did he say it does not exist.

Twewang Topgyal comes from a very different kind of Buddhism. He is a refugee from Tibet; and Tibetan Buddhism, as we shall see, is very different from Sri Lankan Buddhism. But he too said exactly the same, when I asked him if he could tell me what this final goal of *nirvana* is:

> I won't be able to tell you exactly what it is like, because I've not been there. I can just give you my picture, or what I would like to see it as. *Nirvana* is the ultimate goal which every Buddhist aspires to reach. It is a state of being, I would like to think. It is the end of all sorrow, it is the total end of ignorance, and it is the sort of stage where you become all-knowing. Apart from that – how one would feel or anything like that – I can't really elaborate. That's just how I would like to see *nirvana* as being.

There are two main kinds of Buddhism: Theravada (also known as Hinayana) is found mainly in Sri Lanka and South-East Asia, sticking closely to the so-called Pali Canon, the collected teachings of the Buddha; and Mahayana, which is a term covering a multitude of different developments of Buddhism, with more elaborate rituals, a greater number of sacred texts (many of which are also believed to have come from the Buddha), more gods and demons, and also more ways of approaching Enlightenment, embracing the extremes of Tantric and Zen Buddhism. From his Tibetan background, Twewang Topgyal tried to explain the different emphases in Buddhism – and he also went on to warn about the dangers of Tibetan Tantric Buddhism, which is a kind of commando raid on truth:

> Basically there are two parts in Buddhism. One is a much more sure sort of way, but it is a much more gradual process. The other one is a bit dangerous, if all the circumstances and if all the combinations do not work correctly, and that is the Tantric Buddhism. It was originally started by the Indian guru called Padmasambhava in Tibet. And the other part was mainly started by someone called Tsongkhapa who was a Tibetan religious teacher. This came much later than the Tantric practice, and of course in terms of actual practice, there are a lot of differences: for instance, Tantric practitioners are quite often married, quite often they drink alcoholic drinks, and so on, which is totally prohibited in the other way of practising. It is said that someone who is practising in the Tantric way of Buddhism is like someone climbing through the inside of a bamboo pole: it's a sort of one-way tunnel, and once you fall down, you will go right down. I think what it basically means is that the practitioner needs to reach a certain sort of level in order to put it into right practice. Now what does tend to happen is that because the Tantric rules of practice are quite liberal, to a layman, therefore there are quite a number of fakes, if you like, or malpractices, which do originate from all that.

So there are many different interpretations of Buddhism. But where they all agree (and here they are simply following the Buddha) is in *rejecting* the Hindu belief (which we've just heard described) that there is a soul, or *atman* within us, which endures through death, and which is reborn until it attains *moksha*, release. For Buddhists, there is *nothing* which is permanent, not even a soul. On the other hand, there *is* a continuing flow or process of change, in which the present stage immediately gives rise to the next stage, and so on, with the direction of that change being controlled by strict laws. So what the organisation of energy (which is at present 'you' or 'me') does, at any moment, influences what that flow of energy will become at some later date – even beyond death. In *that* sense there is rebirth in Buddhism, but there is no self – no soul – riding along through the process of change: there is only the process itself.

So the idea of no-self, which is called in Pali *anatta*, is one great difference between Hindus and Buddhists. But where, in contrast, they *agree* (and so also does our third religion, Sikhism) is in maintaining that the whole process of rebirth, or of re-appearance, is controlled by a strict rule or law of reward and punishment. This is called *karma* (or by Buddhists in Pali, *kamma*). *Karma* means that any good you do in this life will be rewarded in whatever future form you reappear, and any evil you do will be punished, maybe by going to a place of torment and pain, or by coming back to this earth as an animal.

Kunvergi Dabasia is a Hindu, living in Coventry, and he described, very briefly, how the kind of life you now live depends on what you have done in previous lives:

> It depends what kind of *karma* you have done in a previous life: if you have done good *karma* then you won't be suffering. But if you have done very bad *karma*, then you'll be suffering. And if you are doing good *karma* in this life, then you'll be having a good life in the coming life – say, if your *karma* is good, you *might* come back as a human being. But if your *karma* is very bad, then you might be going to be an animal.

Sikhism

So *karma* and rebirth (or in the case of Buddhists, reappearance) lie at the very root of Hindu and Buddhist lives – and the same is true of Sikhs. Sikhism also began in India, as a kind of reforming movement. It is based on the teaching of ten gurus, beginning with Guru Nanak, who died in 1539. Gurbachan Singh Sidhu, a Sikh living in Coventry, explained to me that a guru is a teacher: 'Prayer establishes a relation with God and a relation with our guru. Guru is the teacher, and by this word we mean, the person who brings us from darkness to light.'

Sikhs place much emphasis on the way they combine different religions: 'We are a combination of all the religions,' said Gurcharan Singh Kundi, echoing the verse of Guru Nanak: 'There is neither Hindu nor Muslim, so whose path shall I follow? I shall follow God's path. God is neither Hindu nor Muslim, and the path which I follow is God's.' 'Mind you,' he then went on to say, 'but we are also different from other religions, because of our preaching, and because that's what our gurus said.'

Two things stand out as making the Sikh different. The first is the reverence they have for their Holy Book which they regard as a *living guru*. The second is the set of five items which the fully commited Sikh must wear, the five Ks, so called because each of them begins with the letter K. (The most distinctive sign of a Sikh, to the outsider, is the turban, though in fact the obligation is to wear the hair uncut: the turban comes in as a part of that, because it is necessary to keep the hair tidy.)

Let's look at these in turn. First, the living guru: before the tenth guru, Guru Gobind Singh, died, he said that after him there would be no further guru except the living guru, which is the collection of holy writings known as the Guru Granth Sahib. This holy book is deeply revered, and it is attended to and treated (both in the home and in the *gurdwara*, or temple) as a living reality, as Gurcharan Singh Kundi explained to me, when I talked to him in Leeds:

> We take our Holy Book as a living guru. It's not a Holy *Book*. Christians take the Holy Book as a Holy Book; Hindus take the Holy Book as a Holy Book; and Muslims take their Quran as a Holy Book. But we take our Holy Book as a living guru. We respect him as a living guru. Now when you go to a Sikh temple our Holy Book will be above the congregation. It won't be on the same level. It's always at a special place in our congregation. In the morning – as in the Army there is a reveille in the morning – so we, at night, take our Holy Book: we close it, we call it *santokh*, and then we take it to the bed, a special place. In the morning, again we bring our Holy Book and put it on the throne; because that itself is a throne. Where our Holy Book is, where we place our Holy Book, that is a throne of a king. So anything which is said from, or read from, our Holy Book, it's taken that these are the actual words of our guru. Because our tenth guru (when they departed from us), his answer was, 'After me, there won't be any guru, and the Holy Book will be your living guru.' So we have faith that the Holy Book is our guru.

I wondered how a Sikh actually goes about consulting this living guru, and he went on to tell me:

> The way we go is this: when we go to a temple, we bow – the same mark of respect – and then we go behind and ask somebody (if there is somebody on the seat already), we ask them to

give a *wak*; 'wak' means, to read the first paragraph of the Holy Book. And that paragraph would definitely coincide with what you had in your mind, because that is the answer.

I asked him if it is the first paragraph that his eye falls on. He said:

Yes, the first paragraph from the left hand side. Some people take it from the right hand side – you know, the bottom right. Some take it from the left. So if the paragraph has started, he turns his page back. And these words – again, it's a question of faith – are exactly what you want.

Then our conversation went on:

'But supposing they're not what you want: can you argue with the living guru? Can you disagree with the advice that is given?'

'No, we don't have to disagree, because guru is a guru.'

'So he has authority over your choice?'

'Definitely. Because nothing could happen otherwise: if the guru wants he can make things happen. That's our belief. I mean, even the wind won't blow unless the Almighty wants it to blow. The rain won't go unless the Almighty wants the rain. So everything is in his hands.'

By immersing themselves in the teaching of the living guru, Sikhs believe that they approach the highest in what Surinder Singh Hyare called 'the easiest way':

Sikhism is the way for perfection, just like all other religions are. But Sikhism is something which has been brought to bear much more on *all* sides of human being, physical, intellectual, and spiritual. This Holy Book is made in the words of the saints – saints who were the fruits of humanity, I can say – the best. Their words are written in poetry; and those we sing in temples and at home. So in a way, the physical side is the best way, because we start from that. But mentally and spiritually also, we get the company of the best. So we approach to the highest in an easy way, not in a forceful way, but easily, just starting from the family.

The second distinctive mark of the Sikhs are the five Ks. They, with prayer, are the mark of what Amritpal Singh Hunjan called 'the practical Sikh':

A real practical Sikh is supposed to get up in the morning, say

> about five or six, to say his prayers. In the evenings, he says his prayers again before going to bed. In the same way, a practical Sikh is supposed to have the five Ks – that is the shorts (that's one of them); and he's supposed to have the steel bangle. He is not supposed to cut his hair, and the fourth one is the *kangh*; and the *kirpan*, that's the fifth – the sword, the small dagger. All these are important. The *kesh*, that is, the hair, identifies a person's spiritual heritage. The *kara*, that's the steel bangle, is supposed to prevent someone from doing bad deeds: it reminds a person that he ought not to do bad deeds with his right hand. The shorts [*kachha*] come from the time when Sikhs were soldiers and the shorts were worn by the Sikhs as a soldier's uniform, really. And the *kirpan* is because in those days, olden ages, when Sikhism was still in the process of being formed, the Sikhs were under threat from the Muslims. So they had to wear this *kirpan* for protection; and the comb (that's the *kangh*) is to remind a person that he's supposed to comb his hair and keep it healthy.

From this one can see what a deep emotional issue it is for a Sikh to be asked to give up one of these marks and messages of his faith – his dagger, for example, because it is an offensive weapon (or could be, in the meaning of the Act); or even more to the point, if he is asked to shave off his beard, cut his hair and abandon his turban, if he is to get a job. Here are two Sikhs, describing what it felt like when they were required to do exactly that. The first is Amrik Singh Dhesi, who had great trouble in finding work, though now he works for British Telecom:

> When I came here in 1961, there were not many people living here. And the jobs' problem was difficult at that time. Whenever we go to the factories for any employment, they looked at our turban and they used to refuse to give us the jobs. And the people who were already living here, they were telling the same stories to the new chaps coming here. So only my uncle was living here at that time, so he suggested, 'You will have to cut your hair.' I waited for a month, I was very, very hesitant to get it cut. Before I got my hair cut, I asked my uncle, 'I must get my photograph taken'; and here's the photograph, taken at that time. I saved my hair. When I cut it, it's still there – I'm still keeping it. I was crying all day on that day I got my hair cut. I did not like it, but that's the thing that happened.

The second is the same Gurcharan Singh Kundi who described

Sikhism as a combination of all different religions. He too had to get his hair cut in order to get a job – but it wasn't easy:

> I went to the barber five times, and every time I came out: five times. There's no lie in it. But the conditions were such that I couldn't do any job. And I thought of the only way to earn more, and that was on the buses. I had to have my hair cut so that I can get my family, and I can achieve my objectives of coming to England.

'But then,' I asked him, 'on the sixth time when you went to the barber, what did you feel? What did you feel when your hair was cut?' He said:

> I have no words to express how I felt at that time. But on the other hand, I had no choice, I had to do it.

But at least in Sikhism, you can always find your way back. And this again is a basic point about Sikhism. No matter how often you fail or abandon the five Ks, you can always come back into the full commitment and practice of faith, through a ceremony of initiation – or of new beginnings – which is known as the *amrit* ceremony. Harbans Singh Sagoo used to be an air traffic controller in East Africa, but now he is a garage owner in Leeds. He described the *amrit* ceremony to me, and told me something also of the basic vows that are made:

> The *amrit* ceremony is conducted by Five Beloved Ones, as we call them, or Panj Pyare. They are people who have already been baptised, and are usually the elders in the community. The ceremony takes place in the presence of the Holy Granth. Members of the public who are ready for initiation get together inside the prayer hall of the temple, where the ceremony is to take place. The Panj Pyare, or the five Beloved Ones, together with two other attendants, and one person in the presence of the Holy Granth, get together round a steel bowl into which water is poured; then specially prepared sweet things (they are called *patasse*; they are special sweets that are prepared for the occasion) are poured into the water by the Panj Pyare, and they use a dagger to stir the water. Then five morning prayers of the Sikhs are said turn by turn. The first prayer that is said, is the *Japji*, the second one is called *Jāpji*, which is Guru Gobind Singh's writing; then the third one is *Sawaiyas*, and then the *Chaupai*, and finally the *Anand*. Those are the five prayers that are said, and the *amrit* is then ready

to be distributed among the initiates. And the initiates partake by sipping the *amrit* five times, and uttering the words: *wahi Guru, wahi Guruka Khalsa, wahi Guruki fateh*, meaning that the *Khalsa*, the Community of the Pure, belongs to the guru, and the victory is the guru's. And the *amrit* is also sprinkled into the eyes and into the top of the hair. This is to purify and sanctify the body and the soul, so that you see, you think, and you do good. And the five Ks of the Sikhs are essential – the wearing of the five Ks is essential before the ceremony starts – the five Ks are of course, the *kesh* which is the unshorn hair, the *kangh*, which is a little wooden comb, the *kara*, which is a steel bracelet that a Sikh wears on his wrist; and then the *kirpan*, which is a small sword-like thing, and the *kachha*, which is a special type of breeches. And then the *amrit* is distributed to all the initiates, at the end of which the four vows are taken. They are basically the 'don'ts'; one of the 'don'ts' is that they will never cut their hair from any part of their body: they are not to eat anything that is fish, meat or eggs; they don't drink anything that's alcoholic, and they don't make use of tobacco in any form; and the fourth 'don't', of course, is that they never commit adultery. And apart from that, the *Gur Mantra*, which is the word '*wahi guru*', is given to them for devotional purposes, and the *Mur Mantra* is given to them as the basic formula. And they are asked to repeat that on a regular basis. They are also advised that the five prayers that were said during the preparation of the *amrit* are to be said regularly as part of the early morning devotion. People who are not in a position to read, or people who are not conversant with Punjabi, can devote a similar amount of time, which works out to about maybe two and a half hours a day, by merely repeating the *Mur Mantra*, or the *Gur Mantra*, which is the word '*wahi guru*'.

Judaism

The three religions which we have looked at so far all belong together: there are strong differences between them, and some of their beliefs contradict each other – for example, is there an immortal soul within us, or (as Buddhists say) is there 'no-self'? Is there One who is the source and creator of the whole universe? To that last question, Hindus (in general) and Sikhs say, Yes; Buddhists say, No (although most Buddhists believe that there are gods to whom they can pray: but the gods are themselves part of the process of change and decay within the universe). So there are differences between these three religions. But despite the differences, they belong to the same general outlook; and historically, as we've seen, Buddhism and Sikhism are derived from the Hindu tradition – in fact, Hindus regard Buddhism, not as 'another religion', but as one of three *nastika* (unorthodox) *darsanas* (interpretations of the Indian tradition).

Our three other religions, Judaism, Christianity and Islam, also belong together in the same kind of way: they have sharp (all too often murderous) disagreements about life and belief, but they share the same general outlook; and both Christianity and Islam are (*historically*) derived from Judaism – though both Christianity and Islam would claim *theologically* that they are also derived from the particular initiative of God.

Jews believe that Judaism goes back to the original creative act of God: 'In the beginning God created,' says the opening verse of Jewish Scripture, Genesis (*Bereshith*) i.1. Genesis goes on, in the early chapters, to describe how men and women have become separated from God and divided against each other. It then tells how God began to heal those separations and divisions by entering into a covenant (a bond of commitment and trust), first with Noah, then 'with Abraham and his descendants for ever'. The terms and conditions of this agreement were finally summed up and entrusted to Moses.

So the Jews see themselves as chosen by God to keep the terms and conditions of the covenant (or at the very least to live in the spirit of the covenant agreement) as a kind of pledge or demonstration – a demonstration in miniature of how *all* human beings should live with each other, and with God, until the day will eventually come when, as their own prophets put it, 'the knowledge of the Almighty will cover the earth as the waters cover the sea.'

Therefore, at the very root of Judaism is this sense of being called by God to undertake his mission on behalf of the whole world, as a Jewish husband and wife, Mr and Mrs Dresner, explained to me:

Mrs Dresner: We are chosen for a purpose of carrying out a mission which he has shown us throughout history. The mission is the responsibility of upkeeping his laws despite the suffering and the non-understanding of the reasons behind them. It's a mission of faith.

Mr Dresner: Specifically, it's been the role of the Jewish

> people, by way of the Ten Commandments, to form the corner-stone of the Western civilisation – in a sense, with the rule of law. The Ten Commandments have formed the basis of legal systems in Western society – and I think that's been a very valuable contribution.

Both Mr and Mrs Dresner referred there to 'commandments' and 'laws'. That is a reminder that the covenant people (the restored and restoring community under God) has to keep *its* side of the agreement, and that includes specific commands and prohibitions. All this is summarised in the term 'Torah', which is often translated as 'Law', but which covers much more than that: it is the term applied to the *whole* of the Pentateuch (the first five books of Scripture), and it is sometimes also applied to the whole of Scripture itself. So Torah is guidance and instruction, which *includes* specific laws and commands. The basic point of this is *holiness* – which means, being separated from all that contaminates and corrupts in order to be close to God. Mr Jack Schild (who was born in Galicia, but who came to this country when he was four, and is now retired) emphasised that 'holiness' is the basic reason for Torah as Law:

> The Bible says, 'I want the children of Israel to be holy, as I am holy', you see. God was supposed to have said that to Moses. He wants the children of Israel, his chosen people, to be holy as he is holy. So from that point of view of holiness, it's believed that the various foods that we're not supposed to eat, and some foods that we *are* supposed to eat, are commanded because of holiness: some animals are clean animals (those that are cloven footed, or cloven hoofed right along, and they chew the cud, those are considered the clean animals), and the others are unclean animals. So the question of holiness is basic; and also there is another reason for the Law. We believe that the Law was passed in order to keep the Jewish people – prevent the Jewish people – from assimilating. It was a kind of fence against assimilation. But actually the main reason is the holiness. It's a lot to do with holiness, you see.

But of course Torah (written Scripture) doesn't cover *every* detail of life. So written Torah was extended in what is known as *Torah shebe'al peh* – Torah transmitted by word of mouth. This 'Oral Torah' is collected in Mishnah and Talmud – collections of interpretations of Torah made by Jewish teachers, or Rabbis. *Some* Jews believe that Oral Torah was *also* entrusted to Moses on Mount Sinai, but that it was only gradually made public, as the changing circumstances made it necessary.

In addition to that, some Jews (a much smaller number) also believe that a third form of Torah was given to Moses on Mount Sinai, the mystical meaning of Torah, which is preserved in what is known as the Kabbalah. One of the forms of organised Judaism, in which this belief is held, is Lubavitch Hasidism. The Lubavitch Hasidim are Jews who are carefully observant of Torah in its traditional form; and one of them, Mr Douber Klein (who is a teacher at a Hasidic, though not Lubavitch, school), described these expressions of Torah:

> When Moses went to heaven to receive the Torah, there were revealed to him all the different aspects of the Torah: first of all, the written Torah, as we can see it today, as it is written in Hebrew, in the sacred text. Secondly, he was given the laws which are known as the Oral Torah. These laws are a deeper explanation of matters which, in the written Torah, are very scantily expressed. For instance, in the written Torah it is explained that the Jewish people shall make a sign on their hands, and between their eyes. It is not explained in very much more detail what this sign should be. The Oral Torah explains that this sign takes the form of what are known as *tefillin*, or phylacteries, and it explains in exact detail how these phylacteries are to be made, and in exactly what position on the arm and head they are to be placed. So therefore it is obvious that the Oral Torah is an essential part of the Torah for our practical purposes. As well as receiving the Oral Torah, which later on was written down in the form of the Mishnah and the Talmud, Moses was also given the mystical explanation of the Torah, which has come down in the form of Kabbalah and Hasidic philosophy.

There are other Jews (in Liberal, Progressive, or Reform Judaism) who do not accept so strong or so extensive a view of revelation, but who would hold that the interpretations of the instructed teachers (the rabbis), which end up in Talmud, are precisely that – interpretations for particular circumstances; and they would argue that this process of interpreting Judaism and making it relevant for life must continue. One Jew, who has moved from the Orthodox to the Reform community, saw the point about *change*, and of Torah remaining relevant for life, as the key issue:

> The idea that Judaism has been the same for thousands of

years is historically false. It's had to change, because society has changed. And although it's very much a religion with a strong legalistic basis, even that legal framework has changed. What Reform Judaism is attempting to do is to maintain that change, out into the twentieth century. Certainly I think it's fair to say that in the early days of reform in Judaism (and we're now talking of the last century, and of Germany, particularly), it almost became a secularisation. Reform Judaism now is much more in the mainstream of the historical pattern of Judaism, but with a strong emphasis on trying to make Jewish law and Jewish practice and worship consistent with the environment in which most people live. And because it's doing that, for people who take their Reform Judaism seriously, it's possible to be a Jew, and a thinking Jew, seven days a week.

His wife added:

I have a great respect for people who honestly keep the laws because they feel that this is a way of preserving a Jewish identity. But as far as I'm concerned myself, it's only a part of Judaism; it's not the whole of Judaism. And if you talk about survival, you have to talk also about, survival for what? The point of Judaism is not just to survive, but to survive for something. And I believe that the laws that have grown up – if you start off with a central ethical concept, the laws grew up as a fence to preserve that central ethical concept, and that central belief in one God. And, yes, they're important to ensure continuity. But you mustn't lose sight of the central message, by making your fences too high.

So Judaism, like Hinduism and Buddhism, is not a single, or simple, thing. But all Jews are agreed that they are *Jews*, and that they live under the command to be holy, even as God is holy; and to be holy, as we've already seen briefly, means being separated from all that is contaminating or unclean – everything, in other words, which might destroy the bond (the covenant) between God and his people. Putting it more positively, the purpose of Judaism is the sanctification – the making holy – of both life and time. This is how Mrs Dresner put it:

For me, Judaism is the practice of an ancient tradition which involves the sanctification (if it's not too difficult a word) of time and of certain aspects of life itself, so that you are living your life in some sort of relationship with your past and with God. There's a lot more to it than that, obviously, but I think that it's summed up in that way, that it sanctifies and makes holy a certain area of your life.

So Judaism is a *practical* religion, worked out in life (especially in the family), and it's much less concerned with theological or philosophical problems, as both Mr and Mrs Levy explained, when I asked them the rather philosophical question, of how they could reconcile the evil and suffering in the world with their belief in God as a wise creator:

> *Mr Levy:* Judaism is not a very theological religion, in the sense that thinking about God and trying to work out the nature of God is in fact very unJewish. Moses attempted to understand God, and was told fairly forcibly that even for him there wasn't any way in which he would know the nature of God; and so Jews don't spend much time trying to fathom out the nature of God. They tend to accept that there is a God. *Some* of us philosophise about the nature of God, but more about the creation process.
> *Mrs Levy:* Judaism doesn't actually distinguish between God and the Devil, and have a sort of theological system, as it were. God is the creator, and he created the world as it is: and why, I don't know, but I accept that basically all the suffering and all the evil must be compensated. That there is a purpose to living, I accept that; and having accepted that, then I have a responsibility to act in a certain way.

So above all else, Judaism is immersed in its past – in its history – through which God has laid his claim upon his people and entrusted his covenant to them. As Stuart Dresner summarised Judaism: 'Judaism is an ethical way of life, set in the particular historical context of the Jewish people.'

It is, therefore, inconceivable for a Jew to betray his or her past, because to do so would mean that they were betraying God. Many Jews made this point to us, but this is how Mrs Jacobs put it:

> Judaism is my inheritance. If I'm going to hand down an inheritance, the Jews have got to keep on going – otherwise, what a terrible waste of suffering for all those thousands of years, if we're going to allow ourselves to disappear – through lack of effort, through lack of faith, through lack of love. I mean, what would God say? What would Abraham say? What a let-down!

Christianity

But one break in that chain of inheritance has been Christianity. Many of the early Christians were originally Jews: and Paul understood what had happened in the life (and death) of Jesus as God's way of extending the family of Abraham – in other words, of bringing all the nations into the promise of blessing, which God had made to Abraham long ago:

> 'In your seed shall all the nations of the earth be blessed, because you have obeyed my voice.' (Gen/Ber. xxiii.18)

So Christianity really began as an interpretation of Judaism – an interpretation of what God had intended the faith of his people to be. But it was an interpretation which saw in Jesus a decisive action of God, through and within a human life, restoring the connection between God and human beings. In other words, it was a renewal or an extension of the covenant – a new testament.

But the interpretation of Jesus was made in Jewish terms in ways which few Jews could accept. Jesus was claimed to be the promised Messiah, or (in Greek) *Christos*, Christ; and he was seen to be, in a unique way, the Son of God, the effective action of God in dealing with sin, and in reconciling the world to himself.

So Christianity divided from Judaism and became a religion of redemption from sin and of atonement with God, passing from death and through death into life. A Christian doctor in Basingstoke explained to me why Jesus was – and is – necessary in dealing with the fact of sin:

> If I do something wrong, I want to say 'Sorry' to God. Because I'm such a miserable sinner, because I do so many things wrong, I'm far apart from God, so I'm sort of not on speaking terms with God, really: God is just too good for me. So I can't even begin to say that I'm sorry. I need somebody to go through, and that's what Jesus is. He's somebody who's identified with your sins, through death. What did he say? This is my body which is broken for you. He didn't need to do it. In the garden of Gethsemane before it, he was really struggling, because he realised that's what God was asking him to do; but he realised how hard it was going to be for himself, because it was going to mean pain and suffering of the biggest kind for him. But he did it so that we could reach God through him.
>
> So if I sin, the point is that he's already paid the price of all

> the sins that are going to be committed in the world. He's not confined to time: so the fact that I sin today can still be transferred to that atonement. So for us, that's what Jesus is, a way of getting your 'sorry' message across.

For another Christian, this basic point (about the seriousness of sin and of the way in which Jesus brings people back to God) is summarised in a reflection on prayer which she keeps by her bed:

> O the comfort, the inexpressible comfort, the feeling safe with a person, having neither to weigh thoughts nor measure words, but pour them out, just as they are, chaff and grain together, knowing that a faithful hand will take and sift them, keep what is worth keeping, and then with a breath of kindness, blow the rest away.

For Christians, therefore, Christ makes manifest, not only the character of God as love, but also the reality of God in human form, and in the Spirit of love which continues from him. As a result there is an urgency among Christians to share the message of that love and that redemption with others, as this young Pentecostal Christian makes clear:

> In this period of time, God is now showing love towards mankind. The Bible tells us, 'For God so loved the world that he sent his only begotten Son.' Now God sent his Son because of his love for mankind. When man fell into sin, God did not have to send his Son, he did not have to do anything, OK? It's because of his love, his compassion. He could not let man die, so he sent his Son. It's because of his love. Now he said, 'I have provided the sacrifice, I have provided the way for you to live a life in the spirit.' And in every day, like even by just talking to you now and sharing the Gospel with you, God is saying, 'Listen to me, I'm calling you, I love you.' And from the very time he sent his Son, he's saying, 'I love you: listen to me.' Christianity is the love of God: that's what it is. The love of God: that's what Christianity means.

There are, of course, many different interpretations of the meaning and practice of Christianity – Protestants, Roman Catholics, Anglo-Catholics, Pentecostalists and so on; but the same basic point comes through them all, that Christianity is (or should be) the translation of the love of God – of God who is love – into this life and this world. And Christians have the sense that God, having participated in human life in the person of Christ, is able to share in their own lives, helping and encouraging them into this life of love, which will keep them safe beyond death. This is how another Pentecostal Christian (who came to this country from the West Indies twenty years ago and who has suffered much during her life) saw it:

> I am a Christian because I'm living in this life, and there's a lot of suffering, a lot of insults, a lot of grief, a lot of pain. And since I know that there's a life after this, I would love to know that after this life, I will live a comfortable life – no suffering, no pain, no torment, and the tear will be wiped away. To me, Christianity is knowing that the Lord is always with me: he knows the sorrow, the fears, the burden, the joy; because, you see, Christianity is not just pure joy. Sometimes there is sadness. But when you are experiencing sadness and little hardships, the joy of knowing that God is with you covers all the sorrow. I really wouldn't exchange this life for anything else. Sometimes I don't feel well, but I don't worry about it – I don't think about it; because Jesus has suffered more than this – and it says, If you suffer with him, you shall reign with him.

Islam

Islam is derived from the call of God to Muhammad to be his prophet, to be one who warns people and calls them back to the truth, that they and all people and all created things come from God and depend on God for their life and being. It is his duty also to warn people that their lives are returning to God who will judge them by an exact balance according to their good and evil deeds.

For the Muslim, Muhammad (who lived in Arabia from 586–632 CE) is the last of the prophets, the seal of the prophets, through whom the Quran, the uncorrupted revelation, has been transmitted into the world. There have been many previous prophets – Moses and Jesus among them – all with the same message. So Islam is connected to Judaism and Christianity, in the sense that God has sent a prophet to every nation. But Islam is different, in the sense that Muslims believe that they are the only community which has preserved the message of God (the Quran) in a pure and uncorrupted form. Mr Abdul Rahman, a taxi driver in Coventry, talked to me about this:

> From Adam to Jesus, every prophet has preached this religion

which is called Islam. Of course, there was no name for it at that time. Then the last prophet came, when the prophet of Islam went on pilgrimage to Mecca. And he called everybody (about 140,000, I suppose, but I don't know what was the right figure) all Muslims in front of him; and then Gabriel came, and he read this verse to the prophet: *alyaum* (that means, today) *akmaltu* (has been completed) *lakum* (upon you) this religion. So 'Today this religion has been completed and you have done your duty. And it is my will that I have named this religion for you, and the next future world; and this religion will be called Islam.' It's not that the earlier prophets have been rejected. They *have* been rejected by the people that never listened to them, but they have never been rejected by God. They did their duty. It's like building a house: one person comes and he builds the walls, and he's called, bricklayer. The next comes and he builds the window, and he's called the carpenter. Then the glazier, then the roof-tiler and everything; so everybody is called by a different name. Adam came with a different duty. Noah came with a different duty. They were doing a chapter, you know. We say they have done a chapter. The Bible does not tell all those things in detail which the Quran does. Those books were for their own time, and Quran is for the whole time until the end – the end of the world.

So Islam is the one – and same – religion which God has always intended, and to which he has continually called men and women through his prophets. Indeed, those earlier prophets foresaw Muhammad as the final prophet and talked about him – a point which Hajji Cassim Mohammad made, while also emphasising that there cannot be another prophet:

God sent his messengers at different times to different nations. Islam is not a new way of life, it is the same old way of life, the same religion of Abraham, the same way of life coming down, Judaism, Islam, right down the line. God sent thousands of prophets. In the Holy Quran God says so (and we believe that the Holy Quran is the word of God, and God does not tell lies). In Deuteronomy, God, speaking to Moses, said, 'I will raise the prophet from among thy brethren, and he shall not speak of himself, but what he shall hear, that he shall speak, for I, God, shall put my words into his mouth.' Now this prophet, we believe, is the holy prophet Muhammad. The holy prophet Muhammad was an unlettered prophet. He did

> not know how to read or write. He was untaught by man, but he was taught by God; the angel Gabriel taught him. In all the religious Scriptures the advent of the holy prophet Muhammad was foretold; and in Deuteronomy, it's very, very clear. Muslims believe that the person referred to there is the holy prophet Muhammad. There is no doubt about it. In the Holy Quran, God says, 'I am its author, I am its protector: no one can change it.' 1400 years have passed, not even one *ayat* [verse], not even one word in the Holy Quran, has changed. How has God managed to protect it? He caused the Muslims to memorise the whole Quran by heart. God has sent his final messenger as a seal of the prophets. And he has sent his final message, the Holy Quran. So there is no more need for any more messages, or any more prophets. What the holy prophet did say was that, after me, reformers will come, *mujaddids*, who will come at different times simply to correct you when you drift away from that straight path. So there is no need for any further prophets or books, because the message is complete.

It follows that Muslims must live their lives as the Quran instructs and encourages them – with the help of what are known as *hadith*: they are the records describing what Muhammad did and said, which can, so to speak, illustrate the Quran, and give practical guidance to the ways in which Muslims should behave.

> The word *Sunni* means that I am following the thing that the prophet has done in his life: the movement of his body (what he has done by his hand, by his foot, by his eyes, mouth, ears, anything), following the movement of his body is called *sunna*. The word he has said from his mouth is called *hadith*. His sayings are called *hadith*, his movements are called *sunna*. So we are following both things.

That attention to detail explains why many Muslims emphasise (like some of the Jews speaking of Judaism) that Islam is not a religion, it's a way of life. As Cassim Mohammad put it, 'We don't refer to Islam as a religion. It's a way of life. The Holy Quran refers to Islam as a *din*, and a *din* is a way of life.'

That way of life is summarised in what are known as the Five Pillars of Islam – the five fundamental affirmations and practices. Mr Mohammed Ali, who works as a guard for British Rail, and who is a member of an interfaith dialogue council, told me what the Five Pillars are:

> The first of the Five Pillars is the *Kalima*: that is, *La Ilaha illa*

> *Allah, waMuhammad rasul Illah* – it is to say, There is no God but God, and Muhammad is his Apostle. The second is the prayer, the five-times-a-day prayer, which I start in the early morning when I get up. It's the most important thing in our life, prayer: prayer keeps us away from lots of things – from all bad things, and bad thoughts. And the third is the fasting [during daylight hours] which we do for a month; I do it anyway, and most of my family does, and most of the brothers and Muslims I know, we all do – regardless of time or anything: this last year we have to keep fast over 18 hours in a day; that's the longest we have. And then the next Pillar is the *Zakat* [almsgiving]: so if we have £1000, £25 is for the poor people. It's 2½% of our earnings – and it's not much. It's like a tax. And then the fifth one is the *hajj*, the pilgrimage – that is, whoever goes to the blessed place (Mecca), that's the *hajj*, and they are purified.

Although Islam emphasises the unity of God and the unity of all life and all creation as derived from God, Islam itself is divided into two main communities, the Sunni and the Shia'. The Sunni claim to follow the *sunna*, or path of the prophet, without adding any new practice or teachings. The Shia' are the party of Ali – the word *shia'* means 'party'; and the Shia' are those who believe that Ali, Muhammad's son-in-law, should have succeeded him, on the grounds, as one Shiite Muslim put it, that it is the close family of a person which knows him best.

The political implications of the Sunni/Shia' divide can still be serious, as we can see in Iran and Iraq. Nevertheless, virtually all Muslims, Sunni and Shia', say that they are Muslim first and foremost – and that being Sunni or Shia' is more a matter of lifestyle and inherited history than it is of being a true or false Muslim.

Houses Divided Against Themselves? Arguments Within the Religions

It isn't just Islam which has divided into different communities. *None* of these religions is a single, undivided community. Sikhs come nearest to being an exception, but Hindus regard them (like Buddhists) as being a part of their own tradition – even though a rather wayward part of that tradition; and even in Sikhism, there have been schisms (for example, the Namdharis) which have produced communities which the majority of Sikhs do not regard as being faithful to the Guru Granth Sahib.

So there's no doubt that the issues which have divided these religions are real and that they matter. The arguments which drive people into different communities within any one tradition tell us a great deal about what matters *in* that tradition. And the issues, in the past, have been so serious that people have fought and died over them. But there seems to be a shift of emphasis taking place – at least among those we talked to: instead of seeing the divisions among themselves as separating the true from the false, the saved from the unsaved, the enlightened from the unenlightened, they see the divisions as occurring *within* the whole truth – *within* the whole community.

What this means is that there is a genuine ecumenical quest going on in all religions, not just in Christianity; and the shift, from seeing division as separation *from* the true community, to seeing it as separation *within* the true community, is a major change in the history of religions. The *issues* remain important – and they still tell us much about the nature of any religion; but the issues are beginning to be held in a different context of understanding.

How does all this work out in practice? Obviously, we can't look at all the major arguments which have occurred – say, between Protestant and Roman Catholic. But let's go back to some of the examples which have already come up when people were describing their own religious tradition.

Arguments Among Jews

One of them was the division between Jews who are closely observant of Torah, and those who interpret it to make it more relevant and applicable to life. At one extreme of observant Judaism, the Lubavitch Hasidic movement has, as one of its basic purposes, the aim of recalling non-observant Jews to the keeping of Torah in its traditional form – as this Hasidic Jew makes clear:

> The Lubavitch movement has been founded on the basis that every single Jew has to be brought back to Orthodox Torah Judaism. And under the leadership of the different *Rebbim*, the followers have gone out in a variety of ways to try and get through to every Jew in the world, to teach him about what it is to be a Jew – sometimes to even let a person know that he *is* a Jew. In recent years the Lubavitch Rebbe has proposed a number of campaigns to facilitate getting through to all the

> Jewish people in the world. These campaigns take numerous forms. First of all (and it was probably the most well-known campaign and visible campaign), was what is called the *tefillin* [see p. 14] campaign. This involved Lubavitch Hasidim going out onto the streets, in all the different parts of the world, going up to people who they think might be Jewish, asking them if they are Jewish, and asking them to put on the *tefillin*. Some people are very pleased to put on *tefillin*: they've no complaints; others, of course, think that you are very impudent, and what right have you got to interfere with their lives. I can only say that one gets a whole range of reactions.

Why is this keeping of every detail of Torah so important? Because God commanded it. There is no option about it. Consequently, Orthodox Jews see any attempt to interpret or adapt Torah as subordinating God's command to human convenience. This is how an Orthodox Jew commented on Reform Jews:

> They *are* part of the Covenant, but the point is this with the Reform: their religion is a religion of convenience. A chap like that can keep his business open on *Shabbas* [Sabbath] and he can go to *shul* [synagogue]; and when the service is over he can come back to his business – they wouldn't forbid it, you see. But the Orthodox view is, you mustn't have your business, you mustn't do any business on *Shabbas*: it's a holy day. And it must be devoted entirely to God, who created the world. That's the point, that Reform is a religion of convenience.

But the point for a Reform Jew is that, since God *did* command Torah, he presumably meant it to be kept in all circumstances; so interpretation and application to changed circumstances are always necessary. Far from betraying Torah, it's the only way to keep it alive:

> There are many people in Reform and Progressive Jewish communities who are very well informed and educated, as far as Judaism in general is concerned, and they are basing their observance, therefore, on an informed view – on an educated view; and they are *not* finding an easy or convenient way out. They are finding a way which is relevant to their lives in the 1980s and is going to be relevant in the 1990s, with modifications. There may be a greater increase still in the degree of observance, or it may not continue; but it will, I believe, be relevant at the particular time.

So the argument here is absolutely crucial to the nature of

Judaism – and every Jew has to come to terms with it. On the one side, a Reform Jew argues that no one – not even the most Orthodox – can keep the Torah (or what is known as *halakah*, the rules by which one walks) without *some* adaptation:

> It's quite impossible to follow *halakah* of 3000 years ago in 1983. And there are many examples, to be truthful, of the way *halakah* has been interpreted even by Orthodox rabbis, which makes it different from what it was as long ago as 3000 years. And that seems quite reasonable: you cannot carry out rules which applied to the way of living of those days, compared with how we live today.

An Orthodox Jew can accept that general argument, but he will claim that necessary adjustments to make the Law applicable are entirely different from changing or adapting the Law so that it isn't so difficult to keep. I asked an Orthodox Jew why Orthodoxy is so important to him, and what he thinks about Reform Judaism:

> My feeling on this is very, very strong. I believe that one of the reasons, one of the only reasons, why Judaism has been able to maintain itself over the ages, has been its very strong rule that we will not change because of the change in the times. I think one of the very, very strong points about Judaism is that it will not change, it will not accommodate to the ages. It won't accommodate. It will say that this is what you have to do, and that's it. I know that Judaism is a strong religion because it's never wavered, it's never changed, irrespective of all the changes. And my God, we've had lots of excuses to change, with all the persecution we've had through the ages. So it's a very strong thing to be able to say it hasn't changed. Now, if you take Reform Judaism, I think it makes people not believe in Judaism at all – because they say: if that is all there is to Judaism, then what is Judaism? And what is truth? Truth is what has been proved to be, or what one has been told to be, so, since the year dot. One has been told that two and two is four from the year dot, and one has believed that that is the truth, and it hasn't changed; and I believe that because Judaism hasn't changed, therefore it is truth. So although people say that in the short term the Reform Movement might help some Jews who are not religious to at least keep them within the framework of feeling Jewish, I think that religion is not a short-term thing, it's a much longer term situation.

But to a Reform Jew, the thought of *no* change is absurd – not to say horrifying. Take the prayer book and what is prayed for there:

> There are large numbers of things in the prayer book which, if I was thinking deeply about the words, I would find in some cases repellent. I don't think it's repellent to thank God for making me a man [one of the blessings, or thanksgivings, in the prayer book: v.p.p222]. But it *is* repellent to suggest that it's a relief not to be a woman! It's equally repellent – I think more repellent – to pray for the restoration of a temple, and temple sacrifice. One of the last things I would like to see is Judaism going back 3000 years, to practices which were appropriate then, but haven't been part of Judaism – certainly since AD 70.

Even an Orthodox Jew made exactly the same point about sacrifices:

> I have questions when I read about sacrifices. There are prayers in our daily prayer book which tell you about the sacrifices which took place. Well, I mean, when you read it through, your mind boggles at what must have happened then. But then, as against that, the rabbis said, Well, at least we sacrificed animals, but we never sacrificed children; or young virgins.

And yet, as we shall see in a later chapter, there are other Jews who not only hope that the sacrifices will be restored: they are actually studying and preparing for that day.

So these arguments between Jews are by no means trivial or abstract. They go right to the heart of what it actually means, in practice, to be Jewish. And yet if you go on to ask, 'Who is the true Jew?' virtually every Jew we talked to, traditional or non-traditional, Orthodox or Reform, believed that to be Jewish comes first: the practice comes second; and even though one side might regard the other kind of practice from its own as disastrous – and certainly as something one would never accept for oneself – at the end of the day it is more important to be Jewish and to maintain the tradition in some form – as this Orthodox Jew says of Reform Judaism:

> When I see so many Synagogues, Reform Synagogues and Liberal Synagogues, springing up all over the world, with a vast number of children attending these classes, at least they are keeping Judaism alive in their own way. And I think I have

> to give them full marks for what their beliefs are: because they do believe in their own way in the one God; they do believe in Judaism. They have their own way, and I think most Reform Jews keep a certain standard; and they call themselves Reform Jews because they want to be able to ride to the synagogue on the Sabbath, they want to be able to smoke on the Sabbath, without feeling guilty. But they're sending their children to classes, and to me when I see it . . . sometimes, on a Sunday morning, they come streaming out of Upper Berkeley Street in their hundreds, boys and girls, little girls, who go through the stages, and the girls become *bat mitzvah* [daughter of the law, the equivalent of *bar mitzvah* which for Orthodox Jews is confined to boys]. So to me I can't see a terrible wrong in what they are doing. To me they are keeping Judaism alive. They will never break away. So although I wouldn't want it for myself – I wouldn't want my children to say I'm going to join the Reform Synagogue – if they thought this was their way, because it was better for them (because otherwise they don't keep the Sabbath), and they thought, 'Well, this is our way', I would never admonish them or anything like that.

And even the Lubavitch Hasid, whose task it is to bring back non-observant Jews to the keeping of Torah, made exactly the same point, when I asked him if he regarded Liberal Jews as mistaken:

> They are certainly mistaken. But this does not mean in any way that they are not Jews; and this is something very, very important which has to be clearly stated. Every Jew, meaning every person who has a Jewish mother, or a mother who has been converted according to the Orthodox law, is a complete Jew in every sense of the word.

Arguments Among Muslims

We've already picked up the major division in Islam between Sunni and Shia' Muslims – and we can observe its consequences easily in the politics of the Middle East. In fact, one Muslim regarded the division as political and not religious:

> I consider Shias a political division which came into existence in the time of the rightly guided caliphs [the *arRashidun*, the first four caliphs, or successors, of Muhammad]; and from that developed the different philosophies of looking at Islam.

> Otherwise I don't consider them to be different from Sunnis.

All the Muslims I met were either Sunni or Shia', but none of them would call anyone on the other side a non-Muslim. I asked Mr Khan, a Sunni Muslim who lives in Coventry, whether the Sunni/Shia' divide in Islam is important. He answered, 'Not so far as I am concerned, or most of us are concerned, because in fact we don't know about the people, whether they are Shias or Sunnis. In Coventry there are only two mosques, and both of them belong to the Sunnis; so there is no separate mosque for the Shias; and they are also entitled, even by the constitution of the mosque, to pray in the mosque, although they are not entitled to appoint an *imam*, or priest.' Even more to the point, about half of the Muslims, when I asked them whether they were Sunni or Shia', refused to answer in that way. They said that they were simply Muslims, and that was enough. And in general and among themselves, both Sunni and Shias agree that the test of 'who is the true Muslim' can only be known to God, who is merciful and who can guide us, if we turn to him, even if – as with Jinnah, the founder of Pakistan as an independent state – a great part of one's life has not been lived in a very observant way. God, Allah, enables us to do good things: *our* responsibility is actually to do them. If we fail, God may still be merciful, if we do one good thing:

> Allah has created men, and Allah knows how men will go about in his ways. But God has given him freedom to do the right thing or the wrong thing; because, if man doesn't have this freedom, there is no sense in having the Day of Judgement; because if we are activated and controlled completely by God, then no action of ours is ours, and, therefore, we should not be responsible. But the Holy Quran says again and again, that in your actions you are at liberty to do good things, as well as to do bad things. And when you do good things, don't forget that Allah has enabled you to do it. Although it is my act, it is with his help; and also if Allah knows how I am going to react in certain circumstances, therefore he can predict, or he knows, how I am going to behave in this world; but it does not mean that we are absolutely bound on one certain path. There is a *hadith* which says that Allah smiles on those people who are going to hell, and he drags them and puts them in heaven. And the reason for that is that there are people who have done lots of bad things, but then Allah gave them the idea and they did a good thing, as a result of which they did

such a good thing, that Allah has sent them to heaven. For example (and this is again, I'm telling you, what I believe personally, because many people may not agree with me), Pakistan was created by a person called Mr Jinnah: he never prayed, he never fasted, he never gave *zakat*. He was like an Englishman: he lived in this country, you could not distinguish him from an Englishman. He was very white, and he drank wine, but when he became old, Allah enabled him to make a country where Muslims could live freely, and to lead their lives according to Islam, if they wanted to. And this act in itself, freeing eighty million people and putting them in a position where they can lead the life of Islam, would lead him to heaven, although all his life he never bothered to know – he never knew what Islam was. At one time, he went to Lahore when this Pakistan resolution was passed, and he was taken to a mosque so that he could pray; and he was taught, very well tutored, how to pray, that is, how everybody else is doing; and after the congregational prayers finished and individuals started prayer, he asked, 'What are these people doing, the prayer is finished now?' And they said to him, 'Be quiet, just stand up with me, and do as I do.' And when he was imitating him, everybody started giggling, because they knew this man doesn't know what he is doing, because he is just imitating the other person. So he was ignorant up to that stage. If we judge him according to the absolute classical standards, he was not a good Muslim; he would have gone to hell. But Allah was kind to him: he gave him the idea that these Muslims, who are such a big community in this country, are still a minority. So they should have their own homeland; and although he was the president of the Congress, he came out of it, and led the Muslims, and fought against the British and the Hindus, and created the country for them. And once that job was done, he died.

So the identity of a Muslim is easy to establish. It is, as one Sunni Muslim put it (explaining why he refused to categorise people as Sunni or Shia'), an issue of whether a person can say with sincerity, the *Shahadah*, the witness, the first of those Five Pillars, 'I bear witness that there is no God but God, and that Muhammad is his prophet.' I asked him who is the true Muslim, the Sunni or the Shia':

It is anyone who recites the *Shahadah*, who says: *La Ilaha illa Allah* [see p. 47]. It is not for anyone else to call him other than

> a Muslim. If he does so, if anyone should call another person who is a Muslim (who calls himself a Muslim, who has recited the *Shahadah*) a *Kafir* or a non-Muslim, then if that proves to be wrong, that will rebound on him. So the Holy Prophet, peace be upon him, has asked his followers never to call another Muslim a *Kafir*. And so I will not, and cannot, call any other sect or sectarian (people who differ in the small principles) a non-Muslim. As long as they recite the *Shahadah*, I shall never do that.

Arguments Among Christians

Turning to Christianity, there's no mistaking the tensions there – particularly in a country like Northern Ireland. Of course there's more going on in all that than religion; but there's no doubt either that Christian rivalry has its part to play – not least in the decisions made by the religious authorities (people like cardinals, bishops and moderators) on mixed marriages (with the promise still apparently required from non-Roman Catholic partners, that the children will be brought up as Roman Catholics), or on separate schools and colleges.

Certainly we listened to one Roman Catholic who believed that his own Church offered more than any other. As he put it himself, 'I don't want to merely be a Christian, I want to be a Catholic, which is being a Christian and some more.' To put it more specifically, he said:

> I think there's one major difference, that we live as the Body of Christ: we believe that Christ came down on earth as a human being, and from that he wanted us to become like him. So when we go to Communion, we actually believe that we receive the Body of Christ, and it becomes part of us. And as a united body, we are the Body of Christ, and we can together live life as Christ wanted us to: and I couldn't find that in any other Church.

But is that really so? When I asked him what the Body of Christ meant for him that it did *not* mean for other Christians, his answer came out exactly like that of many other Christians in other parts of the Church. I asked him how Jesus is really present in the bread and the wine: 'That's a question that everybody asks, really. To be honest, I don't know. It's a belief. There's many things we don't know, that we believe in. It's a mystery, really. But when you do believe in it, you get a lot from it, a lot of feedback from it. I can't put it into words.' In other words, the experience is real, but the mechanism, to put it crudely, of what is going on cannot be described. But that experience can be found elsewhere; and another Roman Catholic, still at school, preferred to see people as Christians, not as Catholics or non-Catholics. I asked her whether she thought Catholics should be educated in separate schools:

> No, I don't think so, really, because at school a lot of my friends aren't Catholics, and we can talk about religion without reverting to 'Protestant is one thing, and Catholic is another'. I mean, we are all Christians; and I think it's good that you should have it mixed, so that you can tell each other your point of view, and not argue about it, but discuss it.

I reminded her that there was a time when the Church used to say, 'Outside the Church, no salvation.' She commented: 'No, I don't believe in that. No. I don't think that's right. That's not looking at it very realistically, because a lot of people aren't necessarily Catholic, but they're very good people.'

Another Catholic said exactly the same, that he was a Christian, but if there *had* to be labels, he was a Liverpool Catholic not a Roman Catholic; he also emphasised how much the old attitudes (including his own) have changed in a very short time. I asked him which part of Christianity he lived in:

> If you'd asked me that question ten years ago, I'd have said, most definitely, Catholicism. But the more I've become involved in the trade union movement and with other Christians, the more I would say that broadly I'm a follower of Christ. Basically I'm a follower of Christ. The Catholicism is the way I was brought up, and it has been and still is the way I find it easiest to follow Christ. In my childhood and in my youth I believed firmly that the only way to find Christ was through Catholicism. I no longer believe that. In fact I see an awful lot of better ways of doing it in other Christian faiths. The more I know, the more I believe that the way I was brought up was totally wrong.

An Anglican also said that he preferred to be called a Christian, and that he accepted all members of other denominations as Christians; but he also recognised that there are differences of belief and practice, and that he himself could not accept a dogma defined through the Pope as binding:

> I couldn't be a Catholic for reasons like the pronouncing of

> the Assumption, just because the Pope has agreed; I couldn't accept it as binding dogma. I see nothing wrong in Christians disagreeing about all sorts of things – it would be amazing if they didn't. What I can't accept is one particular part of the Church saying that this is it, this is truth, and absolutely no one else is right – we're the ones that have found it. It's not just the Catholic Church: the charismatic churches do the same.

So the issue of how Papal authority is exercised remains divisive. But in general there is a process at work among Christians very similar to what we've already found among Jews and Muslims: the differences are real and important, but there is an increasing recognition of a much more important community of *all* Christians, which embraces the diversity in which people live.

Arguments in the East

In the East, as we have seen, Hinduism makes a virtue of diversity, allowing that there are many different paths to the same goal. That does not exempt Hinduism from internal religious conflict – Gandhi, after all, was assassinated by a rigorous Hindu. But it does mean that Hindus are brought up in the midst of diversity as a basic religious fact: 'We Hindus, we have faith in different gods and goddesses, and we are brought up with this idea. And I feel that to have faith in anything, whether it is God Siva, or Goddess Lakshmi, it doesn't matter really. To have some sort of faith, that is the point.'

For the Sikhs, living so closely under the living Guru, the Guru Granth Sahib, the possibility of internal conflict is reduced. The tension among the Sikhs is much more between those who are keeping the Five Ks and the rest of the religion observantly, and those who are not; and one Sikh even made this plea:

> I want to say this to my own people, and to the youngsters who belong to Sikh families; I want to tell them that the fear that many of them have in their mind (about the fact that if they were baptised and if they became the true Sikhs and followed rigidly all the restrictions that are imposed and all the vows that they take during the baptismal ceremony) that it will hinder them in any way in their careers, in their life, is a misconception. Because whatever one does, one must seek the Guru's grace. The success can only come through Guru's

grace, rather than through one's own personal efforts. And, therefore, they should not be fearful of sticking to their faith and asking for Guru's grace for success in their spiritual and material lives. And God will definitely be gracious. That's all I want to say.

But for Buddhists, there are divisions comparable to those in Judaism, Christianity and Islam, divisions broadly between Theravada and Mahayana, though Mahayana, as we have seen, is broken down into many other parts. And certainly one Theravadin said that he could not accept Mahayana because of what it had added without authority. He said, 'I personally cannot accept the Mahayana: I think it's an extension of the orthodox school of thought.' On the other hand, a Tibetan Buddhist claimed that the Tibetan Scriptures and teachings are the authentic ones – though he also made the point that because of rebirth one can – and indeed must – live in both forms of Buddhism sooner or later:

> We have heard through our teachers that Lord Buddha's teachings were fully translated and kept in their authenticity, and full context; and from that point of view, I think that when we are looking for something authentic, something genuine, I think we can say that Tibetans can provide it. But there are you know, two main kinds of Buddhism, Hinayana [lit., Lesser Vehicle] and Mahayana [Greater Vehicle] – Mahayana is the Tibetan kind of Buddhism. But from our experience, and through our teachers, we have heard that we've got to go both of these two ways, if you are going to achieve Enlightenment. Before Enlightenment, we have to practise both of them. Although one is the bigger vehicle, and one is the lesser vehicle, nevertheless we have to practise both of the vehicles.

Another Tibetan Buddhist drew out the differences in emphasis in belief, but he too regarded the differences in practice as superficial:

> What we Tibetans would say is that our form of Buddhism is very authentic – apart from superficial things, like incense-burning and putting out prayer-flags: those sort of things originated quite a lot from Bon religion, which was in Tibet before Buddhism came there. But in terms of the texts, the Buddhist texts which we have, most of them start with the Sanskrit, and then the interpretations or the explanations

> follow in Tibetan. So I think that in many of the texts, it is fairly authentic what came from India. Now in terms of the Buddhism in Sri Lanka or in South-East Asia, that is Hinayana; and I think the basic difference is this: in Hinayana there is more emphasis to achieve the Enlightenment or *nirvana* as soon as possible, but in Mahayana Buddhism there is more emphasis that you want to achieve this Enlightenment so that you can help other people. That is the basic difference. Then of course, in terms of actual practice itself, because of different circumstances I suppose there are quite a lot of superficial differences – but they *are* superficial.

So we are back again with differences in life-style and ways of doing things, but with an essential agreement that the aim is Enlightenment. That is why a Zen Buddhist argued that the *real* differences in Buddhism – and for that matter in all religions – are not between the ideas in the different systems: they are between those who are setting out on the Way as pilgrims, and those who are not. *How* you make the journey depends a great deal on what sort of person you are. The more important thing is actually to set out:

> I think the divisions are not so great within Buddhism. For example, I go regularly to the Buddhist Monastery in Ulverston; and although they are Tibetan Buddhists, and have got a much more Roman Catholic kind of Buddhism than my own, there's always enormous love and friendship between us. And I don't see many schisms within Buddhism. They do occur, but not so much as perhaps in other great world religious systems. The splits are not so injurious. But the difference, the real division lies, I think, between pilgrims and non-pilgrims. It isn't a division between different world religious systems or different faiths that matters: it's between, if I can put it quite hard and boldly, those who talk about following the path and those who follow it. You don't get physically fitter by looking at colour photographs of the Lake District mountains. You actually get physically fitter by walking them. And if you like, my love and affection, with all its problems, is for those people who actually follow the trail and the track. And they come from all world religious systems. That's the real division.

So in Buddhism, it's much the same as in those other religions where divisions have occurred: there is a clear recognition that the divisions exist and that they stand for important issues, but different practices in Buddhism are allowed. That, at least, is how a Theravadin Buddhist put it:

> Mahayana Buddhists are followers of the Buddha, but we consider that their interpretation of his doctrine is not quite correct. There is no place in Theravada Buddhism for the veneration given to the Coming Buddha, or a *bodhisattva* [a *bodhisattva* is one who turns back, on the edge of *nirvana*, to help others still on the way – see p. 262.) So there we tend to differ. I think it's the same in Tibet as well: they have the Maha Dalai Lama, whom they treat almost like a God, but we disagree on that interpretation. But we accept their right to preach that kind of doctrine, and their interpretation, even though we think it's not correct. After all, to attain *nirvana*, you don't necessarily have to be a Buddhist!

In other words, if we go back to those mountains and those hills, there are different ways of travelling over them:

> I was coming over the Bowland Hills not so long since, and as I was walking (I'm a very keen mountain walker), and I was trying to put one foot in front of the other, not being terribly fit at that time, I was overtaken by a man on a hang-glider. And it struck me that the hang-glider was really a visual representation of things like transcendental meditation, and other ways of seeing it. But I personally prefer to put one foot in front of the other and keep my feet on the ground.

Hang-glider, on foot, mountain pony, Range Rover – there are many ways of crossing the rough country. Does it matter which form of transport we choose? *Will* we get to our destination in any case? Does it matter which religion we choose? As well as issues *within* religious traditions, there are issues between religions, and above all the issue of whether it is desirable – or necessary – or right – to move from one religion (or no religion) to another – the issue, in other words, of conversion, and the question: What must a person do to be saved?

To all those questions we will return in the last chapter, when we've heard more about the religions themselves. So far, we've sketched in some of the main characteristics of these religions, and we've heard something of the tensions and disagreements that occur within them. But at the heart of all of them lies, not argument, but the practice of religious life; and at the heart of *that* lie prayer and meditation. In the next chapter, we will listen to what those mean, to those who pray and meditate.

3
A Feeling of Peace: Prayer and Meditation

What Is Prayer?

Prayer is one of the most obvious things that people are doing in all these religious traditions – even Buddhists pray, though (as we shall see) there are real doubts among Buddhists about God and prayer. But praying is certainly one of the things that happens most commonly in all these religions. Even more to the point, the way people describe what they are doing and what happens in prayer is often dramatically similar in the different religions: often, when you read these accounts of prayer, you would find it impossible to know which religion a person belongs to, just from what they say, and without being told. In this chapter, different people will tell us what prayer means to them, and what they actually do, when they pray – or meditate – because the two are not the same. In the next chapter, they will try to describe what the *experience* of prayer (or meditation) feels like to them – on the inside of that experience.

But first, let's get clear from them what prayer *is*. What comes over again and again is that prayer is a way of using your mind and body so that increasingly you are drawn into a union of joy and love with God. Here is a Hasidic Jew describing this amazing union with God – and remember that Hasidic Jews live lives of very strict obedience to the commands of the Jewish law. Out of that deep root of discipline grows this tree of beauty:

> Life, in this world, is a struggle between man's natural characteristics and his divine possibilities. Therefore, there has to be a time when a man can nourish himself spiritually in order to deal with the natural characteristics of his body and mind. Prayer means joining oneself with God; and one of the fundamental ways of joining oneself with God is through, first of all, inspiring the soul into a state of joy; because according to Hasidic philosophy, it is explained that joy is the natural state of the soul. Therefore, before prayer there has to be a pre-

paration so that the soul can prepare itself for this encounter with God, which happens every time of prayer.

I asked him what the point of prayer is, and where he thinks it's leading:

> The purpose of prayer is to realise one's total dependence on God for every single aspect of one's life. The state of joy, which a person can achieve during prayer, is probably the closest connection that one can have with God, and when this connection takes place, one feels a harmony with God and the universe in which one lives. One feels totally under the power of God's control, with a desire to sing; and often during prayer one does in fact sing. In prayer, often the actual song, the specific song which emerges, is an unconscious, unwilled, emergence.

That comes from Orthodox, observant Judaism. But a very similar emphasis on this 'union with God' can be heard in the other religions. I talked to a Sikh, Harbans Singh Sagoo, who is a follower of Sant Puran Singh, an East African Sikh teacher who moved to England; his appeal was for a return to faith and commitment among Sikhs. From that background, Harbans Singh Sagoo describes why prayer has to become the *purpose* of life:

> What we are here for – the purpose of this life – is to work in such a way that the soul merges with the Supreme Soul. And the only way it can happen is by practice, so that you cultivate the same attributes in you which Guru Nanak spelled out in the Holy Granth – the attributes of God which is the Supreme Soul. And this can only be achieved through prayer and devoting your time that way.

He went on to make the vital point that there are two levels of prayer. At one level, you simply make a commitment of time, even when nothing much *seems* to be happening; and at the other level – what?

> There are two aspects of prayer. One is the mechanical aspect where there is the command and there is the obedience. The command comes from the Guru that these prayers have to be said, and the obedience comes from the disciple in the sense that he sits down and says his prayer. He can say this thing mechanically time and time and time again, but he achieves nothing. But what he *has* done is devote the time that is required to – or shall we say for – the Guru. But on the other

> side, when you come to your personal devotion, which is your meditating – now that is an experience which is difficult to explain, because the experiences are related to each person with his own capacity to be able to pray, his own depth of devotion; and it is very difficult.

I asked him what those experiences feel like:

> I can't really explain the feeling; I have no words to express the feeling that one has, or I have, when I sit down to meditate. But I do know that there are occasions when my mind wanders and I feel that at the end of my devotional period, I have sat and meditated and that I've achieved nothing. But there are other occasions when my mind gets in tune with something beyond, and you have a feeling of peace inside, and you can sit in devotion for hours on end, and you are completely oblivious of your surroundings and everything; and what you see or hear is something that I can't describe, but it is a unique feeling; and at the end of the period you have that innermost satisfaction of having been . . . of having achieved something. But how to describe that, I don't know.

All that was said by a Sikh. But a Hindu, Dr Gupta, feels equally strongly that the point of being alive is to achieve this 'union with God'. In fact, he feels it so strongly that he actually left this country to return to India, not long after I had talked to him. Why has he left? Because he has found that the goals in life of money and power and prestige (goals which are taken for granted in the West) are fighting to destroy the far more important goal of achieving God:

> If you have a direct communication or a line of communication, knowing that there is some being, or force, or power that is superior to everything on earth, and you can communicate with him in such a way as to improve your life and get his help to bring this about, then that's perhaps the Hindu word 'philosophy'. The other aspect of the Hindu philosophy is the question, what are you on this earth for? And many a time, in the Western world certainly (and in the Westernised aspects of Eastern life as well), it's become a very materialistic society. Every aim in life is to achieve money, wealth, position in life, power, ego, everything to build oneself up. And this material gain which is striven for is in direct conflict with the spiritual gains which we should be making. . . . So the whole aim in life should be to attain oneness with the Almighty. And

if you can achieve oneness and unity, then the Hindu philosophy says you don't have to come back to this earth time and time again; you achieve it and that's it. You have achieved the utmost.

Thanksgiving

If that sense of union and achievement is so strong, it's not surprising that prayer moves on into praise and worship and thanksgiving: 'Oh, yes,' said Krishan Mittal (a Hindu), 'it does happen – and it's spontaneous: from within you, straight away it comes. And you say, thank God I have achieved this thing.' A Jew put these two sides of prayer very simply and directly: 'Prayer is saying please or thank you. It's almost a feeling of divesting myself of a burden. When you share pleasures or share troubles, the pleasures are heightened and the problems are eased.'

Jews in fact have a blessing for almost anything that happens or any circumstance in which they find themselves, as I heard from Mrs Levy in Manchester, where you certainly need faith to be thankful for the rain:

> Judaism has blessings for almost every occasion you can think of – you have blessings if you hear thunder, blessings if you see lightning; you have blessings on first seeing beautiful blossom in the spring. Basically what it's saying is, 'Gosh, isn't it a beautiful day?' and the prayer bit is when you take the extra step and say, 'Thank you.' So instead of just saying, 'It's a beautiful day,' you're taking something and relating it to the outside – instead of just focusing on you, and you yourself alone. Prayer is a period of time when you stop tearing around; you stop, and you can perhaps assess where you are. One of the meanings of the Hebrew word for 'to pray' is 'to judge yourself'; and perhaps this is a time for self-assessment and meditation, and for thanking.

So prayer is a two-way relationship with a reality beyond oneself – a reality which people have traditionally called God. This is how a Christian, Ray Iles, describes it:

> Prayer to me is when I feel that I want to open up to the experience of God. In other words, I can pray to him – more often than not when I've got problems; and it's strange to say, but somehow or other the answer's there, and it will come to

> me. It doesn't mean to say it comes within the first five minutes or anything like that, but somehow prayer is one answer, a way of getting some sort of response from yourself to God and from God to you.

Listening

So, the basic point about prayer – for those who engage in it – is that it feels most like a relationship with a person; and therefore prayer is as much listening as it is talking. John Callaghan is head of pastoral care in a Roman Catholic sixth-form college. It's a job in which it's obviously necessary to be a good listener; so maybe that's why he emphasises the importance of 'listening' in his own prayer-life:

> People sometimes think of prayer as a very active thing in which they do all the talking; but I would emphasise the listening part; and I think if there's one reform in my own life, it would be to reserve for myself some time each day in which I would be quiet and stop worrying about things – just give myself a chance to listen.

But how does God speak? Another Christian – a young Pentecostal Christian called Michael Stevenson – has been through a teenage period of rejecting God and the Church. But now he has come back to a kind of direct conversation with God in prayer, which he describes like this: 'God speaks in many different ways. One way God speaks is through his word, the Bible; God speaks through a minister while he stands in the pulpit; and sometimes God does speak directly to you: even though you cannot see God, God does speak to you.' I asked him whether God has ever spoken directly to him:

> Yes, definitely. It's a really calming experience, really fantastic – because even today, when I came in from work, I was a bit depressed, and I thought, Oh – you know – I just felt down; and my sister was here, and I couldn't even talk to her. I just went upstairs and I talked to God. And he talked to me because he spoke to me, and then through his word he confirmed to me what he wanted to say. So God does speak.

Other Christians no longer feel that the Bible speaks to them as literally but they also feel that some answer comes through:

> I call prayer a conversation, because I think any conversation is

where there's two people, even if one is talking all the time and one is listening. To me it's a sort of a conversation. And it's a conversation, in as much as I feel that God is listening. I don't get sort of blinding voices coming back, saying, Do this, and do that; but I do get something back. It's hard to describe, but I think you do get something back. You're thinking about what's going on around you, about your life and your work, and your home; and you're saying to God, 'Well, here it is; it may not be much, but here it is, and here I am: and I wonder what you think of it?' I think five years ago, I would have said, 'Well, the way I get something back is, I read the Bible; and the Bible gives me things to do.' That's still true: there's something in there for me. But I don't sort of feel now that it's particularly significant – that I can open it one day and a verse will come out and smack me between the eyes, and that's God talking to me. I think the Bible's there for general principles. So it's very hard to describe. It's just the thinking of your life and everything in that way – saying to God, 'Well, here it is, and I wonder what you think about it?' You actually think about it consciously from that viewpoint, and I would hope – and I think – that you do get something back – probably from within really, not from up there with a loud hailer, giving directions, but really from within.

Dave Phillips agrees that you don't hear voices from a cloud, but an answer does shape itself inside. 'Obviously,' he said, 'there's no voice comes out of the cloud and says, No! It's a sort of . . . you sense . . . you know that there's somebody there, you know that they're listening; and whether it's in the result, or whether it just eases your mind, I tend to think that I am getting an answer.'

The Discipline of Prayer

So prayer *may* be a very direct conversation. But that does not mean that it is always easy. Prayer undoubtedly demands persistence and practice, preparation and work. Mrs Qureshi is a Muslim who lives in Coventry. She describes the self-discipline which is necessary as the foundation of prayer: 'It's will-power. If I don't pray at night, or first thing in the morning, I find myself lost. You are deceiving yourself if you fall out of that order; you feel as if something is missing from your life.'

It is because of the necessity for order and self-discipline that many people choose set words, or set forms, of prayer to draw them into this relationship with God. That is certainly true of Sikhs, as Gurbachan Singh Sidhu describes. He is a founder of the Sikh Missionary Society, whose aim is not so much the conversion of non-Sikhs to Sikhism, as the education of Sikhs themselves in their faith. So he is sensitive to the different levels of understanding among Sikhs, and that's why he believes that a set form of words, in a hymn or a prayer, can carry those with little understanding into a love of God:

> We have set words, set hymns written by our Gurus: these are the hymns that we would recite, with concentration on the meanings of the hymns if possible. And those who don't know the meanings, they would perhaps concentrate on God which cannot be seen – because it does become slightly difficult when you are chanting something you don't understand. But if you ask me this question personally, while I'm reciting my hymns I'm always concentrating on what they mean. And they mean a lot to me.

The same is true for people in other religions. Here a Muslim and a Hindu make the same point, that the repetition of both word and action holds them in their life of prayer:

> We have a pattern – a religious pattern – to each day. We get up in the morning and do our prayers: for me personally, it's a case of being thankful to God for the new day, and thankful that I am alive to be able to serve God for another day.
>
> For me, it's a routine; I have the bath and clean clothes and go in front of our gods and say whatever prayer is to be done, and I start the day with that thing. My husband stays in bed at half past six and says the Gai Mantra twenty-four times: at the same time of day he repeats the same thing; it's in our faith to do these things.

A Muslim is required in any case to pray, in a set form, five times a day – and we've already heard how that creates difficulties for Muslims in this country. But in addition to those set prayers, a Muslim may take on particular devotions and prayers, as I heard from Mr Khan. He is a solicitor and a lecturer in law at a Polytechnic, and he describes a particular devotion of his wife:

> In Islam there are lots of prayers, and they are recommended. The main reason is that if you do all those prayers, you will be concentrating on Allah, God. For example, people are asked to read the Holy Quran, or they are asked to recite *durud*, that

is, the prayers on the Holy Prophet; and the main thing is that whatever you do, you do it continuously over a long period. That develops an internal strength in you, or a particular link with that prayer, as a result of which that prayer could produce wonders for you. It is not limited to any particular one: you can develop any one that you like. But the essential thing is that you must do it continuously – for a period, say, of six months. Now my wife specialised in a chapter of the Quran called *Ya Sin*, and she read it again and again, again and again, again and again; and now, when she is in real trouble, she recites it, and things happen. How they happen I don't know. About two years ago she went to see her mother who was in a coma in Pakistan. When she flew there, her mother was lying unconscious, and people told her that she had been unconscious for a few days, and she will not be able to talk. So my wife said, 'Don't you worry about it, I've got my own answer'; and she started reciting that particular *sura* from the Holy Quran, and before it finished, her mother woke up, talked to her and discussed some fairly important things, and after that, she went again into a coma and remained in that state for several days.

So traditional, set words *are* important for many in making a start in this relationship with God. Yet for others, words seem to destroy prayer: I found that this was particularly true of young people. Nora Chatterji is a Hindu girl who was just coming up to her A levels when I talked to her. She had this to say:

I think you should just pray. Say the things you want to say. Why should you have to say, for instance, Our Father – does it mean anything to people that say it, really? I've got many Catholic friends: I used to go to a convent school, and one of my closest friends was very, very Catholic, and she used to go to church every Sunday, and really believed; but in this last year, the last six months, she hasn't gone to church. It's upset her parents very much, and all that. But she said it didn't mean anything to go there and just chant prayers. She just wanted to go and pray when she wanted, and they couldn't accept that; but I feel the same.

So we're back again with prayer as a simple and direct conversation with God. A Roman Catholic – who knows the tough side of life, having been made redundant from a textile factory in Lancashire while his family was still young – makes this clear.

I talk to God like I'm talking to you. I can be struggling on the car in an awkward position doing a job, and I get a bit frustrated at times, and I'll just say, 'Come on, God, you can see me struggling, get your finger out, you can see what I'm trying to do – come on.' Just like that. I find it very easy to talk to God. I really believe that God is listening to me any time I wish to talk to him.

But in fact there is no real contrast here between those who use set forms of prayer and those who do not. Muslims, as we've just seen, use given forms of prayer: their prayers at five set times each day have fixed gestures as well as words: but prayer is just as much a conversation for them:

> Prayer is a conversation with my Creator, to remind me that I'm standing in front of my Creator, that I have a few days' life in this world, and that one day, today or tomorrow, I have to meet my God. So when I stand for prayer, I devote myself, as much as I can, thinking that he is watching me, my God is watching me, my Creator is watching me; and I express whatever my needs are, my griefs are, my desires are, in that prayer. I ask for forgiveness, I ask for a straight path, and I also ask for blessings in this world and in the hereafter – not just for me, but for my family, and for all the human beings on this earth.

The same is true for those Christians who also use given words to help them into prayer: 'Prayer is talking to God,' said Simon Williams, a social worker in a 'new town' in the South of England. 'It's a conversation. God knows everything, but you consciously say to him, Here I am.'

Distraction

But no matter how repeatedly people in these religions describe prayer as a simple and direct conversation, they also – just as frequently – report how easy it is for their thoughts to be distracted. Mrs Bhupinder Dhesi is also a social worker – this time in Coventry – and she said, 'One thing I will admit, is that whenever I try to see him my mind wanders. I can't concentrate, because if I try to read in the book, I don't stick to one thing. My mind wanders even to things which I never imagined before.'

According to many people, it takes years of practice and discipline to control these wandering thoughts. Mr Oliver is an Orthodox Jew: he was a taxi driver for many years but now he's retired; and he at least has had time to explore the reality of prayer:

> It *is* difficult, you know, to train your mind to cut off from thoughts entering your head while you're praying – it's the most difficult thing. Even rabbis have confessed in some of their speeches that it is a most difficult thing to attune your mind to your prayer and say, 'Well, I'm praying, every word means something and nothing else goes into my mind.' It takes years and years of practice to be able to cut off. But it does get easier as I get older – yes, it definitely does.

Mrs Chauhan is a Hindu holy woman, who, as we shall see, has achieved many of the most complicated forms of Hindu prayer. She emphasises how long that achievement has taken her:

> When I'm praying, I'm keeping in control, I think straight to God, I'm never hearing anything else – I keep in my control. It takes a long time, a long time. When I started in 1947, I got to be successful in 1951; continuance: get up at four o'clock in the morning, take the two hours every day, pray heart to heart, then it's a success.

To help achieve that concentration and control, and to build a wall against distraction, one of the most common techniques is to recite the name of God (or, for Hindus, the sacred sound Aum), until all other thoughts fall away. The sacred sound Aum is so important for Hindus that I asked Pranav Patel, a young Hindu follower of Satya Sai Baba, what it means to him:

> Prayer for me is mostly the recitation of God's name over and over: the name is higher spiritually than the physical form itself. It's like getting a connection with God when you do that, and it also gives you more control of your physical self by doing that. You can actually feel the connection. The Aum sound not only gives you control of your breath, but mentally it gives you that connection. I've never taken drugs, but I suppose, the way I've read about people taking drugs, when they feel sort of high, I suppose it's something like that. You feel like you're in heaven, that's the only way I can describe it.

The overriding importance of the Aum chant was also emphasised by Mr Kalia, when I called on him in Coventry:

> In our Hindu life, the most important thing is the Aum, the chant: that's the most important, because it doesn't hold any note. In English, you can say that every word has its note

> which you can touch – say it physically. But with Aum, you can't touch anything. You don't touch it with the tongue or anything, it goes straight away. It's a prayer to unite you, and the whole universe is enclosed in it. That's what we think – that's what our Shastra, our holy Scriptures, tell us. It's a sound source, not a shout, and it's not being made into anything. So when you say Aum, then you start coming on, coming on like that sound, then vibrations come. So that Aum is the most, most important thing. First we have to say that, with every prayer. Then the prayer starts.

In the prayer, the concentration – and the chant – may then be on the name of a particular manifestation of God, as it is for Mrs Chauhan: 'We chant "Hari-rama, Hari-Krishna, Krishna, Krishna," this is praying. This is what we chant.' Indeed, reciting the name may be all the prayer there is. A Hindu wife describes the persisting, underlying belief of her husband – who protests that he doesn't believe!

> My husband says he doesn't believe in this prayer. When he gets up in the morning, he says, 'My work is my prayer'; but he will first go to the gods and goddesses which I have got, and he will say, 'Kali, Kali, Kali' – because I think he is brought up with this; and if we go on a journey – suppose we are going to London – he is the first to say, 'Durga, Durga, Durga.' But if you ask him he will say, 'Oh no, I don't believe in any one of them.' But he must do.

There are many other techniques for helping this initial – and initiating – concentration: one of the most common is the use of prayer-beads, or rosaries. Christians, Muslims, Hindus, even Buddhists, commonly use a string of beads so that each bead concentrates the mind on one particular prayer, or, as in the case of Muslims, on one of the beautiful names of God. Mrs Chauhan, a Hindu, describes what the beads mean to her:

> Every day I pray the *Gita*, and some prayer for Matangi, also *arthi*, and the beads, 108 beads. The first important beads are the *rudraks*: you say the *rudraks*. It is the story of Siva in starting the worlds, he opened the eye and the waters flooded in, and the trees grew, the seeds grew. These we call the *rudraks*. It's very powerful in the prayer. After the *rudraks* you can go anywhere; but the beads are against any hurt to your body – they help you plenty – they are very powerful.

Buddhists also use rosaries, or prayer beads, and Ugyan Norbu told me how they are used:

> This is called prayer or *mantra*. We read, *Om ma ri pad me hum* – six words; it's very difficult, it's a concentrated formula: it is a Sanskrit word, and this is chanted in the Buddhist world all over. Six words you pray, and then you put one, to count how many you've said; because some lamas, or some high-monks, might say, 'You promised to read 200 a day', or something like that; or you promised yourself, I must do 200 or 100. So you want to count; and I think it is a kind of Buddhist tradition that we have these beads, 108, and usually these beads are blessed by high lamas; and they are always put on a very clean place. You take it when you are using it, but otherwise you place it in a very clean, high place, and always you use incense for purifying.

Tibetan Buddhists have other rituals, including the prayer-wheel – though the risk there is that the turning of the wheel becomes almost a substitute for engaging in the reality of prayer itself:

> Tibetan Buddhism involves quite a lot of rituals, in its practice; and of course there is some basis why these rituals should be involved. I think it is mainly for visualising very subtle concepts. On the other hand – I must emphasise this point – at least half of the people, religious practitioners – what I call professionals – they don't quite realise what they are doing, although they repeat everything in a sort of automatic way.

Life as Prayer

But whether with set words or liturgies, with prayer-wheels or rosaries – or without any of them – all these religions agree that prayer eventually has to permeate the whole of life; or to put it the other way round, prayer – one's relation with God – has to move out to become the whole of one's living. Mrs Emmett is a Christian who makes her faith practical by adopting, or fostering, children. To help her to do this, she said, 'I constantly try to make my life a prayer anyway, a prayer, and so I try always to conduct an imitation of Jesus' life in a situation, as far as I possibly can.'

It is this conversion of every moment into prayer which in the

Eastern religions creates the Third Eye, the inner spiritual eye which sees what our two external eyes are not equipped to see. Gurmukh Singh Bansal told me how you develop this 'Third Eye' – and since he has worked his way up, in this country, from being a car mechanic apprentice to owning a car dealer's franchise, that perhaps explains why he has to do this while driving!

> I can do this more or less all the time. When you drive in the car, you're speaking inside your mind, even though you're concentrating on the road; but inside we call this the Third Eye, where you usually get peace of mind.

'But,' I asked him, 'why call it a Third Eye – do you see something?' He answered: 'If you close your eyes, you see something, which is like, all I can say, is light, or something bright – the more you pray the more light you get, and the more peace of mind you get.'

Prayer for Others – Prayer with Others

Almost everyone we listened to talked of prayer as a way of union with God. But if prayer is only a way of getting *us* to God, then surely it's a very selfish occupation – running away from life in order to escape into God? But that union with God is only the foundation of prayer: out of that union, prayer reaches out sideways, so to speak, to embrace others in that same unity of love. *That* is why prayer is evidently one of the ways – one of the most important ways – in which we can love them. And Mrs Emmett, who talked just now of turning life into prayer, went on to recognise that since prayer *is* so powerful as a way of loving people, some people might resent being prayed for, if they haven't been asked first – though she has never found that:

> For those who perhaps say to me that they don't have a relationship with God – they say, 'Well, I don't really believe all that much, and I've never given it a lot of thought' – when I say to them that I remembered you in my prayers, I often get the remark, 'Well you know, it's nice that you do, but whether it will do me any good or not. . . .' But I say, 'Well you know, the caring bit is my way of caring for you, because I know, I know how much I get from praying and sharing my life with God like that through prayer, and I feel I'm doing it for you, although you can't do it.' And nobody has ever got offensive

> about it. Or said to me, 'You know I'd rather you didn't, it's not what I want – if I want to pray for myself I will.' Definitely not, no.

Muslims also pray for others, as Mr Mohammed Ali, the railway guard from Leeds, told me:

> Whenever I pray I share my prayers – I ask for blessing; you see it's a part of Islam that the country where you live, you're instructed to pray for that people and the country as well. Personally, I know a lot of Muslims who sit down after their [set] prayer and pray to God, 'O God, save us from the devil, and save the people of this country from the wrong path'; and that is the best I could do, and I can do that any time without anyone seeing me. As far as I am in this country, I am obliged to do it, because all good things, I am a part of them, any bad things, I'm a part of the bad things.

I asked Michael Stevenson (the Christian who described prayer as talking directly to God) whether this union with all other people in prayer means that one can take on the problems and anxieties of others. He answered: 'Oh definitely, I think that's one of the joys of being a Christian and one of the very focal points, being able to say, "Father, this man has a problem, I want to talk to you about him." And he hears me, and he does hear on behalf of other people, yes.'

In fact, Mrs Chauhan, the Hindu holy woman, goes even further and undertakes to do ritual prayers for others when they don't have the time or the relevant knowledge of the rituals to do them for themselves:

> There are all sorts of different people; and some don't have time for the prayer, because the prayer takes a long, long time. It's not easy for the prayer. It's like, if you want to buy a house: you don't go straightaway to the house, you go first to a solicitor. I help in that way.

So prayer is not private or selfish: it is a way of enlarging the circles of love in which people live. And it became clear that one of the most important reasons why people pray is that it does literally bring people together – it makes us members one of another. So assembling in one place for prayer – in mosque, temple, synagogue or church – is not done out of a sense of wearisome duty, but because people actually want to be there: For any Jew, like Mr Jacobs, there is in any case a strong sense of community, with the past as with the present, which assembling in a synagogue reinforces:

> On formal occasions at prayer, I suppose I'm linking myself not only with the past, not only with the memory, but I'm linking myself with my fellow Jews, who I know will be doing the same thing in whatever country they are. This is very important to me, and I have a feeling that it is very important to many people, many Jews.

But Christians feel an equal compulsion to join with each other, in a realisation of community:

> Being a Catholic or being a Christian to my mind is a social thing. If there isn't a social element to it then either you're on a desert island with your eight gramophone records, or there is something seriously gone wrong, maybe in your understanding or in other people's understanding of you.

Mr Lakdawala makes the same kind of point, from a Muslim point of view – that 'believing' has to be involved with others:

> I have been saying prayers at home, but I say it's more advantageous as a community, because it's not only your relation with God, between man and God, but when you go to the mosque you develop your social relations as well, and I regard it as very important from that point of view.

So prayer involves others in one's own relation with God; and that can mean asking for things quite specifically on their behalf. At one extreme, the Hindu holy woman, who undertakes particular prayers for others, believes that anything can be asked for and will be given – though she also pointed out that the answer to prayer (whether a prayer is answered or not) is affected by the position of the planets; and another Hindu, Mrs Chatterji, adds, also by *karma* – evil done in a previous birth will be working out its effect and it may consequently block a prayer or prevent a prayer from being answered. Here, first, is a part of my discussion with Mrs Chauhan. She said:

> 'I am from Kenya, but I am in this country to help people, with the prayer to God – anything wrong, I find out what in my prayer.'
>
> 'So people come to you with their problems?'
>
> 'Yes, with their problems, many, many problems.'
>
> 'Such as?'

'Disease, some business, some family problems, some housing problems, many problems.'

'Where do they come from?'

'All over the country – London, Coventry, Birmingham, Southall, Manchester, everywhere.'

'If they come with an illness, does God always cure it?'

'Yes, if you trust God, God will help you.'

'Does he never say No?'

'Never, never.'

'Supposing I ask, "Can I have a Rolls-Royce?"'

'Suppose you have good luck, maybe chances, you pray to God to help you.'

'Could I come to you to ask for the money to go to Spain on a holiday?'

'Yes, why not?'

'Anything at all?'

'Anything.'

'Have you ever known him refuse?'

'Sometimes God refuses because of very bad stars; all people have different stars.'

'Might God say no, because the person is evil?'

'Yes. And I find out in my prayer – I get a sense of evil. I feel something in my ear saying, Don't do this, don't do this – all the time there is an answer in my ear, and I cease to pray.'

And Mrs Chatterji adds:

If the prayer fails, then we believe in *karma*: there are all sorts of logical ways of analysis of this in Hinduism, to the effect that probably a person has been born with this fate; so what I desire, say, for my daughter, she may not have good life as *I* want her to have, so I have to resign to his will.

But as she went on to say, even if bad *karma* is working against a prayer, prayer itself works against bad *karma* and reduces its effect. I asked her, 'Could your prayer push against bad *karma*?' and she replied, 'Yes, this is what we believe.'

So prayer as intercession – as asking for things – is clearly important. But for what sort of things do people ask God? Everybody agreed that it cannot be for trivial or selfish things – though a Sikh, Gurbachan Singh Sidhu, recognised that many people do ask for things that concern themselves:

The Guru's word says that if you are asking for something all the time, then you are selfish. Your prayers should be directed

> to the Lord just because you wish to have a relationship. If it's soiled by your ambitions and your demands, then there is no meaning at all. However, it's always difficult to resist something in the mind when you are saying your prayers. Most of the people would go to the Sikh temples or elsewhere and would ask for certain things – for help, for example, for the birth of a son, or other gifts. But personally I think a prayer is a prayer is a prayer. It's a relationship between man and God, and that's all.

And another Sikh, Gurcharan Singh Kundi, agreed with him:

> I think that prayers should be such that you shouldn't ask for anything. *Niskam* means, 'without demanding anything'. He knows everything, He knows your needs. He knows what you are looking for. So when we pray, we just pray our *bani* – you know, our *Gurbani* – because we have different prayer for the morning, we have different prayer for the evening. So we pray and in the end we do the *ardas*, after we have concluded our prayer, and in that *ardas* we ask for the well-wishing of everybody, not for me as an individual. *Nanak nam chardi kala, tere bhane sarbatt da bhala* means you are well-wishing for the whole universe, not for yourself. If the Guru wants, he can make things happen – that's our belief: even the wind won't blow unless the Almighty wants it to blow; the rain won't fall unless the Almighty wants the rain. So everything is in his hands.

And that includes ourselves, as Mrs Pancholi, a Hindu, makes clear – and the longing to be with God is the only real prayer for her:

> No, I don't want little things; I have all the happiness I want in my life. I've got all materialistic happiness: I want to be with him when I die; and I want his help. I want to be with him. And that is all I require, I don't need to ask for any worldly happiness. He has given me everything – good home, family, everything that I wish for.

It is out of that desire and longing for God that prayer for things or for other people arises, as a Jew describes the prayers in the Jewish prayer book:

> There's a lot of things in our prayers: there's prayers for sickness – for anybody who's sick; there's prayers for thanksgiving, for what the Almighty does for us; there's prayers to save us from dangers; there's prayers that we shouldn't have a bad neighbour – that's right at the beginning, that one; and

> there are also prayers that we're grateful that we've got the Torah; and there's prayers for forgiveness of the iniquity of sin.

The all-important thing is to ask in absolutely simple trust, as Mr Klein, a Hasidic Jew, emphasised, remembering an old story about answered prayer:

> The story is about a very great rabbi, and this rabbi could see that there was a terrible decree hanging over the Jewish people; and there was no way, through the prayers of all the people present, of breaking this decree, until one very simple man in the synagogue said, Well, let me try and see what I can do. He said, I can't read Hebrew, I can't put the words together, but I do know the letters of the alphabet. So the simple man just read out the letters of the alphabet; and he said to God – Here are all the letters of the alphabet: now you put them together into the proper prayer, and may my prayer be answered. And this prayer broke the decree which was hanging over the people.

Prayer – Answered or Unanswered?

Listening to these many different people in different religious traditions, it was clear beyond doubt that many of them have seen, and do see, answers to their prayers – sometimes very dramatic answers:

> I have been at a service where there's been a woman with one leg shorter than the other, and she walked with a limp. She was prayed for, and her leg did grow an inch – or between half an inch and an inch, during the service, while people were watching.

A Roman Catholic Christian described himself as a big believer in prayer, and tells how he gets down to praying in a very direct way:

> If I'm ever stuck or ever in trouble with a car, any problem whatsoever, I have a standard saying. I'll say three Hail Marys, and I will say ten times out of ten the problems are solved. Never misses: I'll find an answer. Never ever has missed yet. I've stuck by that, three Hail Marys, and I've never gone far wrong. I'm a big believer in the power of prayer.

I asked him whether he had some examples of prayer being answered:

> A couple of years ago my wife's father went on a holiday abroad and he was taken ill, and he came back, and that man was literally dying, he was dying, and the whole of the family were round that man's bedside; and I am convinced to this day that the power of prayer pulled that man back. At one time I said to my wife, 'I don't think he'll see through the night', I was that convinced he was that far gone. And I am convinced that the power of prayer pulled that man back.

I asked: 'If he's going to go to heaven, what's the point of bringing him back?' He answered: 'Oh well, he might not have done all that he's supposed to have done – yet.'

In Basingstoke, a doctor told me that she had seen some unmistakably dramatic reversals of disease, but that usually such healings work themselves out over a longer period:

> I *have* seen a baby's club foot put straight. But usually the things that happen are over a slower period of time – to people with some sort of disease, usually some malignant disease, or some manifestations of it.

But if prayer is so powerful, why isn't it *always* so powerful? Why don't we empty the hospitals and keep our loved ones alive by prayer? The same doctor went on:

> I've prayed with Christians, particularly when I was doing my house job – a lovely lady who had the most awful cancer, forty years old, two children growing up, and you know we were convinced she was going to get better; and she didn't. So it didn't happen the way *we* thought it would happen, but out of that came something else. For one thing her husband began to enquire more about the faith, and he contacted me a couple of times afterwards. But because I was a doctor and she was a patient, that didn't develop into a great deal, because it's just something one doesn't do. But I'm sure, through that, he came to a faith that he might not otherwise have done. But it *is* hard to see how good comes out of things like that. But all the nurses on the ward, for example, saw what a wonderfully calm lady she was and how she wasn't afraid of death – and that she was praying and those sort of things. Now if she'd just sort of got better, OK they might have heard that she'd got better, they may not have believed that she'd got better – they may not

have seen her afterwards. But they saw something else. I still think that good can come out of these situations, although at the time there is hurt; but God's big enough to heal the hurt and make something of it. And you know, our ways aren't always God's ways, and his thoughts aren't always our thoughts, because his ways are higher than ours. That's what it says in Isaiah. So if you've asked and the answer is, No, God *has* answered your prayer.

It was clear from listening to all these people who pray that they are equally well aware of the question of why some prayers are answered and others not – or at least, are answered with what appears to be a No. Part of the answer, given by people in all these religions, is that we can only live our lives in the ways allowed by the world, a world which is controlled by scientific laws, including the fact of death, without which there would be no universe. But within the conditions of this world and this life, the experience of prayer and of union with God is as unmistakable as the scientific law of gravity if you step off the roof of a house.

So prayer is to live and work within the circumstances and conditions of this planet, and to unite those circumstances to God. That union is in itself a true reality for those who experience it, and it may have surprising results. Here is another doctor, a Hindu hospital consultant, describing this cooperative process between the conditions of life and prayer. First he said: 'I ask God for help and guidance so that I'm able to help the patient that I'm dealing with.' I then asked him what that added to his medical skill. He said:

I'm not entirely sure, I can't really define how much that adds to my skill. It gives me that much more confidence to deal with a patient, and I don't think I've done anything harmful, touch wood, so far. So that it really gives me that much confidence. There are times, numerous occasions, when you know that things happen to patients in spite of what we do. They get better overnight, when they have been at death's door one moment. They die when they have been very well. You realise time and time again that there is something else that is conducting affairs, more powerful than we will ever be and become. That (for want of a better word) is God or the Supreme.

Here, on the receiving end, is Ray Turner, a Christian, describing how his wife's recovery from cancer seemed to be a consequence of *both* prayer *and* medical skill, when I asked him, 'Does prayer work?'

> Most certainly. Eight years ago, just about this very time, we discovered my wife had breast cancer. Now you know, you can put it down simply to the skill of the doctors, but I wouldn't. I was told two days before Christmas that she had six months to live. And here she is. And if ever anybody is an example, as a Christian, she is. She has sort of developed my Christianity for me. And the work that she does now is tremendous: she has a self-help group for people who have had breast cancer. So yes, those prayers were answered by God. She still goes for her six-monthly check-up, but there has been no recurrence of the cancer. So that's just one of the examples of my prayers being answered – and nobody will convince me otherwise, that it wasn't an answer to a prayer. She was in a very bad state afterwards, both physically and mentally, but she's tremendous now, she's great, she's a tower of strength.

So asking for things in prayer is not a *substitute* for practical help: it's an *additional* way of helping. Above all, it's a way of helping in circumstances where otherwise it is hard to see what can be done. Christopher Gajewski's family came originally from Poland, so his own feeling of impotence in relation to Poland is not surprising. But prayer is *something* he can do:

> What else can we often do for them personally? For example, the people in Poland? I mean, what can the man in the street do, what can he do to help those people who are starving? It's a way of giving your time to those people, ten minutes, or a quarter of an hour, give a bit of time and you can pray to God. I mean, we believe that God does exist, and I believe that he will help those people to bear the suffering. Now you can't buy that, that isn't something you can go out and give a donation for. Or you can pray that they will have the courage to help themselves. That isn't something that you can give to them directly.

In *that* context, it becomes possible to see why many of those we listened to believe that prayer always *is* answered – always does make a difference – but not necessarily on our time scale or in the exact ways that we want:

> Allah knows which is the right time that prayers should be

answered, but you shouldn't expect so soon. You should pray, pray all the time and we really know it, we are sure that Allah will answer our prayers; and he answers them when it is the best time for us.

Even so, it does *not* seem that all prayers are answered even on a long time scale. Tibetan Buddhists pray to return to Tibet, even though it does not seem likely to happen: 'This puzzles me, yes,' said Ugyan Norbu: 'Tibetans have been praying for world peace and for peace in Tibet. Well, maybe our prayers are not strong enough, not dedicated enough – not living up to what we say. Maybe Tibetans are not perfect, but I find that Tibetan people are praying and prostrating, and they have a full faith and unshakeable faith in the teachings of Lord Buddha. But still the problem is there.'

So there are puzzles. Perhaps as a Muslim, Mr Lakdawala, suggested, we're sometimes like children asking for what isn't good for us:

A child asks for so many things. Sometimes he looks at a fire and asks for it; but the father doesn't give it to him – he knows what is good for him and what is bad for him. It is for the child to go on striving to ask, but it's for the father to deny or to accept his request – it all depends.

Of course, it seemed a bit odd to me that if the father is going to make his own mind up anyway, the child should be encouraged to go on asking:

Yours is to strive and make an effort as long as you can, and leave the result to the will of God – just as the Quran says, 'Man gets that for which he makes an effort.' Can I tell you a small incident from the life of the Prophet Muhammad? There was a time when one of the Bedouin came to see him. When he came into his house, the Prophet, may peace be upon him, asked the Bedouin what happened to his camel. He said, 'I've left the camel outside to the care of Allah.' Then the Prophet said, 'It's not right – you must first go and tie that camel and *then* leave it to the care of Allah.' So this is what I believe in, the effort.

So *is* God working his purpose out, even through the changes and chances of this life, so fraught with accidents? A Christian – a wife and mother – answered:

That's a difficult one – it is a difficult one, that, because I have

> a friend who lost her son recently who was killed on a motorbike, he was only 17. She's such a sweet girl and she always has been, and it was very, very hard for me to accept it in the beginning. I thought, 'Why Bernadette? Why did it happen to her, her of all people?' And yet when I'd got over the initial shock and come to terms with it, I realised that God must have had a reason for taking her son. Not because of Bernadette, but for her son, he had a reason for wanting her son – perhaps to save him from something worse; we don't know that. He knows best, because he said, 'If you trust me, let go: I will look after you regardless of what happens, and I know what's for the best.' We *think* we know what's for the best, but he actually knows what's best for us. I think it's sad, the suffering, the cross that Bernadette has to bear now, I think that's hard. It's a hard cross to carry to lose your child, but I think God took him for a reason, and that it was the best for him.

Even so there is no doubt whatsoever that suffering tests this faith. Jack Schild, an Orthodox Jew who came long ago from Europe, and has a strong memory of all that has happened to the Jewish people by way of persecution through their history, can believe that God does know what he's up to – but only just; and he cannot see any answer to the question why prayer seemed to be unavailing in turning aside the Holocaust:

> According to the *shema*, the second part of the *shema* tells you that if you don't keep the *mitzvot*, the commandments, of God you will suffer – so perhaps we should put it down to that: due to the sins that the Jewish people do, wrongdoings of the Jewish people, they are suffering. But whether we can always say that I don't know. It's very difficult to understand that.

But, I asked him, what does *he* really feel about it?

> If you are a believer in God, you would say, Well, God treats us like that, I suppose he knows what he's doing; but I find it very difficult to explain. I remember a Chief Rabbi, Dr Jakobovits, wrote a marvellous article once in the *Jewish Chronicle*. And he was asked – he said, 'The Holocaust? this is such a terrible thing, you know, babies being thrown into incinerators and things like that, and there was nobody to take their part to stop it.' He said, 'It's something you can't answer, something you cannot answer.' They asked our rabbi at the *shul* about this, and he said it was a decree from God. He says, 'We don't know why he did it; there are some people in this

> world who do such wickedness that maybe mankind deserved this kind of thing.' He says, 'We can't answer it.'

It is clear, as this Hindu, Mr Ladd, puts it, that words provide no answer to questions as deep as these: there is only the persistence of faith:

> You have to be quiet at that time, not to get excited, just wait and see. That is what I believe: you will get the reward – that is, God will help you. After all, if you believe, or if you pray – pray to God with conscience – he will be there.

So why go on praying? Because God is there. God *is* a part of human experience, just as much as the suffering is. People pray because God *is*, not in order to get rewards or to get off the hook of suffering, as Mr Krishan Mittal, a Hindu, put it very succinctly: 'I worship, I do my prayers, without any reward from God. God is there, yes; and he has given me strength to face this world and live a peaceful and normal life.'

Meditation

Prayer, then, is one of the most important things which people do, day by day, to mark and affirm their faith. So too is meditation. Meditation may overlap with prayer, if it means becoming quiet within oneself in order to realise the presence of God, as Ray Iles, a Christian, describes:

> It's really being quiet – completely quiet – and as it were sort of listening and putting your problems to God. It's very similar to prayer, in a sense, but just thinking, thinking things over in your mind. So, as I say, I'm not very good at it at the moment, but I seem to get some sort of comfort from it. And when you speak to other people who are doing much the same sort of thing, you find that it's not just you that's going through these sort of experiences, other people are in their own way, and that's a great comfort as well.

It says something for meditation that it is more important – more significant – than homework from school, as this young Hindu has discovered:

> I believe that in saying prayers with love and faith you can get near to God, instead of just doing your maths homework – which isn't really going to get you anywhere. When I'm pray-

> ing, I'm meditating, trying to forget everything that's around me, and just concentrating on God – hopefully he's listening to me – and hopefully he answers my prayers.

Meditation and Enlightenment

But meditation may have no reference to God at all. It may be a quest for the realisation of peace and enlightenment within oneself. It's a kind of self-discipline in order to transcend, or get beyond, one's self.

It leads to relaxation – the most common word we heard to describe the results of meditation; and it clearly helps one to ignore the minor irritations of life – including mosquitoes. I liked very much the way in which Mr Wickramaratne (president of the Sri Lankan Association in North London) could see Buddhism as a kind of 'preventative' against mosquitoes, of rather more secure effect than Flypel – and it depends on the deep Buddhist renunciation of killing any form of life:

> When you do meditation – and Buddhism stresses meditation is the main path leading to *nirvana* – you experience that complete relaxation, that complete purity of mind. I must confess I haven't done the advanced schools of meditation, but even in simple meditation, when you concentrate on an object, you can experience it – it's not very difficult. But I believe in the practical side of Buddhism also, like no killing of a living being. I myself never ever killed an animal, or even a butterfly or something like that, in my life – or a bird even. The only thing that I've ever killed is a fly or a mosquito. Even then I feel sometimes guilty towards them. Recently when I went home on holiday, there were mosquitoes in my father's house, and I was just about to kill a mosquito, and my father said, 'Why do you want to do that?' I said, 'Because it's going to bite me.' But he said, 'I don't kill them and they don't do any harm to me.' And we all got bitten, but not him, actually; and he said, 'I haven't got any marks at all on my body from a mosquito bite.' So if we share good-will in that way, they also seem to react in that same way.

So an important part of meditation for a Buddhist (far from being escapist) is to cultivate and extend exactly that compassion for all living creatures. One technique for that, within meditation, is to realise that, because of rebirth, *any* living creature may once have been the form of a loved person – say, for example, your mother. This is how Twewang Topgyal, a Tibetan Buddhist, explained it to me:

> Compassion doesn't arise suddenly: it needs to be cultivated, in very gradual steps. In Tibetan Buddhism the concept is this: because we believe in rebirth, we believe that the Buddha who lived about 2500 years ago has been reborn almost innumerable times in various stages – maybe in terms of human beings, maybe in terms of birds, and fish, and all sorts of living creatures; and therefore each time he has taken birth, he has been a son, a member of a family or a tribe; so we believe that there isn't a single creature which has not been your mother at one time or another. And that is the basis on which one can build up some sort of compassion. And then, of course, you need to practise it all the time, and that will reinforce it.

But what do you actually do in order to meditate? There are many different ways – different paths – but a key to all of them is: concentration. Here a Zen Buddhist describes what he does:

> Meditation is of course a very pretentious word – I use it because it's easily communicable; but now that I've used it, let me attack it. We prefer in Zen (which itself of course means 'meditation' – it's a Japanese corruption of a Chinese word), the word 'sitting'; and so one of the things I'm doing is sitting. And if you like, what I'm doing is, simply sitting. Which is very hard to do. It sounds so easy, it's rather paradoxical. Well, I have a blue platform cushion, a flat cushion, and on it is a black Zafu, it's a sort of kapok stuffed cushion, rather round. And I sit in half lotus for half an hour, and then change over onto the other leg after half an hour. And that's all the hour is. I'm mainly counting sort of silently to myself with every breathing out, counting a number. And every time my thoughts intervene, I go back to one. So I'm finally focusing, with a great amount of physical effort – the Buddha always talked about his own faith and structure in very physical terms. If you look at the Sutras he repeatedly, time and time again, talked in those terms – so it's a very physical activity. And even in this terrible cold weather we've been having recently, I meditate with just a shirt on, and there's no problem, because it is such an intense physical sort of effort to concentrate and to bring the mind back again, from the wandering to the numbers, and from sensing what is happen-

ing around to sensing the activity within the mind and getting beyond thought.

It's one thing to say that you concentrate: but on what object or thought do you concentrate? Mr Wickramaratne replied:

It could be anything. I mean, I could concentrate on looking at my toes or some object in front of me, a book or something like that. It's just complete concentration on that; and then everything outside doesn't really exist for me at the time.

But for a Buddhist, concentration is likely to be on the Buddha; and for that purpose, many Buddhists have a shrine and an image of the Buddha in their homes. Dr Fernando, a Theravadin Buddhist, talked to me about this, and this is a part of our conversation:

I attend to my devotions in the morning and I attend to my devotions in the evening – they are called devotions, not prayers. It's a form of showing my gratitude to the Buddha for showing us the Way. There are other Buddhas who attained the same state on their own, but who cannot teach. The Buddha had a mission.

I asked him whether he actually talks to the Buddha. He answered:

I can't, he's not there any more. He's not there any more. He's attained that state of *nirvana*. He's not there any more. That's why we have no prayer. Prayer doesn't exist in Buddhism because there's no one to talk to. In my devotions I say to myself, 'To the best of my ability I shall try to emulate the life of the Buddha.' So I have my shrine-room, and even my children, before they go to work or their colleges, they do their devotion, and only after their devotion they set out.

But why have a shrine room devoted to the Buddha if the Buddha is no longer in contact with us and has simply left us his teaching? Dr Fernando said:

It's almost the same as having a portrait of your parents, to remind you of the love that they had for you; when you visit the grave of your parents, they are not there any more, but you are saying thank you to them for having looked after you when you were a child – placing their hand on a fevered brow, comforting you in moments of stress. What other purpose is there for visiting the grave?

Buddhists and Prayer

Other Buddhists, though, do pray and ask for various things. They believe in the existence, not only of *devas*, but of other superhuman realities, gods and goddesses, who may perhaps come to human aid; and then one of the purposes of meditation is to visualise what those realities may be like. Tibet is particularly ritualistic – that's to say, it translates belief into practical and visible forms, so that people can *do* something as well as just think something. It's no good saying to your wife, 'I love you', if you don't give her a kiss and express your love in a practical way. A Tibetan Buddhist told me how prayer and symbolic action are tied together:

> In Tibet (and Tibetans in general) we always pray in the morning and in the evening, and always also we put and burn butter lamps every evening and every morning – and also burn incense.

I asked him what these prayers are:

> Well, there are so many prayers: prayers for the truth, prayers for long life, or for certain eminent lamas, or for all people, prayers for world peace, and prayer for one's health; prayer for forgiveness for one's own wrongdoings, and to promise that I will not do any bad things in the future – try not to do it, at least, in the future; and I will try to do, or try to promote, good things in life. At the moment, we, as Tibetans, pray a lot for world peace; and I feel that Tibetans are the only people who day and night, pray for world peace; and yet we find our country is in jeopardy. But also we pray for Tibet, for freedom for the Tibetan people, and for the happiness of the six million Tibetans in Tibet.

At this point, I remembered how often I had read in books written in the West that Buddhists don't believe in God and so cannot pray. So I asked him to whom he was talking when he prayed:

> Talking to? Talking to what we call *Gunchok. Gunchok* is the holder of the *dharma*, the one who sees, the one who is all-knowing of the situation, the one who has got the power, a certain amount of power. And who is he? Well, any Buddhist enlightened persons, or enlightened person, you can call God; there are many, and they can be anywhere. The Lord Buddha is one. We don't have to go to the shrine where there is a

symbol of Lord Buddha. You can pray anywhere, and you can put any object, and if you think that this is Lord Buddha himself, you can pray there, if you have enough faith – and there could be Lord Buddha there. If you are deeply praying, yes, you have to visualise: you have to visualise strongly that he is there, and the contact between you and him is very close; and there are various stages of visualisation, I think, but I am not good in these things.

The same Buddhist went on to emphasise that Buddhists do most certainly believe in God – they even believe that they may become gods through rebirth – but it all depends what you mean by God:

It depends on the meaning of God. I was puzzled by anyone saying 'God', but Tibetans may not be saying God in a Christian sense – that is, Jesus Christ's Father, or the Lord, and Jesus Christ is the Son of the God. It is not in that context. Now in Tibetan Buddhism (maybe it's similar to Theravadin – I feel it is the same) the point is that after having achieved Enlightenment, and if you are completely enlightened, then you are what we call 'all-knowing'. There is nothing left that you have got to achieve. Everything has been achieved, you are fully enlightened. And you have the potential and the power, and you have the wisdom. And that is in turn sometimes, I think, translated as God. And if that is God, I think we have got thousands of gods. And that's why we are talking about you being able to be a god, because potentially that Buddhist nature, the kind nature, compassionate nature, or the very good nature, what we call 'Buddha's seed', *is* in everybody's mind; but also the bad qualities are in the mind. So, 'which one we should cultivate', is the issue. So I don't think that Tibetan Buddhism believes that God is solidly somewhere, and that it is one. But we believe that everybody has got potential to be a good and enlightened and all-knowing being – and it could go the other way round.

So meditation, like prayer, is a very natural activity: it's one of the things that humans are able to do if they choose to do it; indeed, it's *so* natural that some young Hindus do sponsored meditations to raise money for good works, rather than sponsored swims:

What we're trying to do now is build hospitals in India, and for that we hope to raise a lot of money by doing sponsored walks;

> and I did a sponsored meditation for twenty-four hours, and we raised £500 almost, for sending to India for the flood relief.

In one other respect, meditation is like prayer: it requires long practice, and it does have to be learnt. Early Christians anticipated Keats in seeing this world as 'a vale of soul-making'. So it is also for Ugyan Norbu, a Tibetan Buddhist – though of course, since he is a Buddhist, it is not a *soul* that is being made, but a good progression of the life that we have while it lasts:

> It's a long process, and you have to learn through books and through teachers – and you *can* learn from many circumstances. In fact, going to different teachers all over will not really help. Buddhism is, to have certain information; but mainly you have to practise yourself. All the difficult questions you have to ask yourself and try to digest, and then see step by step. Everything takes time. And to make a good human being, like making a good programme or something, it always takes time. When we are going to do something good it always takes time. And if we are expecting something to happen very quickly, I am sure this will be mistaken.

Nor is it a matter of 'book learning': there is a deep religious difference between information and insight. Mr Poey, the Buddhist originally from Malaysia, made this clear:

> Being intellectual will not enable you to understand. All the books in the world – on philosophy, on religion – will never bring anyone to happiness. I've learnt, all these years, that there is only one thing in life which can make us happy and contented, and that is what the Buddha has taught, the one-pointedness of mind. In other words, like the yogis of old, you must practise concentration, meditation and contemplation. So, since that early time, I tried and tried and tried to concentrate on what I do – but that is a difficult thing to do in this world.

Times of Prayer

So although, like prayer, meditation and its effects spread out and fill the whole day, there are many people who try to find a particular moment for meditation or for engagement with God – and it really is surprising how many people in this country are up at five or six in the morning (or earlier) for this deliberate time of quiet. We've already heard this from a Sikh, a Hindu and a Christian. Here are a Muslim and a Jew:

> Today I got up at six o'clock in the morning. I had a wash and then I prayed my first prayer. During the hours of work, sometimes I miss my prayer, but I do try to the best of my ability to carry out the prayers if I can. As soon as I get home I continue my prayers. You see it's prayer which brings me closer to my belief and to the memory of my Creator, and without that I don't think I can survive in this world for one minute or one day. It's just impossible to survive. It's an everyday duty for me, that when I go to bed I think of *fajr*, and how I have to get up in the morning; not just to work, but most important, above all, for my prayers; *then* I think about my work.

> I get up in the morning – when I don't oversleep – I'm a human being who does oversleep sometimes – but my general pattern is that I get up in the morning at about a quarter past six. I put on the *zizith* – that's a garment that a Jewish person wears to remind him of the 613 commandments which he has to fulfil. He's obliged to wear these *zizith* at all times. They're a sign to the outside world that he is a Jew.

Daily Prayer

Already this is beginning to make the point that daily prayer, in some of these religions, is not a matter of *choice*: it's a matter of *obligation*, as a part of belonging to that tradition. Muslims have five obligatory times of prayer each day, as we've already heard.

Sikhs have a comparably set programme, which I asked Harbans Singh Sagoo to describe:

> It's a very set programme that I follow. I generally get up round about half past four in the morning and have a bath. Then I sit down to say the five prayers that are being set aside as the Sikh morning prayers. I also have a copy of the Holy Granth at home, but before I sit down to say my prayers, I have to instal the Holy Granth on its place, and conduct a small ceremony which is really a sort of personal devotion. As soon as I've done that, I sit down and say my five prayers. If I've got any more time left on my hands, then I just sit down and meditate – which normally takes between half an hour to three-quarters of an hour before I get up to get dressed and prepare myself to go to work. This is the morning. In the

evening, the programme is not so organised, because of my social involvement – I'm all over the place. But if I'm at home, or if I'm at the temple, then of course the evening prayers are said, and all the normal ceremonies are taken care of. But in my absence, my wife takes care of that part of the daily course.

For Buddhist monks the daily obligations are also detailed, but for the lay-people they *may* be less so – it's a matter of choice: though if you do choose a daily obligation, then it was a Buddhist who used the strongest word – 'straitjacket' – to describe the necessary discipline involved; and he talked also of two 'mill-stones' of grinding discipline:

> There are two disciplines within Zen. The one is the daily meditation. That's exactly the same time in the same way: it's a straitjacket of meditation – there's no deviation from it. It's laid down very, very clearly, to the minute and to the position, how it shall be done.

Since it is often claimed in the West that Zen Buddhism is a very free and liberal philosophy (not even a religion), I asked him who lays down the detailed obligation:

> The teacher usually, but there's a tradition anyway – there's many hundreds of years of tradition about Za Zen and the way it can be done. But that is only one of the disciplines in the millstones. The other millstone is the acceptance practice: acceptance practice is a minute by minute – and every minute – meditation in accepting life as it is – accepting it as it deals the latest uncomfortable fact – that it's snowed so you can't go out, or, you were going to have a nice summer's walk and it's raining. All kinds of things happen. The Buddha is delight-fully generous: he sends a thousand frustrations a day to hone our practice of everyday life.

For Hindus, it is equally a matter of choice. After all, Hinduism believes that there are different paths, through many different births, leading to the goal, so it cannot be a religion of *one* obligation for *all* people. Chitra Pal Singh made this point very strongly to me, when I called on him in Leeds:

> In Hinduism there is no compulsion that you should do one thing each day, or (what do you call it?) some kind of a ritual prayer, as in Islam; in Islam they say that five times you have to pray in a certain way. In Hinduism, fundamentally this ritual element doesn't play much part. The point, the whole point, is

> this: the honesty of a man should not be limited to five or three minutes. No. It must persist through his life. Every moment of the life should be honest, it should be selfless. I should think of higher things, less of myself, more of others – and of improving my life, so that it becomes without desire. Serve others more, think of others more, and think less of yourself.

But of course many Hindus do choose a daily obligation, though what it is and when it happens will obviously vary.

In the same sort of way, Christians may undertake daily prayer, but it's not laid down as an obligation. A typical description is that of the union worker and maintenance fitter, Ray Turner:

> Without fail I begin my day by saying prayers. And at this point I'd like to say that I regard saying prayers as different from praying. I was brought up to say prayers, but until very recently I hardly ever prayed. So more or less out of force of habit I begin every day by saying prayers. I'd like to say that I spent a few moments of every day praying – my intentions are always good – but no, I'd be dishonest if I said I did. But I try to put a few minutes aside just to sit and try and communicate with God – and I'm only just learning how to do that.

All of us – in prayer and in meditation – are learners. True, you meet some people who seem to have been carried into distant discoveries far beyond the territories that you or I have yet explored – and I met several such people while making these programmes. But what are those explorations – and discoveries – like? What does it *feel* like to be on the inside of prayer and meditation? That's what we're going on to ask, in the next chapter.

4
God on a Bus: Experiences in Religion

In the last chapter, we looked at some descriptions of what people do when they pray or meditate – and we began to learn something of how deeply those activities (or sometimes inactivities) belong to the heart of religious life. But it's one thing to hear people describing what they do; it's quite another to try to get inside those activities and understand what they *feel* like, on the inside of the experience. And that's what we're going to attempt in this chapter.

There are two dangers in doing this: first, it can't be done. You can't put deep experiences of this kind into words. 'How can you describe the indescribable?' as Dr Fernando put it, in Chapter 2. These experiences are real, but they are so unlike anything else that no words can really catch hold of them. Look back at what Mr Harbans Singh Sagoo had to say in the last chapter (pp. 63–4), and you can see that he is certainly talking about *something* (he can recognise when things are or are not happening), but 'how to describe it, I don't know.'

The second danger is that religious experience is not really so important to the believer as it is to the outsider who is interested in what goes on in religious life and behaviour. In fact, teachers in all these religions warn explicitly that too much religious experience may be dangerous for your spiritual health – or even the *quest* for such experience, as an end in its own right. A great deal of prayer and meditation is entirely without dramatic experience, and it is not undertaken to achieve it.

Still, the fact remains that prayer and meditation do have consequences in the inner life of those who engage in them. And several people did try – usually reluctantly – to give some idea of what it feels like to be on the inside of these experiences.

Prayer and Presence

The most common comparison was to say that it is like the

emotion you sometimes feel when you listen to music. In fact, Mr Jacobs (a Reform Jew) finds that the experience of feeling God's presence is not simply *like* what may happen when listening to music: it can *happen* in that way. As he put it: 'The feeling of God's presence is different from the ordinary living day by day. It can happen on unexpected occasions, and also on surprising occasions. I think I can feel it sometimes when hearing music. I happen to be part of a very musical family, so perhaps this is one of my blessings, a natural blessing.'

I asked Ray Turner, a maintenance fitter and trade union worker from Liverpool, what it feels like to him when he's praying:

> I try, first of all, to relax and to make my mind blank, so that I have no thoughts – get rid of the problems that go through your mind all the time – I try first of all to do that. And then in order to think of God in a way that God is within me, is inside me – I try and float out of myself and join God inside me, and just say, 'Look, you know, I'm here: if you don't want to come, OK, but I'm here'. I found it *very* difficult at first. My thoughts were all over the place. But the longer I've done it, the easier it becomes. It's just a strange sort of sensation that I used to only get on very rare occasions – perhaps when in church, or perhaps listening to a piece of music. And it just feels as though all the worries and turmoils of the world go. They soon come back of course. But it feels as though I'm not really me, that I'm looking down on the body, that I'm there. I get this tremendous peace. But I'm never very articulate, and I can't express in words what I feel, and I find it most difficult to explain what it's like. It's like you're looking at the most beautiful painting that you've ever seen, or listening to the most wonderful piece of music, and putting it all together. And that's about as close as I can get to it. And no words; I don't use any words except when I start off; and I don't think that God ever uses any words; and yet I get the feeling afterwards that God wants me to do something. I've read of different people who've had some tremendous experience – people who've visited a shrine; or I remember reading a book about Padre Pio who had these tremendous experiences. And I've read and I've heard about this charismatic movement where people join together and they speak in tongues and they get this. . . . To tell you the truth it frightens the life out of me, and I've fought shy of going to charismatic movement meet-

> ings. I don't know why: I just feel as though it's not for me. I get these moments of being close to God at a meeting with people, talking to people. I get it occasionally at Mass, at the Eucharist, but I can get it listening to a piece of music. I can get it playing with a little baby, you know. I can get a tremendous spiritual uplift from seeing particularly one of your own babies, one of our kids when they were small, but even other people's children; or even looking at a field. But I've never had this thing, I don't know what you call it – this spiritual 'seeing the light', if you like – the Holy Spirit descending upon me.

On the other hand, some people have had much more specific and dramatic visions – including Mrs Lynch, a West Indian Christian who has suffered much illness and pain:

> I remember one night, I wasn't very well really, I was in terrible pain: it was about three or four o'clock, and I started to pray, you know. I love praying. I will just pray for a few minutes, and then I was just thanking God for giving me grace – you know, grace and courage and strength to stay with him and to know that he is with me. So I was praying, and I was there thanking him, you know. And after a while I can remember just seeing the words of God written, and I can remember plain that they were all gold, and golden colour. The background was like blue, pale blue, and I could see the words, 'Let not your heart be troubled, neither let it be afraid.' And you know, I felt so happy, and I began to praise the Lord, and thank him for hearing me and answering my prayer. And you know, it's funny enough, but I could feel as if somebody was just hugging me – just embracing me and hugging me. It was so lovely and I felt so good.

For others, the vision they see has no detail: it is simply one of presence and intense light. For a Muslim, this is not surprising, because God is described in the Quran as *nūr*, light. One Muslim described how he helped his wife into prayer by encouraging her to concentrate on light as the basic image:

> When a person starts his prayers he breaks his contact with the rest of the world, and he is in a direct communion, or communication, or contact with the Creator of this universe. I feel myself to be in front of him, and in a position that I can express my problems to him, I can communicate to him what I want to, I can seek his help. And at one time, soon after the

> wedding, my wife said that she found it difficult to concentrate on God. When she wanted to pray, she could not think about God. And I told her that my own experience is, that, if you are unable to concentrate, you should close your eyes and think that you are in front of a lot of light, a lot of energy. And then you will start a feeling about it. And she said, 'Well, I can't; even if I close my eyes, I can't see things like that.' And I had to advise her that in that case she could look towards the bulb, just for the initial experience; and once she gets used to it, then she will be in a position to concentrate. In the Holy Quran there is an *ayat*, a statement, which says: '*Allah nuru samawati wa'l'ardi*' [xxiv. 35]. It means that God is *nūr*. *Nūr* is like light or energy, very powerful.

The image of light is one we've already met among the Sikhs. When Mr Gurmukh Singh Bansal was describing how Sikhs cultivate in prayer a 'Third Eye' through which they see God, I asked him what he saw with this inner eye. He answered: 'If you close your eyes you see something, which is like – you could say, Light; or something bright. The more you pray, the more light you get; and the more peace of mind you get.' He went on to say: 'When you are really close to God, you get an injection through your body.' I asked him if he could really *feel* it. 'You can feel it, yes,' he said. 'It's like somebody giving you an electric shock – like somebody touching you with an electric shock, and it goes straight through your body and relaxes you.'

Another Sikh, Sarbjot Singh Hyare, who is a doctor in a blood bank, emphasised the physical reality of this third way of perceiving, when I asked him how, in prayer, he could be sure that he wasn't just talking to himself. 'It's like having a third sense,' he answered, 'a sense that there *is* a presence. When you're talking to yourself, you know that there's no presence around you. But when you're praying, you know that there's something else, and that you're getting some rebound.'

For Dr Pancholi, that 'presence' beats against him in prayer, in a way which is as realistic as the rough-and-tumble of his daily work as an engineer:

> Because I am an engineer, in my lifetime I have met a lot of rough people, and all they talk is very bad language. And I have to deal with them at various levels. On the job, I have to be very, very strict with them. I have to swear at them even at times, to kick them, to push them out, because we are losing a lot of money. But once we have done that, once we go away

> from that, then I always think the one real thing is our God – Aum. And I pray to him, 'Please guide me, what I should do in the circumstances?' So that is really beating me, like beating waves. It's really hammered into me that he is there. So whenever I'm in trouble, or whatever I do, I must think of him, and just ask for his help. And he somehow gives me help. He directs me what to do, you know, even in distress.

For Jacqueline Rapson, that presence became real as a love surrounding her daughter when she was very ill – and her daughter *also* felt it, even though she was scarcely conscious, and even though she herself was not looking for that 'encounter with love' in prayer. It was as though a second person was present:

> My eldest daughter was quite ill; and when you're on your own, as I was, you tend to think, How am I going to cope? For five days I stayed in the hospital with her, and it was just through prayer, and knowing that I *wasn't* on my own, that I was able to cope with each day as it came. Prayer showed that there are *two* people who loved her and cared for her – which also made me feel better. I know Christ was working in her life, even though she couldn't see it for herself. Sister Charity [an Anglican nun] went in to see her and held her hand all day, and Gillian said later she felt a very warm glow, a very warm feeling; and she's never forgotten it. Only a few months ago, she said to me, 'It wasn't just a warm feeling, Mum, it was a feeling of love.' And I said, 'Love for Sister Charity?' So she said, 'Well, no, not really. It was just a feeling of love that surrounded us.' I've never told her that you can feel that feeling in prayer. It was just something that she experienced herself.

It's not surprising, therefore, that Hindus deliberately cultivate this sense of physical presence in prayer, by creating as many visible representations of the Divine as they can, in their temples and shrines – and by treating those images as being themselves alive. Dr Gupta, another distinguished engineer, engaged in high-level research, told me about this in Bradford:

> Every Sunday I go to the temple, and I hardly miss any Sunday. So on that day particularly I have very good thoughts, very good feelings. God lives everywhere but still the temple gives a feeling in you – and that feeling cannot be expressed in words.

I asked him, 'What do you do, when you go to the temple?' He answered:

> When you go to temple, first of all (according to the Hindu

> traditions) you can't take shoes inside the main hall, where the idols of Lord Krishna and Rama have been installed. . . . As soon as you enter, you feel that you are in front of Lord Krishna and Rama. So automatically the feeling comes: I'm not praying because I *have* to pray, but when you go in, you feel yourself that you should do this. So actually, when you are in front of the Lord, in that hall you can find that all your five senses can be satisfied: that's why we are having a very beautiful idol of Lord Krishna and Rama, so that you can concentrate. So your eyes are busy, your ears are busy listening to very beautiful music and hymns and songs. Your tongue is busy in chanting the name of the Lord. So in this way your senses are well occupied. So now your body is there, and now you have to realise *why* we are here. Sometimes I feel such a joy I start crying. So that fills me with extreme enjoyment.

'Do you find that you're taken almost out of your surroundings?'

> That's right, that's right. I feel that this is indescribable joy which one can achieve.

'Do you get that experience of intense joy outside the temple? Or is it that special place which helps to create it?'

> This is the most important thing: this joy *can* be achieved anywhere, but it depends upon the sound you have there. If you go to the pub, the atmosphere is very different. So you can't say that if you go to the pub you can concentrate and have the same type of joy. In the temple, it's very difficult to say that bodily I'm there. Physically I'm there, but mentally I'm maybe somewhere else.

Detachment

That last reference, to going 'out of the body', connects prayer with meditation. Meditation, where it has no reference to God (see pp. 86–88), is obviously not going to produce a sense of presence. Its aim is complete detachment from your surroundings and even from your own thoughts. But it does have unmistakable consequences, including 'out of the body' experiences, as Mr Poey, a Chinese Buddhist originally from Malaya, told me – though he also emphasised how important it is not to *aim* for those consequences, since that would be a form of attachment to this world and its experiences:

> I will get up some time before my breakfast. I'm a man not

strictly bound by dogmas of tradition and so on. And I will go there and chant. As the Buddha has taught, there are two vibrations in this world: one is good, and the other one is not favourable. The one that is not favourable relates to things like the noise from aeroplanes, motor cars and so on. The other one is good; and, therefore, he has taught the monks in Pali what to recite when they are chanting, so that the good spirits, the gods, the deities will help them, and so that the bad spirits will not disturb them. And I discussed it with the famous monks, and they said, 'Yes, it's good for you to learn how to chant.' And from a scientific point of view I can definitely say that it is a fact; because if I'm angry with you, then my voice is different and you also will be angry. But if I could talk with you softly and in a gentle voice you will help me: you will be very friendly with me. So, therefore, I learnt how to chant from the monks. When we chant, this produces good vibrations, and it's believed that the good spirits will come to you, to your house, and this will help you to the good. And, therefore, I wish my wife, my children, my family, and people all around us to be happy, to enjoy long life and so on; and after that I spend a few minutes to contemplate – to reflect what I've done and what I should aspire to do in the future. You see, our minds are like wild horses, and even if we keep them down, they still keep on running. But sooner or later the horses will tire. And so the same thing with chanting, with meditation. When we try to meditate, that is, to still the mind (and according to the Buddhist concept there are forty objects which you could meditate on) – the best, as I was taught by a famous Thai monk and also by a Sri Lanka monk, is to meditate on our breathing. So: we sit down quietly and let our breath go naturally. Sometimes we breathe fast then slow, deep then shallow. And we must be conscious of it all the time. Well, of course, sometimes my wife will talk to somebody, but we're not supposed to be disturbed by it. You say, Yes, I hear them talking, but it doesn't matter; keep on and on about our breathing; always thinking that now I am breathing longer, slower, shorter, deeper and so on. And eventually I found that if I could do that long enough, there are days when I find that my breathing becomes so very shallow, I feel as if I'm floating. Of course I'm not floating, but I do feel very light. And I have confirmed that myself by practising yoga, by doing what we call the dying pose: you just lie down flat and completely relax your muscles and all that, and your breath will

> become shallower, and shallower, and you feel very light.

It occurred to me to ask how he can be sure that he is *not* floating. After all, several meditation movements claim that it *is* possible to fly around the room. He laughed and said:

> I'm not ready to confirm that! I'm aware I'm *not* floating, but I feel very light. I feel as if I'm floating, but I know I'm still sitting there. But I feel I'm very light, and I do not breathe hard; my breathing is so smooth, it makes my body very light. Well, that is a good sign. But the Buddha has warned people of course (you might know that), that we are not supposed to take delight in developing our psychic powers in doing miracles. There are no miracles. There are no miracles today. Nobody is performing miracles. Jesus Christ performed miracles, Buddha also performed miracles; but there are no miracles now: in those days science was in its infancy. Nowadays the magicians do tricks: they understand the tricks, but the laymen do not understand. So there are no miracles. All we know is that by meditation we want to improve and purify the mind.

And that's exactly what a different kind of Buddhist – a Zen Buddhist – also said. He began by distinguishing three different kinds of human activity: first, there's everyday living, aiming to get particular things done. Then, he went on:

> There are other activities like running bare-foot through the grass, which are not, as far as one can see, task-centred activities. To make that a task would be to ruin the situation by being conscious of it. Meditation is a third kind of activity. I think the peak experience for me was when I was about twenty-nine: I had this stiff, this rather stiff Quaker *persona*, and this 'respectable-citizen', rather Ibsenian view of the world; and I had also, as a child, suffered a lot of poverty. We lived in County Durham, in a colliery village, and things were scarce. But in addition to that, my father was a very, very violent man, and I was a battered child – systematically sort of battered; and this had a tremendous effect, I think, on me, and was one of the reasons I was in Quakerism, I think: it was a sort of container, a sort of metal container, and the pacifism was very important to protect my own violent feelings – because I'm a terribly passionate sort of person by nature. And I had really been wrestling, going to some meditation groups and some sensitivity groups, for some time; and at one of them, I felt physically sick at, revolted at, the whole experi-

ence. I was up against something I couldn't deal with. And I had been really touching, remembering, reliving the violence that my father had done, the fist across my head, the kicks, and my wetting the bed when he would attack me in the middle of the night, when I was asleep. I think the worst thing was when he would club me with his fist when I was actually asleep; and I would wet the bed, and the shame of that I was reliving; because I used even then to wake up in the middle of the night, in the late twenties, and hear a door, or a gate, and sweat with fear. It has a very deep imprint on you, such an experience. And I was up against all this, reliving it, and I was frightened stiff and I was physically sick and vomiting almost; and I decided that I wasn't going to go back for the last session. I wasn't. I couldn't stand it, it was too difficult – I was busy, I had all kinds of excuses, I had all sorts of things. But I was really afraid. And then on the day of the experience (the meditation group was that night), I decided I was going to go. Come hell or high water, I was going to go. And I had the most amazing religious experience. I really was no longer afraid. And I was bathed in love, and everything seemed exciting, and everybody seemed marvellous; and they were loving, and there was so much attention and affection. Only an hour before, everything had seemed a tremendous harassment. And I remember walking down the road to the group, just skipping along, you know. It was pouring with rain, but it was like a summer's day. And I remember seeing the bricks in the wall. I'd never noticed bricks before: they were fantastic, the patterns of them, and my visual sensation was like an artist; I wanted to get some paint and a brush, and just sit and paint it. There weren't any worries, I wasn't being pressed to go anywhere, I felt totally complete within myself, relaxed, loving. And it still feels that way now, although it's twelve or thirteen years ago. I was aware of great forces outside myself, benign and benevolent forces, rather like lying in a warm sea, you know, and you're struggling against it. Suddenly you realise, that if I stop struggling, I'll simply float. And that experience remained with me to this day. It went away gradually over the weeks, so it was less intense. But I still have it, and I still feel the lightness of it, and I've felt it again several times, since that time.

So experiences generated in religious contexts may be very dramatic indeed. But the suspicion, which Mr Poey expressed, of psychic whiz-kids – and of fraud – was shared by Pandit Pandya – who, in order to *be* a pandit, has to be well-trained in all aspects of Hindu life. I asked him what he made of the so-called *siddhi* powers. These are the eight supernormal powers, which include the power to postpone the moment of your death, or to leave your own body while still alive. He said:

> I don't believe that thing. I don't believe that in India people have got powers to go from this body. I don't believe in that thing. Some people say that they see *pictures* like that, and something comes to mind and they don't get to sleep all night – some pictures come, like on the TV, and they don't look at it even, because they think that by night they will get up and something will happen and they will be afraid. But I have never experienced that thing. And there's no thing for the body so that the soul goes out and comes back, never.

I asked him how he accounted for the many stories that one hears about this happening. 'They're stories,' he said, 'just stories. Never in my fifty years of life have I experienced such things.' But what about the rather less spectacular things – like healing the sick, or finding objects which have been lost (both of which *have* been claimed by other people we talked to)? 'All magic tricks,' answered the pandit: 'All magicians. You might have seen it on TV – magic. They keep the cards up here in their sleeve. These are all magic tricks.'

Well, that's a healthy scepticism, when you remember how easily people can be exploited religiously – and what big business religion has now become. But even without those extraordinary powers, meditation *can* be a dangerous thing to do: you can, for example, go as lifeless as a stone; and if you don't have the right knowledge (if you are too young), you may not be able to come back. Mrs Chauhan is a Hindu holy woman, who has learnt and practised many of the most far-reaching Hindu rituals and prayers. Here she describes the very difficult prayer through which she makes contact with the dead:

> Yes. That time I will pray, and it is a different prayer, and I will give you the answer [to the question of what has happened to a dead person – in what form, for example, have they been reborn?]. This is a very special cycle for the prayer: it's very difficult: it takes a long time for the prayer. So if I want to find out, if a person has died, which way he has gone, it takes plenty time. Then I give the answer. God gives me the answer. If God refuses, then I stop.

I asked her, 'How long does the prayer take?' She said:

> It takes three hours. Before I was married, I used to do this prayer. One woman came to me at home and said, 'My father has died three months ago: I want to find out why he has died, and what his end is, but he won't talk to me.' So I take the three hours of prayer, and I find out what her father won't say, then I give exactly the answer. After I got married, I have no time to pray this, so I stopped. But when my children are all grown up, then I do this again. But not now. You see, if you want to give the answer for the dead body, it's a very bad prayer. So my child will sigh and say: 'What is wrong? My mother does not give me any answer.' Because when I'm starting my prayer for the three hours, my body is like a stone – a dead body; and the children will have a lot of worries about it. So I stop.

So the experiences in prayer and in meditation may be dramatic. Far more often they are not. In the case of prayer, they are a simple, steady adherence to God, in which, as this Muslim says, the attributes of God are worked *into* life:

> Prayer is communion with God. You are talking to him. God says, 'I am nearer to you than your jugular vein.' He lives within us. In fact he says, 'I dwell in your heart: your heart is my temple.' And when we pray, we do *dhikr* (that is, remembrance of God). *Dhikr* doesn't only mean saying, *Allahu, Allahu* [O God, O God]; it means living it: living the qualities of God. When the holy Prophet said, 'Embue yourselves with the Divine Attributes,' what he meant was, 'You must live the quality of the attributes.' *ArRahman* is one of the attributes of Allah; so is *arRahim*, beneficent and merciful: that means that *you* must show compassion and beneficence to others. That is what the holy Prophet says.

In a similar – though also very different – way, a Hindu learns to see and experience God in all appearance. As Mr Singh put it: 'The One says, I am in the mountains; I am the Himalayas, the highest of the mountains; among the shining ones, I am the sun; at night, I am the moon, and the light that comes from the moon. I am everywhere.'

Is Prayer Talking to Oneself?

So prayer is to confront and talk to the Divine – to God, however imagined or described. But the question obviously arises (and I asked it of everyone I met who engages in prayer), 'How do you know that you're not just talking to yourself?' After all, many people (as we've just seen) describe prayer as a conversation with God – Mr Mohammed has just said that: 'Prayer is communion with God: you are talking to him.' But as I put it to him and to others: 'You don't actually *see* God, so how can you be sure that you're not just talking to yourself?'

We've already seen one answer to that question, in chapter 3. That was the answer which said that there seems to be an answer – a come-back – which is not created by oneself, and which is entirely different from thinking things over or talking to oneself while doing the washing-up.

But apart from that, there were two other main ways of answering that question. The first was to say, 'Well, maybe I *am* talking to myself; but does it matter?' The point is that something does seem to happen, whatever's going on – as Mrs Iles, a part-time catering assistant, said:

> I *could* be talking to myself. I mean, that's the first sign of madness. But it's inbred in you – you know, you've gone to church – that there is someone there. There's been several times where your faith, I think, pulls you through. There really has been. As I've said, we've been really short of money, we get paid at the end of the month – and I don't earn a lot, being part-time. You've got to the stage where you've thought, you've barely two ha'pennies to rub together, how on earth are you going to manage? Then all of a sudden someone gives you back the money that you lent them – on the very same day that you hadn't got any money. And you think, That's impossible: how did they know I didn't have any money? And that's the very day they give you something back returned. You've run out of bread and someone says, 'Oh, I forgot to pay you back.' I've got one of those everlasting cupboards that people borrow things out of – or I've got a kind face. And it comes back in a measure that's so precise, the very thing you need is what's given back to you.

Ray Turner also thought, when he first started praying, that God couldn't be 'there'; but then he found something different was happening. I had asked him the same question, whether he thought he was talking to himself:

> When I first experienced, I did think that to myself. And I thought, Really, it's only like those slumber moments when

you're going to sleep, when you're neither awake nor asleep, and all I'm doing really is relaxing – it might be yoga or whatever you call it; it's not really God. But if it wasn't, if it's not God, then the things that I do besides praying – now – that I've never done before, it doesn't make sense: those sleeping moments, this yoga and relaxing things, they don't instil into you to *do* things. You asked about my faith. I used to think that faith was something you had. I don't believe that any more. Faith is something you do. To me now, faith is a verb. It's not a noun, it's a verb. These moments that I spend in prayer make me different. Sometimes it doesn't last very long, and I drift back into the sort of lackadaisical way I was before; but there's something – I keep saying that I spend too much time doing things and not spending enough time with my family but go on doing the things I'm involved in. And I can't really say why I do it, except that something's pushing me. I'm convinced, though I can't prove it in words – I couldn't write an equation that it points to God – but I'm convinced that he's there. If you could prove it you could convert the world, I suppose. I can't prove it. I just know.

But there was another, quite different, answer to the question, 'If you haven't seen God, how do you know, when you talk in prayer, that you're not just talking to yourself?' And that was to say, 'But I *have* seen God' – including God on a bus:

It was in India. I was coming to England. I was going to board a bus, and there was a naked person, and he didn't have any fare. He wanted to travel in the same bus. The conductor said, 'Listen: until you pay, you can't travel on the bus.' I said to the conductor, 'Look, if he wants to go, let him go, I will pay for him.' So I paid for him. We were only about two miles from the place where we set off; the driver lost his control of the bus, and the bus turned over sideways. There were only six or seven passengers in it – and myself and my wife, and we had a little baby. And believe you me, the bus went in a tunnel sort of thing, on the side of the road, for nearly ten to twenty yards – about twenty to twenty-five yards, this way. It was all dust inside, all full of dust. But nobody was hurt. We were taken out by people, those who were nearby. And I was asking everybody, 'Where is that naked person?' Now it's not that I have listened to this story from somebody; no, I have seen it, because I paid his fare. And that guy wasn't there. That is the proof which I can say, that God is there.

Mr Gurcharan Singh Kundi, to whom that happened, is a Sikh. For Hindus, the idea of 'seeing God' is just as literal and natural, because the Divine becomes manifest in *all* forms of appearance. That's why (as we've just seen) Dr Gupta is in the presence of God when he is in front of the images of Krishna and Rama in the Temple. Those images are *more* than photos or signposts pointing to God: they become the manifestation of that reality within human range. The art and iconography of Hinduism are the cultivation of this transfer, *from* representation *to* becoming what is represented. This was explained to me by Mr Ladd, the headmaster of a Gujerati school, attached to a Sri Krishnan temple:

> We concentrate our mind – or, say, heart – with the image of the idol. We believe that that Krishna is in my heart. So we pray like this, concentrating on the fact that Krishna is in my heart. In fact we believe that in every person, God is there – in every person, whether old or young, or anybody; every person has God in his or her heart.

But since, for Hindus, *Brahman*, the true reality which underlies all forms of appearance, becomes manifest in *any* form of appearance, it follows that God can become visible in human form – or in other words, can become incarnate. Whereas some Christians at present seem to be puzzled about how incarnation (in their sense) can happen, for Hindus it happens all the time. Therefore a Hindu may literally see God in front of him, and talk to him in a way which is concentrated in a particular human person; and that's exactly how the followers of Satya Sai Baba regard him. So when they pray, they often get a visible appearance of Satya Sai Baba – and others may also see God in that literal way, as Pranav Patel remembers:

> You can actually feel the connection. The Aum sound [see p. 71] not only gives you control of your breath, in the sense that you can breathe in more deeply and so on, but mentally it gives you connection. I had a friend of my friends, in Sheffield, Dr Guriya: he went down to Sheffield, and one of the congregation (it was a church) tried doing Aum, and he got the connection, in the sense that he saw Sai Baba. And he didn't know who Sai Baba was. So that's how I see it. If you've got strong enough faith (and of course, back to your past life as well [*karma*]), you can get the connection.

What does an incarnation of God look like, and what does he do?

Vismita Patel, a library clerk in Bradford, recalls the first two times she saw Satya Sai Baba:

> The first glimpse I got was a little bit of his hair while he was sat in the car, and I thought, 'What is so important about him?' It was a lovely atmosphere, the crowd was all happy, and they were all cheerful and they were all very happy to see him, and I was happy myself, and I could not understand it. I thought, 'He just looks like everybody else, the same human body' – that's what I saw. The next time I saw him clearly was when he was walking through the crowds. We were all seated outside. We waited very patiently; and as my doubts grew, they were washed away; and I had the feeling that he knew what I was talking about, and he was answering back: if I said, 'He's not really materialising *vibhuti* [manifestation of superhuman power], it's probably up his sleeve', all he did was look at me directly in all these crowds, and he said, 'I'll give it to the person next to me and not me.' So I had a very good view of this, and I thought, 'Well, it can't be magic.' The next day I had another doubt, and so he kept on coming on, and my doubts were washed away one by one.

I asked her what *vibhuti* is. She said:

> It's a wave of his hand: one minute it's not there, and the other minute it's there, in his hand. And he gives it as a little *prasad* – a little gift for you to take. It's to show his love. He gives people pendants, lockets, rings, saris.

But that literal way of 'seeing God' depends on the whole Hindu understanding of the relation between this universe and *Brahman*, which other religions don't share. Even Sikhism, which arose out of an Indian context, denies the regularity of incarnation in that sense, because the living Guru, the Guru Granth Sahib, makes any different kind of manifestation of God unnecessary. Surinder Singh Hyare made this distinction between *avatar* (incarnation in and through a human life) and the continuously living God in the Guru Granth Sahib, when I asked him the same question – how can he know that God is there, when he never sees him?

> In our prayer we concentrate on the Almighty who is everywhere, who hasn't got a shape – we just remember his attributes. You can say it's a third sense, or something like that. You can't see him. We can see the Book all right, but the

> force that is working through that Book, that you can't see: that you can only feel. Because we think that our Holy Book is the sort of living God who can give us advice on every matter.

I asked him whether that is at all like the Hindu idea of *avatar*, of God becoming manifest in the world. He responded:

> *Avatar* is in human form, you can say, but *avatars* are very few – there are only a few in the whole of history. We take the Book as living: an *avatar* is gone. They are only for certain times and they are gone. But we take this Guru as living, and we get guidance from that thing.

Still, despite the contrast, Sikhs do, in a sense, see God in and through the Holy Book, as Mr Hyare said. But for Muslims, the very possibility of seeing God in *any* sense is not simply unnecessary, it is impossible – indeed, it is a serious blasphemy to suppose that God could come within the range of human senses. This was made clear by Hajji Cassim Mohammad:

> To be a Muslim, in the first place one must have *iman*. *Iman* means belief in God – belief in an unseen being. Now we are told that we must worship God as if we see him, but we know we cannot see him. But he sees us. So we are conscious that he sees us. Not only that, but we're not even allowed to have an idea of what God looks like. If we did, we would be limiting him to time and place. And God is limitless and placeless. In fact he is time itself.

As a Shia' Muslim put it very briefly, 'You can see God by the *iman*, by heart, not by sight.' Yet even Muslims can see, quite literally, the splendour of God – the sort of after-glow of his glory. We've already heard Mr Khan describing God as *nūr*, light; and Mrs Khan agrees with him: 'God is One. He is the extreme power. He gives us everything. He is just light, pure light.' I said: 'I notice you use the word "he": do you think of God as more masculine than feminine?' She answered: 'I don't think there is any question of thinking "masculine" or "feminine" about God; because God is light.'

It might seem equally impossible for Buddhists to see God, since, as we are often told, Buddhists do not believe in God. But to say that is to make the mistake most commonly made in the West about Buddhism. As we've seen, most Buddhists *do* believe in a god or gods, but not as the One from whom this universe is derived, and who remains independent of it. But in *their* sense of

God, some Buddhists do see God – and many other spiritual realities as well. In fact, for Mr Ugyan Norbu, a Tibetan Buddhist, the air is so full of spirits that he has to use a knife slowly in the kitchen in case he cuts a spirit in half:

> At home, in my mother's place, we always fill seven bowls of water, every morning and every evening; and I have heard that we do that because we believe that there are spirits everywhere, and some of the spirits who are living there are feeling they are thirsty. In reality – in truth – they are not thirsty, but they are feeling their own thirst. And if you have the water available there, then even though they are not drinking, they have the satisfaction of drinking there, and the feeling that they have drunk and that they are no longer thirsty.

I asked him whether he had ever seen or sensed one of these spirits:

> No, I haven't. But I believe there are six realms of spirits – so some people believe in ghosts, and ghosts are one kind of spirit; and there are many kinds of spirits. Tibetan Buddhists believe, for example, that if you whip your knife across, like this, you mustn't do this, because this harms certain spirits. We can't see; but we can't see the wind: but we know that the wind, if it's strong enough, we feel it. The fact is the wind is there. Wind is an element which can be proved. But I think maybe the spirit is more refined. But we think the spirits have their senses, and therefore we've got to be very careful.

So not surprisingly, the very purpose of many Tibetan religious practices is precisely to give visual form to what are otherwise subtle concepts – including God – as we've already heard from Twewang Topgyal. But he went on to make the point that Buddhists need to see, not only God, but also his opposite, the punishment of hell, in order to live a realistic life. I had asked him whether the gods and demons, so vividly portrayed in Tibetan monasteries, really exist. He answered:

> A lot of these pictures are for the purpose of visualisation. Presumably we want to have some sort of a concept of hell, and therefore one has got to have some sort of ghastly picture of a physical environment, and so on. They are portraits of what hell is all about.

I asked him why we have to have a picture of hell. He said:

> There are two levels: if one is at a very elementary level [in the

> process of reappearing], then I think one really needs to be frightened of doing something; and therefore there must be some sort of penal restriction; whereas if one's ideas are slightly more developed, then I think that hell itself is a creation of the mind. *I* would like to think that it really doesn't exist – it is a creation of one's own, whatever you call it, *karma*, or lack of understanding, or ignorance.

Other Experiences in Religion

So far, in this chapter, we've been exploring what happens to people in the experiences of prayer and meditation. But there are many other so-called 'religious experiences' – profound moments which people remember. As we shall see in the chapter on family life, for some Jews the most important religious experiences occur at the times of transition in the family – when a boy becomes *bar mitzvah*, or at a wedding. Some Christians have their own 'time of transition' which they can remember, when they were baptised as adults, not as infants. For one Christian, it was a fairly general memory of a happy occasion:

> I can remember it very vividly – it was such a lovely feeling, such a restful feeling. I was only about fourteen, and I just felt so nice, and so much alive, and so happy, and I think that's been with me. I was so fortunate to feel that, you see, so fortunate.

But for another, it had a more distinct content:

> Well, when you come up [out of the water], it's a bit like – light, I suppose. The first thing is just a great sensation of light. But apart from that, it was very ordinary – I mean, it's like getting thrown in the swimming pool. It's wet, and you're under water for a few moments, and if somebody wasn't holding on to you to pull you back up again, I suppose it would be pretty horrible.

And then, beyond Baptism, there is the experience of receiving the Holy Spirit, which some Christians call a second Baptism, and which may result in speaking with tongues or in seeing visions – or in a kind of transition to another level of joy. We've already seen how Mrs Lynch described one of her experiences in prayer: here she describes what it feels like when she is speaking with tongues:

> It's something you can hardly explain because you feel so

> different. You feel as though you were transformed – as if you weren't in this world at all. It's something special really. For me to explain and for you to have the experience is two different things. You feel just happy, you feel as if you weren't in this world, as if you were transformed – as if you were taken away out of your own body – as if you were in a special place. And you know, you felt just happy and joyful. And even when that feeling is over, you still feel that joy within you.

The after-effect was also remembered by a young Pentecostal Christian, Michael Stevenson:

> For me, after I was filled with the Spirit, it was one of the happiest times of my Christian life, because I felt so much joy in myself, that I really – I got filled, one night in my bedroom, and when I went to bed I was so happy that I couldn't sleep. I was tossing and rolling, you know. I was really happy. I think being filled with the spirit initially brings great joy, OK? And then after that it begins to give you strength to live your Christian life.

Sikhs, with their devotion to the Guru Granth Sahib, have their most powerful religious memories associated with their living Guru. But they may also have a comparably deep experience when they meet a particular teacher. This happened to Mr Harbans Singh Sagoo, who, as we've already heard, is a follower of Sant Puran Singh, an East African Sikh leader who was then living in England. I asked Mr Sagoo what he felt when he first met Sant Puran Singh, whom he calls Baba-ji, as a mark of respect:

> The very first day when I went to visit him, I was virtually speechless. There was this aura around him, and there was one other person with me. He was in the room, and we went and sat close to him, and the influence that he radiated was so strong that I was not only speechless, my ears were burning, as if I had blood-pressure and I had a frog in my throat. I just could not utter a word, and inside me, I had a very, very strong feeling of guilt. It sort of made me look inside me, and I thought to myself, 'You've wasted so much of your time and you've done nothing.' That 'nothing', I could not define at that time. But as I thought about it, that 'nothing' was that, in the religious sense or in the spiritual sense, I had attained nothing, so that twenty-five or thirty years of my life had just wasted away. Then, of course, when I started going regularly to his company, there was one thing that came very strongly to me,

> and that was that all the material wealth, all the material things that one strives for (and these are also the teachings of the Holy Granth), all the material things that people strive for, people fight their wars for, are going to stay *here*; there's nothing to go with you, and nothing to benefit you in your life hereafter. And the only thing that is to benefit you is the name of God, upon which you must meditate. It wasn't a sermon that was preached to me in particular. This was something that I picked up in his company. Whenever we met him, the things that were talked about were always religious. There were certain of these things that made such a strong impact on my mind that I was, shall I say, transformed overnight to give up striving for this, that and the other, and to devote some time to religious activities, and that led me to baptism, and that has led me to taking a very active part in the religious life here in Leeds.

I asked Mr Sagoo if he still goes to visit Baba-ji, and if so, whether he still has the same feelings in his presence. He answered, 'Oh yes, though the feeling is not as strong – I'm saying that, probably because the guilt is not so strong: having chosen the path which he advocates, the guilt is not so strong.' Then he went on:

> I still find one thing, that I sometimes have problems in my mind that I want to discuss with him. There is guidance that I need, and I go prepared with these questions, but when I go there, my mind goes blank, because of his very overpowering personality. And then sitting with him, in the company of other people, many a time the problems that you have in your mind are answered through a discourse with questions and answers from other people, people in the *sangat* or congregation, and I come away having learnt more things than I actually wanted to, or that I might have learnt by asking the questions myself.

So the range of emotion and experience which gets entangled with religious life and becomes religiously important is enormously diverse. Dreams are religiously important, especially in the Eastern religions: to give just one example, Mrs Chauhan, the Hindu holy woman, remembers a dream as one of the key events in directing her towards her eventual way of life:

> When I started my prayer, when I'm nine years old, I saw a very nice dream: I followed the dream, and I reached success.

In the dream, first I saw a lion: on the lion I saw the one lady just sitting, very beautiful, and she gave her hand into my hand – when I'm nine years old. I've never forgotten that dream up to now.

Pilgrimage

But in the midst of all this diversity, one single event stood out in all these religions as the one most likely to produce intense and vividly remembered experience – and that event is pilgrimage. In all these religions, going on pilgrimage is an important way of being religious. For Muslims, every man must try to get to Mecca at least once in his life. For Jews, when the Temple was standing, it was equally an obligation to try to get to Jerusalem for the pilgrimage feasts – it is not an obligation now, but the journey to Jerusalem (especially to the Western or Wailing Wall, a surviving part of Solomon's Temple) is, as we shall see, an overwhelming experience. So is the journey to the Golden Temple of Amritsar for Sikhs. For Christians, pilgrimage is not an obligation; but the effect of a pilgrimage to Walsingham or Lourdes or to many other holy places is profound. Buddhists also have their places of pilgrimage, associated with the Buddha – in Sri Lanka, for example, the shrine of the Buddha's tooth and the Buddha's footprint. Hindus have many holy places – and holy people, to whom pilgrimage is made; and in the end, the end of death, Hindus hope to make the final pilgrimage of their ashes to the Ganges.

Here then are people from each religion describing their experience of many different kinds of pilgrimage:

Jews

Israel I love. Jerusalem is on a plane of its own. Jerusalem, I really feel, is (to coin a phrase) spiritually uplifting, absolutely. It's the feeling of the richness and the wealth of history and God, and of everything that has ever happened there. Going to the Western Wall, knowing that that is really the epicentre of what we have got left, that immediately brings back all the suffering the Jews have gone through, through the ages. I did break down – tears do come out from one's eyes – though I think I broke down more at the Tomb of the Fathers.

When I visited the Kotel, that's the Western Wall, in Israel for the first time, I was quite young – I was about fourteen, I think. And at that age and in that place I really felt that this is something important to me, and that this is something I will hang on to. It was a kind of certainty that I hadn't felt in any other way before – that this is me and this is who I am, and this is the thing that matters to me.

Going to Israel is like going home. The heart of it for me is to go to the Kotel, the Western Wall, to what we believe to have been Solomon's Temple (or a part of it). I think I probably gasped when I saw what I was looking at; tears poured down my face, and I wished that my father could have been there too – because Jerusalem was not a united city in his lifetime. Although I didn't put the little piece of paper into a crevice with a wish on it, I did put my hand on the wall. I did feel that, not only was I there, but I was there for him and a lot of other people who are outside our world now.

Christians

Five or six years ago my husband was sent home to die. And it was a miracle: he got over it. The first thing I did when he had his operation (this was in the middle of the winter) was come to Walsingham that same night. The Slipper Chapel was opened for me, and I spent about half-an-hour in there. And from then on, with the prayers of our friends, and Our Lady's intercession, he was cured, and he's well and fit today. Everyone says that they don't know how he got well. The doctors don't know. And I say it was through prayer; mainly Our Lady, and I have to give St Jude a little bit of thanks as well – you know, patron of hopeless cases; but without Our Lady he couldn't have done it. I went to Lourdes a few years ago, and the first thing I did when I came back from Lourdes was to come to Walsingham, and walk the Holy Mile, just to get back to sanity.

Muslims

The first pilgrimage to Mecca is an obligatory one. The rest is all on a voluntary basis; I'm grateful that by grace I went to that place. I can't express the feeling and emotion and the blessing – it's something each individual has to go and find out for himself. Regardless of what happens in the whole universe, that place will be always protected. There is no doubt whatsoever, and that is the promise from God.

Every Muslim's life ambition is to be part of the big '*umma* [the whole Muslim community] and to kiss alHajaru 'lAswad [the Black Stone], and go to Masjid alNabi where the prophet lies. And when you go there, the whole history of Islam comes before your mind's eye. I mean, you walk in those streets and find where the prophets have walked. And the whole history just comes like it is before a mind's eye; you feel sublime and you feel great.

There was a time when I stood there near the Ka'ba [the central shrine containing the Black Stone], and I felt that I wasn't on earth at all. I was on a different plane completely separated from earth. It's an experience you get there that you can't explain, really, in words. You feel it, you experience it. It's really difficult, because the pilgrimage, the *hajj*, is not easy on the physical body; but the experience that you get is so different, so beautiful.

Hindus

When I went to India to see Sai Baba, I think that was one of the most beautiful times of my life. I don't think I will ever forget it, even though I was too young to understand the real significance of Sai Baba. I felt there was something there, even though I was very young; and I knew then that he was God.

I feel more at home in India – although I'm very Westernised. You have to go to India for a whole year really, to know what the festivals are really like. I've seen *Holi* in Indian films, and it's great fun – but I'm missing out if I don't join in the real thing.

Buddhists

For us, a pilgrimage is to hear a lecture – as a pilgrimage: to hear the Dalai Lama, to hear some eminent Buddhist scholar. It's not just listening to a lecture, but a pilgrimage, because in Buddhism we talk all the time about the transmission of the *dharma*: and the transmission for us is not just a talking, or a communication, but almost a literal, physical, passing across – rather like the transubstantiation: it is a physical feeling of vitality that you get when you go to someone who has gone very far along the path. It is a finding and a being found.

When I was even a boy, we were taken to Nepal, where Lord Buddha was born. Near Nepal, there are two very high temples, Bhalyoulchoten and Phapashingon. I don't know when they were constructed, I can't remember; but they are very famous. So we go there for the pilgrimage, and we go there with full conviction, with no money – we just go very simply. When I was there, I felt that I've got to do a little bit more: I've got to do more. 'Yes,' I felt, 'this is worth doing, this is something good happening: I must do a little bit more.' Then it teaches me that always, when something good is happening, it tells that I've got to do a little bit more.

I went to Sripada, the Footprint of the Buddha, only about seven or eight months ago, and the feeling I have is complete peace, and as if nothing can harm you. And you are there, and the whole place is filled with peace and love, and loving kindness, that kind of thing. And I feel, What am I doing as a person? I should be trying – I mean this is my own feeling: I think, Oh well, I must do something to eradicate poverty in the world: I must do something worth while. I am here now, and I'll be just gone the next day and I have not fulfilled what I should do, or I have not made use of my opportunities that I have had. And then the same thing I experienced at Radipura, which is the ancient capital of Sri Lanka, where there is a statue of Buddha, the *Samadhi* statue, of the time when he was meditating; and I think it's Pandit Nehru who came there when he was Prime Minister of India: whenever he used to come to Sri Lanka, he used to always, evidently, come and stand in front of the statue; because he said that gave him absolute peace for the time when he was there. I have quite often stood in front of that statue, and I think to myself, Well, this is complete peace; and you are quite oblivious of everything else, the whole world as such. And this is complete peace.

Sikhs

I think the only time that I can remember feeling, as an adult, quite content, and actually feeling that it had something to do with religion, was when I went home for the first time after I'd been in this country for three years. And I went to visit the Golden Temple; and I think that was the only occasion on which I felt really good and happy. That felt like being close to, you know, close to that superhuman power, and it made me feel content: it was peaceful, just being there. I was only there for a couple of hours, in the temple, and it really did make me feel good.

So these moments of intense experience are clearly memorable and important for those who experience them – so memorable that the first part of an answer to my original question falls into place. I asked at the outset what it is about religion which makes believers all too often so angry and divided from one another – creating, or helping to create, so many of the social and political problems of the world. Part of the answer, paradoxically is simply this: religions are the contexts in which people discover dramatic consequences of peace and presence. No amount of outside reduction or even ridicule (describing, say, the neurophysiology or the psychopathology of what is going on) will ever make unreal the discoveries which people claim in the exercise of contemplation, meditation and prayer. And that's *one* reason why people would rather die than abandon their faith.

But that's only part of the answer. Equally important is the fact that religions have to be *organised* if they are going to make sure that those routes toward discovery are going to be handed on to another generation. The strong and often intransigent authority of religions, demanding obedience over such issues as abortion (to pick up the recent example of the Spanish bishops), has *its* part to play in creating passion and divisive emotions. 'We are,' as Shaw once put it, 'overrun with popes' – and in saying that he was *not* thinking particularly of the Bishop of Rome!

In the next chapter, we shall look at the part which Scriptures play in religious life, and at the more general issue of authority and obedience.

5
The Word of God and Guru: Authority in Religion

Religious belief clearly releases people into dramatic and often overwhelming experiences – moments which are literally unforgettable. But religious life does not *depend* on those experiences – indeed, dramatic experiences, of the kind described in the last chapter, are rare. The foundations of a particular religion are much more often laid in a basic teaching or Scripture. Whatever our own individual experiences may be, the fundamental beliefs and practices of a religion rest on an authority which lies outside the individual. In its strongest form, that authority is regarded as *the* Word of God, a revelation from himself, which we have not created or invented. In its weakest form, the authority may be that of a teacher or guru, who instructs the individual but then leaves him or her to make out of that instruction what he or she will.

For Jews, Scripture consists of Torah, Prophets, and Writings (*Torah*, *Nebiim* and *Ketubim*, in Hebrew, hence, from those initials, it is often referred to as *Tanach*). For Christians, Scripture embraces what they call the old covenant, the old *testamentum*, or testament, but to it they add the new covenant, the new testament. Muslims believe that God did reveal his word in Jewish and Christian Scripture; but Jews and Christians have corrupted what was revealed to them, so the Quran revealed through Muhammad is the final seal of God's Word, confirming all that has gone before and correcting the corruptions which Jews and Christians have allowed to creep into *their* Qurans, their Scriptures. Hindus have many sacred writings, but lying close to the heart, for almost all Hindus, is the Song of the Lord, the *Bhagavad-Gita*. Buddhists cannot have the same ideas of revelation, and they are more likely to attend to a particular teacher; but they too, as many Buddhists have already said, have their devotion to the written records of the Buddha, in, for example, the Tibetan Scriptures, or in the Pali Canon. And for the Sikhs, their Scripture is a still-living guru, to be reverenced as such, the Guru Granth Sahib.

So all these religions have a resource of wisdom, strength and authority in what we can loosely call 'Scripture' – though each religion has a very different idea of what a Scripture, or a revelation, or a word of God, actually is. And even *within* each religion, there are very different ideas about the status of its own Scripture. Take the Bible, for example: did everything happen literally as it is described?

Scripture and Revelation

For some Jews, Torah *was* given, exactly as described, to Moses on Mount Sinai: millions saw the event, and it is confirmed anyway in experience. Mr Klein put this side of the argument about revelation, when I spoke to him in Manchester:

> First of all, there were about three million Jewish people present at this event, and they have handed down the news of this event through the generations. It is more of a fact that God appeared to the Jewish people at Sinai than any scientific imaginings or calculations about what might have happened in the last few thousand years, because any scientific theories are only based on certain constants. There is an assumption that certain things have remained constant, and this is only a theory which cannot be proved; whereas if a person comes along and says to you, 'I saw this', that is much more an acceptable criterion on which to base one's life. That's one side of it. That is connected with why we believe that the event happened. The second side of it is in the practice of the actual religion; because in the practice of the actual religion (in other words, in the practice of these laws which have been handed down to us, and in the study of the whole realm of Torah which has been handed down), we can feel in our lives, and see in our lives that this is the truth. The Torah is absolute and eternal. The Torah is the instrument with which God made the Universe and therefore the Torah is a link between the Universe and God; and therefore the laws of the Torah are the link between man and God.

But for other Jews, even a word like 'revelation' is suspect, let alone an acceptance of the literal transmission of Torah from God to Moses on Mount Sinai. Mr Cowan, a Reform Jew, put the other side of the argument:

> We have the Torah, which is the five books of Moses, and

each week (and I go regularly to the synagogue) we read from the Torah; and this is the basis of the Judaism which I believe in, which is natural for Jews; because within it, although the five books of Moses have got many stories which one is not obviously asked to believe happened exactly, there is something there which at least has a moral aspect, it has something behind it which is even active today. But 'revelation' is a word I don't often use, to be quite honest. I don't think in terms of revelations, so much as what I hear, and how it circulates through my mind, and through my feelings, and without perhaps giving it a name, it makes me do things, it makes me think in the way I do.

Probably the majority of Jews live somewhere between those two extremes, believing that something *did* happen on Mount Sinai, but not pressing too far for a historical judgement on exactly what, in detail. As a business journalist, Stuart Dresner no doubt has some sensitivity to the problems of getting accurate copy while on the move!

I think that the account of the giving of the Ten Commandments on Mount Sinai signifies that something big did take place then. I don't believe that the whole of the five books were given at that time, and in fact that's not even required – it's not even part of the official ideology that that was so. It's rather that the official theology, if you like, is that God revealed himself to Moses and dictated the Torah to Moses, stage by stage, throughout the wanderings of the children of Israel in the Wilderness.

The same sort of changes in attitude to Scripture seem to be happening also in Christianity. The days certainly appear to have gone when (as one person we listened to remembered) one couldn't even drop the Bible on the floor without getting into trouble. For some Christians, like the Pentecostalist, Mrs Lynch, the Bible certainly *is* the word of God in a strong sense:

The Bible, which is the word of God, wasn't written or printed, just as a person would take up a book and say, 'I'm going to write a book'. The Scripture tells us that the Bible was written by men of God who were inspired; they couldn't just write anything. As God led them through the Holy Spirit, they would write what God wanted them to write.

For a person like that (who happens to have suffered pain and illness for many years) reading the Bible, even reading single texts, can be very powerful in life:

> There was a time, about five years ago, and I remember I was a bit restless, you know, I wasn't feeling too good, and I was a bit anxious really; and I took my Bible to read. I couldn't find anything in it to read at all. I just couldn't find anything in the whole Bible to read, and I put it down; and after a while I took it up again, and I said, 'Right: anywhere I open it, I'm going to read it.' I opened the Bible and there was Corinthians, and I remember I was reading this Scripture where Paul was praying, when he was praying that the Lord would take away his infirmities, and he was praying, and the Lord said, 'No, my grace is sufficient to keep you.' And I read just that verse, and I read over, and over, and over, and over. And it meant so much to me, and I got up and I prayed; and I came downstairs, and I went in the kitchen and made a big breakfast. For weeks I hadn't made any breakfast; my husband always made the breakfast, because when I got up in the morning I felt so bad – the children going to school – so he always came down and made the breakfast, and then he calls me down, or sometimes he brings it up. And that morning he was in the bathroom, and I crept downstairs quietly, and I went in the kitchen, and I made a huge breakfast, and I shouted, 'Come down!' 'Oh,' he said, 'I'm coming down, I'm coming to do your breakfast.' And when he came down, the breakfast was on the table – I felt so good, because I knew then, I couldn't find anything to read, but the Lord gave me something at that time; and when I read it, it consoled me and I felt good, and I came down. And it was good.

Bible-reading is therefore a very important part of Christian life for many Christians:

> That plays a very important part, because the Bible is food – the Bible is like what food is to every human being. To a Christian the Bible is food because it strengthens him, helps him to walk – you know, makes him stronger. It encourages him, builds him, so the word is a very prominent part of every Christian life.

But for others, the Bible is a guide not far off a historical novel, as Peter Thompson told me:

> The status of Scripture is a guide; not really a historical novel,

> but I don't hold it as fact; I don't hold it as a book that you can't deviate from. It is a glimpse into the way life was 2000 years ago; and the way one person struggled to exist and to live, and how he affected other people.

So I asked him in what sense, for him, the Bible is inspired:

> I don't think they're inspired to the point that God was over the hand of the writer, and took the pen over, and wrote it out. But I think the people were inspired through the action of Christ. They saw something in this man, and this is why I think I'm attracted to him now: they saw something in him that was so marvellous, so inspiring, and so full of vision that they had to react and they had to do something about it – they had to put it down as they saw it, and this is a very individual thing. You know, you get ten people and they would each see it in ten different ways.

Peter Thompson is an Anglican. But Christians in other parts of the Church hold very similar views. Ray Turner is a Roman Catholic, and for him the Biblical record is a bit like the differences you experience when you've been to a football match and then see it on TV:

> I believe that it was written by people some seventy – or fifty, sixty – years after it actually happened, and that it was influenced very much by the fact of the Resurrection. For instance, some of the things in it, the Nativity, for instance, in my mind, probably was a humble cave where it happened; and Mary had the baby; and probably a couple of shepherds came in. There were no angels – I don't believe there were any angels singing; but after the Apostles realised that Christ was God, they said, 'Oh yes, remember? and all the angels came down – must have been, we knew who he was, didn't we?' The same with the Transfiguration – you know? I believe that they had a spiritual experience. I believe that when they went up the mountain to pray with Christ, they were so overwhelmed by his prayer, that they experienced this, just as I do when I go to Mass. But after they'd realised that the Resurrection had taken place, they probably sat down and said, 'Remember when we went up the mountain? and we saw Jesus with God on one side and Elijah on the other, remember?' They were only ordinary guys; and I've done it myself at the football match: I've seen it on the television afterwards and I've thought it was a different game. It's what influenced you at the time.

Therefore, many Christians we listened to use the New Testament to guide their lives into an imitation of Christ – and that, for them, is its importance. Mrs Emmett, for example, said: 'Almost all of my life, I try to keep in line with God, so as soon as I'm doing something wrong, I'm aware that it's wrong, and I'm already into trying to get it right: I try and think "How would Jesus handle this?"' However, as I said to her, surely Jesus didn't have four lively children to handle?

> No, he didn't; no. But he handled other things that perhaps weren't that much different really. It's just perhaps the circumstances are different. But the main thing is there. You know, crises, he was always in the midst of crises, which I seem to be in the middle of a lot. He always had such a nice approach about it all, a nice way about it all. And I tend to go for the most warming way out of it, when everybody's left with perhaps a little bit of warmth, really. I try to warm the thing up. Which I think is what Jesus did. Try to just keep the coldness to a minimum. I know, I definitely know, when I'm out of step with God's whole feel for his world.

Quran, Law and Order

For Muslims, as we've already seen in Chapter 2, the Quran really is *the* Word of God. So the Quran has a much less disputed authority and status: God has spoken through previous prophets, but only the revelation through Muhammad – who himself, according to Muslims, could neither read nor write – only *that* revelation has been preserved unchanged and uncorrupted. Mr Mohammed Hassan described the inimitable miracle of the Quran to me, emphasising its connection with all other revelation that has gone before it:

> God had spoken to Moses before; he'd spoken to Adam. God speaks beyond them all. The word of God has been sent by the Ten Commandments before. It's been given to Jesus, the Prophet of God, in a book; and the last one came by the Quran; and the miracle of the Quran is that it hasn't been changed; and God has said it's not going to be changed. The challenge to be able to change it was given to the genies and all other creations, to get together to make something similar – not even the same, similar; and they said, 'We can't.'

So strong is this sense of revelation – of what God has given or sent down as a whole 'package', so to speak – that it should ideally be read in its original language, Arabic, and it should certainly be recited in Arabic in prayer or liturgy, even though the worshipper does not understand that language. Mrs Qureshi, a road safety officer in Coventry, talked about this:

> The Quran came to the Prophet Muhammad in Arabic, so we are really reading something in its original language. That is something noble as well, that is a part of praying, or worship. But to be able to understand is even better, because Islam is not just reading Quran and learning the translation; Islam is a whole way of life.

So there is not the same variety of attitudes in Islam towards the status of its Scripture. What *may* be in dispute is the extent to which it is necessary or desirable to enforce traditional laws or penalties which are derived from the Quran or its interpretation in tradition – penalties such as cutting off the hand of a thief, or death for adultery, to give just two examples which have become familiar in the English press. There are two points to bear in mind here: the first is that Muslims do not expect their laws to be enforced for them in non-Muslim countries, though some would *like* the laws of this country to coincide with Islam – that point was made repeatedly; and second, those penalties are in any case extreme penalties – ultimate deterrents in social life. Since Mr Khan is a solicitor and a lecturer in law at Lanchester Polytechnic, this is obviously a matter to which he has given much thought:

> The whole idea of punishment is that the society is facing a problem with one of its members; and the society finds an answer which is best from the point of view of the individual as well as from the society's point of view. So Islam has laid down certain punishments, and those are the only punishments which can be given, and no more crimes can be invented by the state, unless they are implicitly covered by the provisions. Now there is one thing which is very much misunderstood in the West, and that is the question of amputation of the hand of the thief, that the hand would be cut off. So, the punishment has two aspects: one is whether it is to act as a deterrent, and the second is whether it will improve the individual as such. Now I have been to Saudi Arabia I think four times, and it was my intention (it has been, in fact, my intention all the time) to find people with amputated hands. And during those four

> visits, although I am very fond of walking and meeting people, I have never found a single person who had his hand missing. The reason is that when you have imposed this punishment (and again, don't forget that the punishments which are laid down by law are the maximum; they are not the minimum, that you must amputate the hand of a person: you have to find out why he has to commit theft), the deterrent aspect comes in. If you go to Saudi Arabia, you won't find any thefts. People would leave their shops open – the people who are selling jewellery, gold, all expensive things – they just put a net in front of it and go to the mosque. Nobody is watching it, nobody is guarding it, and nothing goes away from that shop. The reason is that the deterrent effect is there.

But if Islam has produced this 'better means', does it follow, in his view, that Islamic punishments should be introduced in this country? Mr Khan replied:

> I think it is a good idea. If the Government accepts it, fair enough. As long as the punishments are there, they may be under *any* name. You don't have to say that we are introducing them because they are Islamic punishments.

And what about capital punishment?

> If somebody has killed another? Capital punishment – killing a man – is allowed in Islam in two situations. One is when a person is fighting in self-defence, and the other is at the time of *jihad*, in the war. Other than those two situations, Islam does not accept capital punishment. If somebody kills another, the other, the persons who are the relations of the deceased (the dependants), they are given the right, either to seek compensation, or ask for his execution. If sufficient compensation is provided, obviously they will be more interested in compensation; because the man is dead, he can't come back. It is only in the case of revenge that they would insist that he should be killed. So Islam is rather in favour of not having a capital punishment, but it has not said that you can't have the capital punishment.

Remembering the film, *Death of a Princess*, which caused so much disturbance and upset after it was shown in this country, I asked about capital punishment for adultery:

> There is the punishment for the man. And the reason for that is, that the person who is married and has got his wife and

children, and he commits adultery, he *should* have been faithful to himself, to the Creator, to his wife, to his children. If he doesn't want his wife, he can get out, there are provisions in the law, but he doesn't want to utilise them, he wants to commit adultery. He can marry again if he wants to. But in society, all the problems start from a very small thing. And if the person is allowed to indulge in adultery, it would be difficult to control others, and therefore the best thing is to stop it in the beginning. And a person who commits adultery has to be punished, and, of course, as I said, this is the maximum punishment.

Hajji Cassim Mohammad is also professionally trained, as an accountant, and he now runs his own practice in Leeds. So he too has given thought to Islamic law and its application in the UK. And he agrees with Mr Khan that it can't be applied here, but that it does act as a deterrent in Muslim countries:

If this was a Muslim state, I would say that that law would have been applicable – for this reason; in England it's a Welfare State, and there is no need for a person to steal. If that person steals, he should be punished. And he isn't punished immediately, his hands are not removed immediately; it's only after many offences; it's a deterrent, an ultimate deterrent. And you will find that there are very few: I went to Mecca and Medina, and there are very few people walking about with one arm; because nobody wants to have their hand removed.

So the really basic point is that Islamic law can only be for Islamic countries: its authority cannot cover countries in which Muslims are in a minority. Most Muslims believe that the Quranic punishments *are* a deterrent, though a Shiite Muslim, in Manchester, added the comment that the Islamic requirement of a just society needs to be enforced just as much:

This country is not an Islamic country. The law which is laid down as Islamic law is for Islamic countries. We are talking about a country which is so secular, with so-called democracy, freedom, and so forth – it's not possible to have Islamic law applied in this country. Islamic law applies only for the Muslims in Islamic countries. And anyway, it's no good cutting the hands of a person when the masses are starving to death. You see, some countries have brought this Islamic law in front of the other nations so badly, it's unthinkable. For example, take Saudi Arabia, the richest country in the world.

> The wealth is in the hands of a few persons. Although the population is only a few, there is still a lot of poor people in that country. So when a poor, starved person, out of need steals because of starvation, then it's no good cutting the hands of the person. The person who governs, the Government, or the King, or the Ruler, whoever they are, they should find a solution by providing the food for the person.

There is, of course, a question here in Islam: as we shall see, repentance *after* death is not possible; so would it not be more just to imprison people, in order to give them a chance to repent – because the alternative is not simply the death penalty; the penalty may be one of eternal punishment? The answer we heard most often was, No, because the preservation of society is more important:

> The ideal – the aim – of man behaving is to make the perfect society, or the happy society – which everybody should strive to achieve; so the laws are to encourage the good and get rid of the bad. The punishment is for protection, not for revenge. The idea is to make law and order in society; this is why we use the punishments.

And in the same spirit, another Muslim added: 'I don't think punishment for adultery is *that* important, but I think punishment for rape, and crimes of that sort, should be tough and brutal.'

So there is no basic disagreement among Muslims about the high status of the Quran – as the word of God; but there *may* be disagreement about how literally it must be applied, or how much it can be interpreted – and that's an issue which is being worked out politically throughout the Islamic world.

The Living Guru

But these religions, Judaism, Christianity and Islam (which Muslims call 'religions of the Book') are not the only ones which have Scripture (to use that general word) as a fundamental resource of authority to help people in their daily lives. The deep devotion of Sikhs to the Guru Granth Sahib has already become obvious. To study the words of the living Guru *is* to worship God – hence the insistence that it should be five times a day: as Surinder Singh Hyare told me: 'Five times a day we have to study Scripture, which is a sort of praying to the God, and feel ourselves uplifted, you see, by coming close to nature and God by speaking through the prayer.' But in fact, *how* much it is studied does vary a great deal, as Jagat Singh Nagra observed:

> Some people can read the whole Guru Granth Sahib and they keep the Guru Granth Sahib in one of their rooms. And there are some other people who have learned a bit of it, and they can recite that part; or some people even haven't learnt a part: they recite only one or two words – *satinan wahi Guru, satinan wahi Guru.* But as long as they are saying it from the core of their heart and remembering God, even that is considered just the same thing.

As we've already seen, a Sikh can go to the Guru Granth Sahib with any problem: it is opened at random, and what is read is always relevant – especially in the naming of a child, where the first letter of the first word opened becomes the initial for the child's name. Otherwise, there is variation among Sikhs about the status of what is heard from the living Guru. For some, as we saw earlier, its authority is absolute, because, like the Quran for Muslims, it comes from God. For others it is advice which they must then decide about. I asked Mr Nagra, after he had described the different levels of study, where *he* would go for advice or decision if he had any difficult problem:

> We would go to a person, actually, or seek the guidance of the Guru Granth Sahib. We do that because it's a book full of all sorts of information; and then, if sometimes you cannot read, then you ask a granthi or a priest who will help. What happens is that they open the book at random and read what is on that page: specially sometimes there are some solutions.

When I was in Coventry, I also met Mrs Bhupinder Kaur Dhesi. She is a social worker for the Minority Group Support Services of the Coventry Education Department, so she is well accustomed to giving – and receiving – advice. I wondered how important the Guru Granth Sahib is for her, in her work, and how she uses it:

> I go to the Scripture – my Holy Guru Granth – because when I came here, that was a present given from my mum to me; and she said that whenever we need something, pray. So I've got that one. So whenever I'm worried about something, I just open that and read it; so that's the way I do it; and actually it's not really advice, it's the moral strength which I am looking for, and I get it from there.

I asked her whether she could open the book to find the winner of a horse race. She said:

> No, oh no; no: not for any selfish reason, because I think we accept these things: money comes and goes and it doesn't matter; and the many things we think of as natural things, we accept that. For my moral support, I get that from my religious book.

The Song of the Lord

Hindus have, not one, but many Scriptures, but close to the heart of almost every Hindu is the *Gita*, the *Bhagavad-Gita*, the Song of the Lord Krishna, declaring that much more is required than the ancient way of sacrifice to lead towards *moksha* or release: Mrs Pancholi, a primary school teacher in Leeds who has made a deep study of Hinduism, summarised what is for her the central message of the *Gita*:

> My favourite God is SwamiNara, but I also believe in what Lord Krishna has said in *Bhagavad-Gita*, 'Keep working, but don't expect any fruit.'

The *Gita* contains within it the answer to all problems – or at least all problems that really matter – though it is recognised as being difficult to understand in depth. It may require a guide; and the reliable guide can only be picked out or discerned by his or her own behaviour, not by some external qualification. Dr Gupta made the point that such guides are not easy to find in this country – and he, you remember, has *left* this country and returned to India, because of the problems of being a Hindu in this country:

> Our Holy Book is the *Gita*; and if you read it, and if you can understand it, you'll find the answer to all of your questions. The only question is, whether you can understand what is written there.

But if you *can't* understand it, to whom do you go for guidance?

> In this country, I think, the question is difficult: it's very difficult to find an expert person. But when somebody who comes from India or somewhere else and has authority, and has achieved or reached that level, we used to ask him.

But, I asked him, how do you recognise such a person? He

answered: 'Let me tell you: the person who does not want anything for himself, he is really a saint.'

So the *Gita* may exercise a strong authority and guidance in Hindu life – and many Hindus told us that they read it, and other Scriptures, every day. On the other hand, some Hindus reject strong controls of 'do this' or 'don't do that', and turn to Scripture, only as the mood takes them – as Mr Krishan Mittal told me; and since he is President of the Hindu Cultural Society in Bradford and spends much time teaching Hindi, Urdu and Punjabi to young children, he certainly can't be accused of being casual about the Hindu tradition. The point yet again comes home, that there are many different ways of being a faithful Hindu:

> I'm not one, I should say, to perform any definite worship, any particular act of worship, as in other religions where there are sometimes some 'do's and don'ts'. But I do remember, I do say some *shlokas* and *mantras* from my Scriptures whenever I feel like it. It depends on my mood – on my temper, I should say. Sometimes you are under strain, and then you remember straightaway. Sometimes you are thinking about some of your personal problems, say financial problems, say you had some slight row with your wife, or in the family, and you are a bit upset; then you think. And when you contemplate in that way, straightaway you realise and go back to your religious teachings of the Scriptures, and then suddenly something comes up, and then it resolves this problem.

Precept and Promise in Buddhism

Similarly Buddhists may respect particular writings as Scriptures with authority – for example, parts (or even the whole) of the Pali Canon. But they are just as likely to find the Buddha-nature (the trigger to Enlightenment) in any object, or even in the Scriptures of other religions. David Brandon, the Zen Buddhist living in Preston, explained this to me:

> The Pali Canon is important, but *many* things are important. I mean, I still regularly read the New Testament, and I see much Buddhism in the New Testament. In fact, I think the New Testament is a much more oriental book than most Christians actually have a credence for. They don't realise, I think, how far east Palestine, Israel, is. And the meaning of the

> book is in that fact. So what I'm saying to you is that all kinds of things are important – in my mental health work, in social work, in religious work. The books which outline the *dharma*, the principle of the Way, are important for me, but so is everything: all life, all books, all experiences, the television, even BBC Radio, can unfold the *dharma* and make it visible. We have a saying in Zen: When you are ready to learn, a thousand Buddhas spring up from behind every hedgerow.

So a Buddhist may well read texts and teachings of the Buddha, but they clearly do not have the same kind of authority over him or her, as does the Quran, for example, over a Muslim. Mr Wickramaratne, a Buddhist originally from Sri Lanka but now living in North London, made this distinction very clear to me, when he said that he does read and reflect on the Five Precepts (the basic Buddhist rules of life – see p. 29) every day, but they are not *commands*: they are promises he makes to himself:

> I promise to myself what I will do. The basic thing in Buddhism, the main doctrine – well, it's based on the Four Noble Truths, suffering, the cause of suffering, cessation of suffering and the path leading to that. But the very basic things are the Five Precepts which anyone can follow, like not killing any living being – not just human beings only, but even animals. And that has influenced me so much. It's not a rule or a commandment. It's a promise I make to myself. One thing I do every morning when I get up is to recite the simple Five Precepts: each morning I say them to myself – a bit loudly, but to myself: I take the view that I will not do such a thing. And then if I broke the promise I made in the morning, I'd feel a bit guilty, that I couldn't keep that promise today. But if I kept it, I'm quite happy that I did it. And then at night, just before I go to sleep, I tell again a stanza, which means that I have done such a thing, and I thank the Buddha for this doctrine, which I have learnt, and I have kept that side of it today.

Authority and Conscience

From that account, it is obvious that Buddhists give strong priority to individual conscience and decision: it is the individual's responsibility to take up the precepts and the teaching, or to ignore them. Thus Tibetan Buddhists have a deep respect for the Dalai Lama, as Mr Twewang Topgyal explained to me:

> Dalai Lama is an incarnate Lama and there are, you know,

> many incarnate Lamas in Tibet. The incarnate Lama means, those who have the will to choose either to be born again or not. Rebirth is that necessary chain through which we must go. But incarnate Lamas choose whether they want to be born again or not. So Dalai Lama is the incarnate Lama and he is the head of the, if you like, Tibetan Buddhist Church, or Tibetan Buddhists; and also he has been the political head as well.

But, I then asked him whether he would accept the Dalai Lama's word, not as having authority over him, but as advice. He replied:

> Oh yes, yes, very much so. That is a very important point, because Buddha always said, 'Don't take what I'm saying, just try to analyse as far as possible and see whether what I'm saying makes sense or not. If it doesn't make sense, discard it. If it does make sense, then pick it up.'

Other religions have a much more organised exercise of authority – though that authority may be very much disputed within the religion in question. This is particularly obvious in the case of Christianity, where the nature and scope of the Pope's authority, in matters of doctrine and morals, has divided Christendom. It even divides Roman Catholics. Some of those I spoke to give the Pope an extremely high status:

> We believe that the Pope is the next to God on earth – that he is infallible in all his teachings on the Catholic Church, on religious matters. We believe that God gave him this infallibility, though he is just a man like any other, but he was given that gift from God because he was specially chosen by God to become the Pope. We also believe that they *are* chosen by God, through the Cardinals and the various things that they do, that God actually chooses them. And we also believe that he has the hardest job to get to heaven.

But others believe that the Pope's authority – and that of the hierarchy in general – has to be justified by its own quality of life and example. That at least is what Mr Callaghan argued in Liverpool – and for him the impossibility of the hierarchy setting any kind of example in marriage (because no Roman Catholic clergy can be married) nullified their advice in that area. In his view the hierarchy should listen more and pronounce less:

> Authority is a problem for Catholics and the Church has set itself a task of self-understanding, of reinterpreting, what it

means by authority. And it's set itself that task very explicitly at the Second Vatican Council. It didn't resolve it, and it hasn't resolved it yet. And it will be very surprising, and perhaps it would be very dangerous, if it resolved it too quickly. The Church, I believe, is the Body through which the Spirit speaks. He speaks through other people as well, but we are people who try and listen to the Spirit and to echo his words as clearly as we can. The point is that my devout Catholic neighbour, who may influence me, will influence me because of the sincerity, the charity, in a word through the obvious *service*, that he is prepared to give to his fellow men because of his love of God. That is what the hierarchy aims to do; and if they are obviously seen to be aiming to serve, out of love of God, then they will carry authority. If they are not seen to be aiming to do that, they will not carry authority. Now take the area of sexual morality: marriage is an underrated sacrament. The people who know about marriage are the married, provided that they have listened to the word of God spoken to them through their marriage. If we could have confidence in ourselves, and if perhaps (if I could dare to say it), if the hierarchy generally could have more confidence in the married, then some of the problems, that we are in, might disappear – because we actually would be able to tell them the answers, if everybody had confidence. But we are put into a false position of not feeling sufficiently confident about what we really know is OK and right and good.

And in fact the majority of Roman Catholics I listened to seemed to be moving in a similar direction – to a reassertion of the traditional position of the Church, that while the Church has a responsibility to teach and advise, in the end the individual conscience is primary – as this Roman Catholic put it, even more directly:

I don't feel bound at all by the ecclesiastical authorities. I certainly look to them for advice in the things that they write and the things that they say. But I firmly believe that all these things, the Scriptures, the encyclicals of the Pope, the letters of the bishops and archbishops, are there, not as rules for me that can't be bent or broken: they are there for guidelines, because in the end, no matter what rules and regulations you keep, it's all down to your relationship with God and your relationship with other people. And if we call ourselves followers of Christ, Christ was the biggest breaker of rules of

> anybody, you know. He bent them, and never ever did he give anybody a direct answer. He always made people make their own minds up on how they should get to his Father. He never ever said, 'Do this or do that.' He told them the alternatives, and said, 'Well, look, you know, I'll show you the way, but in the end it's up to you.' I think the Second Vatican Council did a lot, as the Pope at the time said: it was a wind of change. We in this country have been a long time feeling that breeze, but certainly it's there.

So not unlike the Buddhists, there may be strongly authoritarian advice or even command (it was a Buddhist who used the word 'straitjacket' to describe the necessary discipline in Buddhist meditation), but in the end the individual conscience is responsible. The same is clearly true of Hinduism. In general, a Hindu would go to a Brahmin or pandit for direction on how to perform particular rituals; there the authority is absolute, since no one else knows, from the tradition, how to perform them. But for advice on spiritual progress towards *moksha*, a Hindu can choose one of any number of gurus – or none, as Mrs Chatterji explained:

> In India you have a priest who advises you on rituals, like how you put the betel leaves, then how you put the betel nut, and things like that. But it is only the practical aspect of that, you know, putting things in the right order. From the philosophical point of view, you have a guru; but not everybody has one.

Pandit Pandya explained to me what sort of questions and issues are brought to him:

> Whenever anybody wants anything to be asked in a ritual way, they come to me, or they phone me, and I will guide them through the religious books, and I'll give them the correct reply and the correct way. There are certain things where they require the priest. First of all, when they open a new shop, they will see what time and what day is suitable for it; then when they want to buy the new car, they will get the service of the *yantra*, which is a kind of machine. From that they see that their God is there. Even in the case of wedding, death, and haircutting, every type of ceremony they want to do or perform, they consult the pandit. Above all, they consult about the date and time – which is all right, which time is all right. And on the particular day and time they will do the ceremony.

The pandit was referring at that point to the strong Hindu belief in the influence of the stars and other planets in their conjunctions. So I asked him how he finds the propitious days and times. He said:

> That is from a book. You can see the book, it is for the full year, all the days and times according to each month, which days are right and which are not – it's shown here. And from this I explain to them, and I tell them, 'Oh, this is the suitable day for you.'

I asked him why the people couldn't look it up for themselves in the book. He replied:

> Because they have not studied in the college or religious group or anywhere in our faculty of religion; so they also might be getting the book, they can buy it from the market. But they can't read it properly, because some mathematical calculation is drawn. All our religion is more or less based on the mathematical grounds. It is like a calculation, which only a priest who has studied can do. The movement of the stars is the most important thing.

I then asked him whether his decision would have authority over those who came to him, or whether they would simply accept it as advice. He answered:

> I explain our way, and sometimes they accept, but not always. Let me give you the example: drinking [alcohol] and eating meat is prohibited according to Hindu religion. Whoever comes round here, I explain to them, 'You are eating the meat at the cost of the death of somebody – killing somebody. And whenever anybody kills anybody, chopping them, it hurts: the voice comes out from the body, "Oh, oh", like that. So the life comes in the blood, and when you eat that type of flesh, meat, it will come in you also.' So I tell them, I explain it to them; and some English people also have left eating meat nowadays. But some Asians don't believe this, and they say, 'No, no: when we are come in this world, let us have full enjoyment: eat, drink, and be merry.' So I say, 'Well, good enough, it is up to you.' Because our religion is a moral binding, not compulsory. It's not like Iran. In Iran they made them throw away bottles of wine and whisky. They were very strict. But we are not so strict, we always explain to the people voluntarily: 'See!' we say. 'Voluntarily' means saying 'See'. The Hindu religion

> puts it like that: we explain: whatever we eat, our brain and our thoughts become like that also. So we ought to explain to them to eat the good food.

For Jews, Muslims and Sikhs, the issue of authority may be as acute as it is for Roman Catholics, because they have (or may have) strong views on revelation coming from God. Thus a Lubavitch Hasidic Jew will submit to the Rebbe in New York the name of the girl he ought to marry:

> A Hasid would ask first of all for the agreement and the blessing from the Rebbe before he would marry the girl he wishes to marry. In this modern age, we have the advantages of the telephone, and often a question, such as whether one should go ahead and marry a certain girl can be quickly answered by telephone. In other words, one telephones New York and one leaves a message with the secretary, stating one's own Hebrew name, and the name of the girl, and then one asks for the agreement of the Rebbe. The followers of the Rebbe see him as a very special soul which has come down into this world. The Rebbe has very special spiritual powers. And therefore the Rebbe has these powers to decide even by just knowing the names of the two partners – because the name of a person is connected with his soul.

Orthodox, or traditional, Jews are also likely to accept the word of the rabbi as having authority over them. Mr Jack Schild said:

> The rabbi has got his diploma, and he's supposed to know all the laws – the Jewish Laws, anything pertaining to the Jewish religion. I accept this word, because that is the *Din*. He's only stating the *Din*: he's not stating his own opinion, you see. If it was his own opinion, I might question it; but it's not his opinion, it's the Law: it's deduced from the Bible, and we've got to accept it.

But other Jews are by no means so certain, and they made it clear that they would only accept the rabbi's words as advice, not as a binding authority. As one husband and wife put it, it's the difference between issuing guidelines and passing an Act of Parliament. And as many Jews pointed out, on any *major* religious matter, no practice could be altered without what is known as a Sanhedrin from all Jews around the world – and that is scarcely likely to happen, considering the continuing divisions in practice among the Jews.

The Sikhs (who are also, as we know, a people of a Book) have a similar system. The final authority lies with the Guru Granth Sahib, but on major matters of interpretation, a Council of Five in the Punjab make the decision:

> If a decision has to be taken nationally or internationally, then this is taken by a body of five people, appointed by the whole community. They are the heads of our five temples in the Punjab. Their decisions are binding on any Sikh anywhere. Even if a Sikh goes to the moon, he would still obey the decisions taken by those five people. We didn't have any edict for the last two or three years but there are certain things that are happening these days that didn't, or couldn't, have happened in the times when the Gurus lived. For example, abortion or nuclear armaments: supposing the Sikhs are facing the problem of whether to have a nuclear bomb, or not to have it, then these are the things that an individual cannot decide. They would go to the council of the Sikhs, those five people; they would invite the learned people from all walks of life among the Sikhs, discuss it, and then finally give their decision. It would then be communicated to all Sikh temples, and to every Sikh wherever he happens to be and that would be binding on him.

But for more local or individual decisions, a person would go directly to the Guru Granth Sahib (as we've already seen), though he might also seek advice from the granthi, the reader and leader of the temple community. Unlike the rabbi in Judaism, the granthi has no formal training or test, so his advice would be respected, but it would not have binding authority. In the same way, for Muslims the Quran has absolute authority. The imam leads the prayers and gives instruction, but he cannot supplant the authority of the Quran. So for advice, Muslims might go to anyone – even a non-Muslim. But in general, much advice or guidance comes from Sharia', the organisation of life and practice in a school of law, rather than from an imam.

So in these religions, there is a different emphasis on authority and on the extent to which individuals must conform and obey. In fact, *within* each of these religions, this is in itself a divisive issue. If there *is* a point of agreement, it is that the religious enterprise is too serious in its ultimate consequences, to be left entirely to chance, or to individuals alone. Too much wisdom and too much experience has been accumulated in the past; and in the future a great deal depends on what we do – or fail to do – now. Religions, therefore, preserve and transmit the resources from which individuals and communities can construct their lives with hope and courage, with holiness and wisdom. How far they insist on conformity, to a particular pattern of such life, is precisely the issue of authority and conscience.

The problem here is not unique to religions: it is impossible to make progress in anything worthwhile – whether playing the piano or learning physics or even playing football – without accepting authority and discipline; and it is equally impossible to make progress in religious life without the same. In all cases, it is the initial acceptance of restriction and discipline which enables active exploration and achievement, whether in science or in religion.

But terrible and evil things are done in the name of obedience. 'I didn't know,' says the Soldier, in Max Frisch's *Andorra*. 'I only did my duty. Orders are orders. What would the world come to if orders weren't carried out?' And evil things have been done by religious believers with exactly that same word of 'obedience' on their lips as their reason. Yet religions have also asserted (at least in theory and sometimes in practice) that the individual conscience is *paramount*. The reconciliation of authority and conscience has to be solved in practice, in life and decisions day by day. So what guidance do these religions offer to people, as they live their lives day by day, week by week, year by year? These are the questions we'll take up next.

6
Day by Day: Religion in Daily Life

Marks of Belief

In the last chapter, we saw how religions guide and control believers in the way they live their lives. The religions differ in the way authority is exercised, and they differ also in the extent to which a believer is expected to fall in line and conform to a particular pattern of behaviour and belief. Obviously, religions like Judaism or Islam which have a strong sense of God's command being contained in Scripture, will have a correspondingly strong sense of how to live, day by day, week by week, and year by year.

We've already seen how, in the case of the Jews, Torah (and its extension in Oral Torah) contains detailed and specific commands. Jews (as we've also seen) may disagree on how literally each command must be obeyed, but they still recognise the existence of the command. The most fundamental commands require a particular ethical style in life; but they also require particular marks of belief, which a Jew must observe every day. Thus a Jewish man must wear each day the *zizith* and the *tefillin*, and his home must have the *mezuzah* on the doorpost (a scroll, following the command of Deb./Deut.vi.8f., containing the basic command to Israel to love God). This is how Mr Douber Klein described their importance:

> The *zizith* is a garment which the Jewish person wears to remind him of the 613 commandments which he has to fulfil. He is obliged to wear these *zizith* at all times. They are a sign to the outside world that he is a Jew; and it is something which a Jewish person should be proud of. The *tefillin* are a bond between man and God, and that is why we tie the *tefillin* around us. It is as if we are binding ourself up to God. According to Hasidic tradition, when one puts on *tefillin*, one should do so with great joy, because even though one might not be aware of the actual revelation of God which is being

> brought into the world through a Jew putting on his *tefillin*, he is assured that this revelation is very, very great; and when the Messianic age will come, he will see the effect of all his actions in this world in their true sense.

Mr Oliver described in more detail what it means to 'bind on the *tefillin*':

> The *tefillin* are the phylacteries which one puts on. One is for your forehead, and one is for your arm. It is wound round your arm seven times, and it is then bound into your middle finger to make the letter *shin*, which is the beginning of the word *Shaddai* – which means the Almighty God. And the other part goes on your forehead. The *tefillin* are one of the three manifestations of knowing that God is with you all the time, so they are the three most important things to a Jew: the *mezuzah* on the door, your *zizith*, which is like a small prayer shawl, and the *tefillin*, that you put on every morning.

Even more insistent in their demands on daily life are the requirements of diet. Some of these we've already heard about: no alcohol for Buddhists or Muslims; fish on Fridays for some Christians (rapidly disappearing though that is); no meat for Buddhists; only meat that has been slaughtered in a prescribed way for Jews and Muslims. Any of these may be ignored by individual believers; but the requirement for Jews to observe the rules of *kashrut* (cleanliness) and to eat only kosher food goes very deep into daily life, as Mrs Dresner makes clear – and since she is a teacher in a Jewish primary school, it's not as if she has much time or leisure for her shopping:

> I am constantly aware of having to buy kosher food and not to buy non-kosher food. It is very easy for me because it is totally automatic. I know exactly what is permitted and what isn't permitted, and it wouldn't occur to me, for example, to go into a non-kosher butcher to try and buy meat. I just wouldn't do it. It's something that I've grown up with from childhood; and usually, even with the Jewish person who practises the least, it's the last of the laws to go. It's one of these basic things, I mean, food and childhood, they are closely interlinked. It's all so very deep and very complex that I don't question it too much because it doesn't cause me any inconvenience. I question it at times when it does cause me inconvenience: for example, if you're in an unfamiliar place or going on holiday, I do ask myself, 'Why is it that I keep these laws?' And the only

> answer really is that it's part and parcel of everything else that I keep, and if I were to let that go, I would feel myself hypocritical in doing almost anything else.

The real point here is that every detail of daily life is converted into a religious act – into a recognition of God, as another Jewish wife and mother, Mrs Klein, put it:

> All the daily chores of a woman become, for a Jewish woman, religious acts. For example, shopping, cleaning, cooking: when I go shopping, I have to remember, and because of our dietary laws, I have to be very careful about the food that I select in the market; and the cooking for example: we have to check vegetables, fruit, rice, because we are not allowed to eat insects. And of course, I have to be very careful about the separation of milk and meat. So, we elevate everything to God – even, for example the cleaning: we have to clean before Shabbat and before the Holy Days, and that is actually a positive commandment. And even the spring-cleaning has become a religious act: we are commanded to clean the house before Passover, to remove any trace of bread. And of course, there is looking after the children, which is very, very important. We stress the importance of the family, and the importance of education too. So that's why we are so particular about being around when the children are at home, to teach them all about *mitzvot*, about the commandments, and teach them about the Bible.

But what is the *reason* for keeping all these commands day by day? Mrs Klein answered:

> Just because God commanded it. It's not like people suggest sometimes, because of hygienic reasons: there isn't any such reason, we don't believe in such reasons. We do it because God commanded it. It's a positive commandment. There are a lot of commandments we don't understand. We can *try* to find reasons for them, but lots of them we don't understand.

Even a Reform Jew, who is certainly not keeping the Torah in all its detail, will not give way on the basic rules of *kashrut*:

> Anything connected with pig-meat is just not on, and that I don't eat. I don't eat any of the fish, or shell-fish, or anything of that kind. And this is not totally logical, I'm prepared to agree to that, it's not totally logical. I was brought up that way. I've never felt very strongly about wanting to eat any of that, so I avoid it, I just don't eat it.

The laws of *kashrut* may not be logical, and there may not even be reasons of hygiene to support them any longer; but, as Mr Benaim insisted, they enable a Jew to turn an ordinary animal instinct into a human act of thanksgiving:

> One of the important things, when you are eating an item of food, is that you can differentiate yourself, make a difference between an animal and a human being. Instead of getting a piece of cake and putting it to your mouth, which is an animal instinct, a reaction, you are turning it by saying a blessing on it; you're turning an instinct into an action which makes you a much more higher sort of level of animal.

Muslims also have a strong sense of the word of God being uttered to them through Quran, and this leaves its characteristic mark on daily life. For a start, as we've already seen, Sunni Muslims are following the *sunna*, or path, of the Prophet – which means, so far as possible, the imitation of his behaviour, since he was the first to allow the Quran to control and inform his own life. Equally, the Quran commands Muslims to pray daily, and the five daily prayers form one of the basic Pillars of Islam. Like the Jews, they can only eat meat which has been slaughtered in the correct way. This is *hallal*, and we have already seen (p. 15) the problems this, together with the ban on pork, causes for observant Muslims.

Equally familiar to the outsider is the prohibition in Islam against alcohol, or any other intoxicants. Not all Muslims observe this, but most do – and a Muslim wife and mother feels so strongly about this that she will not even buy groceries in a shop which also sells alcohol:

> We don't go to those shops. One day I was doing my shopping and I wanted to buy some vegetables from an Indian shop, belonging to a Hindu person from India, and my son stopped me. He said, 'He sells alcohol: I don't want to go and buy things from his shop.'

A bit like the Jews, the food laws are the last to go in daily life. I asked a Shiite Muslim in Manchester whether he did anything each day as a Muslim. He answered: 'Not really. We are not that religious. But you can say what we *don't* do which marks out that we are Muslim. We don't eat pork or bacon in our breakfast! So clearly you can say that we are Muslims.'

But for those who *are* observant, daily life for a Muslim housewife is very like daily life for a Jewish housewife, in the sense that she has to be careful to remember what God requires:

> Muslim people can't eat any pork or ham; and we can't just go in a shop and buy anything: anything like animals, it depends how you slaughter them: you have to read something out of Quran, and that becomes the *hallal*. And we can't eat any fat, or anything like that: we've got to be careful what we eat. And we've got to be careful what we wear: we can't wear very thin clothes which will show our body. We can't wear short clothes which will show part of our legs. We've got to be covered.

At the opposite extreme from Judaism and Islam are religions which do not lay down detailed requirements for daily life, but require that the spirit and character of belief should be translated into life – the Christian, for example, who talked of trying to make her life an imitation of Christ (p. 73), or the Buddhist who saw the Five Precepts, not as precepts, but as promises to himself which he tries to keep each day, and which he reviews each night (p. 133).

Week by Week

But people in at least some of these religions don't only live from day to day: they also live from week to week. Sunni Muslim men are required to assemble in the mosque each Friday (as we shall see in Chapter 9, Muslim women don't *have* to attend mosque each week, though they may); and Jews must keep the Sabbath from sunset on Friday to sunset on Saturday. Once again, the detailed requirements are much more elaborate for Jews, since the Sabbath is a day of absolute rest: no work and only very limited travelling is allowed. Jews should attend synagogue on the evening of the Sabbath, and they too have an issue over the separation of women from men – as we'll see in due course. But basically, the Sabbath is a day of tremendous *joy*, as Stuart and Merrill Dresner describe:

> She: It's the day that keeps me going for the rest of the week. Without the Shabbat, I feel that the week would have no shape. And I know this from experience: at times when I didn't keep the Shabbat, life was just continuous and there wasn't any shape to the week. The week builds up to a kind of climax for the Shabbat. It's certainly a very, very happy day. It's composed of many elements: prayer is one very important

> one, both at home and in the synagogue. We ourselves can't get to the synagogue on a Friday night, because we live half an hour's walk from the synagogue, and it's difficult. So we pray at home, which is very important, and provides a lot of the atmosphere. And food is terribly important. There are three meals that you *should* eat on the Shabbat: one on the Friday evening, and two more main meals during the day on the Shabbat. And accompanying the meals there are songs to sing, table hymns they are called; preceding the meals you make a *kiddush* – you make a blessing over wine, and over bread; and after the meal you say a grace, which involves again, plenty of music and singing.
> He: Yes, music only for singing, because we are not allowed to play instruments.
> She: Right, that's quite right. The other aspect of the Shabbat that's particularly important is the word *menuhah*, which means rest: that involves the complete ceasing of all everyday things: we don't use electricity, we don't travel, which is very important.
> He: I think I should clarify that: we do use, we do have the benefit of, electricity: that is, our lights are on, and we have heating, but we don't switch lights on – which I think is rather important, otherwise people might get the impression that it's dark and cold, but it's not. We switch the lights on before the Shabbat, as part of the preparations. And if the telephone rings, it has to just ring.

For observant Jews, therefore, the work in preparation for the Sabbath is very considerable as this account makes clear:

> We have to really begin by the preparations we make before Sabbath, because there is no way one can spend Sabbath without making full preparations in advance. The house has to be thoroughly cleaned, all the everyday machinery has to be put out of the way because we are not allowed to use it on Shabbat. Special Shabbat table cloths are brought out. The table is decorated with flowers and other more ornate vessels; and of course, all the cooking has to be prepared in advance. This is because on Shabbat cooking is forbidden, and therefore, what we do is to prepare all the food before Sabbath, and then leave the food on a metal board. Then this metal board is put onto the stove, and in that way the food is kept warm without us actually having to turn on or off the light. So the Shabbat is such a different day from the other days of the

week that we should make this noticeable in as many ways as possible, not only in the house but also in our dress. And therefore, all one's better clothes one keeps and only wears them on the Shabbat. In this way we show that it is a holy day and different from the other days of the week. So basically we keep the Shabbat because on the seventh day God rested. It is explained that on the Shabbat every Jew receives an added dimension to his soul. And in order to appreciate the full revelation of this extra part of his soul he has to conduct himself absolutely according to the orthodox laws, which are prescribed regarding the keeping of the Shabbat. On the Shabbat I feel a different person. I feel more alive, more bright, more cheerful, the house seems to be a different place. In fact when one keeps the laws according to the Shabbat, it is like being in a different world. So in no way could one think of it as being a restriction. It's only positive. On Shabbat we sing, on Shabbat we dance, on Shabbat we have time to study without any interruption. We have time to pray.

So the rules seem strict: but they clearly set Jews free into a new kind of happiness, especially in the way they bring the family together. Mr Jack Schild is an Orthodox Jew who came to this country (from Poland) before the First World War. He remembers the strong Jewish community of the East End, and regrets the disintegration of that way of life:

Shabbat is a very beautiful day. In my younger days, when I went to the Yeshiva, I used to move around a lot amongst Hasidim. I used to go with my father (*olav haShalom* [peace be on him]); he was a member then of *Jickaver Stiebel* (*stiebel* is a room, you know) [*ie* the assembly room of those who originally came from Jickaver in Galicia] in Dunk Street. He joined that particular place because a lot of his *landsliet* belonged to it. *Landsliet* means people who came from his town, from his country – from Galicia. They used to get very famous rabbis, Hassidischer rabbis, coming there, and it was very jolly – very jolly. I remember, some of them were very well-off, you know, very comfortable, good business men, and one of them used to donate a crate of beer, for Shabbat; another one used to donate whisky, another one wine. And the Ladies' Guild, they used to make beautiful *gefilte* fish. And the rabbi, he would sit at the head of the table there, and he was giving everybody a portion, and everybody considered it a most wonderful thing to get a portion of fish from the rabbi –

> the most marvellous thing, nothing could be more wonderful than that. And I used to enjoy the singing, and the dancing, and the clapping, you know. I used to enjoy it; and I loved the Shabbat, because they didn't have that during the week. But now we haven't got that; and I might tell you I don't feel as much as I did in those days, because around here, I wouldn't say it's exactly dead but you can say fifty per cent dead. The Shabbat has a very poor attendance in the morning. At night when I had *yahrseight*, for my mother, the anniversary of her death, when you're supposed to say Kaddish, I couldn't say it, there was no *minyan*, there was only 7 people.

At the opposite extreme, Buddhists may go to their temple weekly, but it isn't a general obligation; and a Tibetan Buddhist, Twewang Topgyal, makes the point that going to the temple is only necessary for those who need it – for those who need instruction on the long road of rebirth:

> It depends on the level of understanding. You need teaching if you don't know something. It's the same as in life: let's take the law, for instance. It's needed when people cannot quite refrain from doing wrong things. But as soon as we reach a situation where we don't have any of those problems, then there's no need for civil law. In the same way, we need walls around prisoners to stop any escape; but once they stop escaping, then you don't need that wall. And it's the same if one is learning a new subject: you need a teacher until you reach a certain level, and after that you don't need him any more. And therefore, going to the temple depends on the level of one's understanding. Initially, teachers are extremely important, but gradually I think one would need less and less teaching. Ultimately what Buddha really said was that, once one is ready to achieve the ultimate state of being, or reach *nirvana*, then, he said, one's got to discard his teachings as well.

In between the extremes are the Hindus and Sikhs and Christians. Hindus don't *have* to go to temple each week – life is lived, as we saw earlier (p. 14), in four stages, and one must meet one's obligations as a householder first, if that's the stage you've reached – as a young Hindu husband and father told me:

> The point about the Hindu faith is that it does not insist that one should be a regular temple-goer. Our lives are divided into certain stages, and we have to fulfil those to the very best of our ability. For example, when you are a student, you have

to be a good student; when you are a father, you have to be a good father; when you are a mother, you have to be a good mother; and only when you've discharged your family duties, then you are required to devote the latter part of your life to prayer and to salvation for yourself.

He is clearly at the stage of 'householder'. Asha Pancholi is still at the stage of 'student'; and she added the point that as a teenager, brought up in this country, the natural experience of the temple has not been part of her life:

I've just been to India, and we went to various temples, but I wasn't all that drawn towards them. I suppose I haven't been brought up in them. Whereas my Mum, she lived there, and she used to go there every day, and it became part of her life. But here there's nothing, so we became used to just trying to pray to God as much as we could, in the house or wherever we were. We didn't have to go to the temple or things like that.

But many Hindus *like* to go to temple regularly, not least for reasons of society and friendship; and if they go, then it becomes religiously important, particularly if the temple has its own pandit. Any shrine can have images and photos of the gods and goddesses, but only the pandit can bring the living reality of the image into what would otherwise remain its dead form; and after he has done so, the image is treated with respect, as a living being. All this was described to me by Pandit Pandya in Leeds:

When there's a photo or an idol, we put life in it by speaking the religious *mantras*. We speak them in the photo, in the idol, and make it live, we make it alive. So when we make it alive, it is called *pranapratistha*: that means we are putting the life in the idols. So when we put the life in the idols, we can't keep it just as it is. Every day we have to give the food, we have to give the milk, and everything that a human might wish, every day.

For those who do go weekly, what happens? This is how Dr Gupta described it:

When you go to the temple, first of all (according to the Hindu traditions) you can't take your shoes inside the main hall, where the idols of Lord Krishna and Rama have been installed – I think another reason may be the hygiene, and it's advisable that you don't take your shoes in. So we have the rack there, we put the shoes there, and then go in the main hall. As soon as you enter, you feel that you are in front of

Lord Krishna and Rama. So automatically the feeling comes. Therefore I'm not praying because I *have* to pray, but when you go in, you feel yourself that you should do this.

And as Mrs Chatterji added, the praying, or worship, is not silent: it takes the form of chants and hymns: 'We have devotional songs,' she said. 'And when you join in, it helps you to relax.'

For Sikhs there is the same strong pull to go to temple weekly, but no compulsion. However, long programmes are organised, and people come and go as they will: there's no absolutely fixed beginning and ending for all those attending – though the end is more important than the beginning, as Gurmukh Singh Bansal told me:

Every Sunday morning we go to church. We always have a programme, myself and my colleague Damun Singh, have a programme. It may be a wedding, or a counterpart, or a *gurupurb*; or even in the temple, people invite us to give a programme for a couple or three hours. There's no restriction for anybody. Whoever goes to church, providing he comes in and stays there for even a couple of minutes, or five minutes, he's still being present; then he can go again if he wants. To have a set time, to start and finish, is not in our religion. It doesn't matter when you go. You can go in, obviously, if there's a proper programme, like a wedding, but otherwise you can go and come. But when actually they are finishing the programme, the end of it, that is the very important part: you've got to be there for that.

So Sikhs don't *have* to attend weekly – indeed, as Harbans Singh Sagoo told me, it's only in this country that Sunday has come to be marked off as a special day:

People generally go to the temple on Sundays, because Sunday for some reason has become, shall we say, the auspicious, or the religious, day. But there are many people who go to the temple twice a day every day. But for me it's the distance: if I lived somewhere near the temple, I might do the same myself. But because of the distance involved, I perform my religious duties at home; and I go to the temple when I can find time to do that.

For those who do go, I asked Jagat Singh Nagra what happens:

We have a religious ceremony every week on Sundays. They

start with the reciting of the hymns from the Holy Book, Guru Granth Sahib; and after the ceremony, there is free food, which is served to all, whoever has gone there, and we share that as well. In Sikh religion, children are allowed to go there as well, even young children. And you can go at any time you like, and come out any time you like. There's no compulsion, there's no fixed time, that you have to go at 9 o'clock or 10 o'clock. You can go any time during the ceremony, and come back when you like.

I asked him how long it might last if he stayed the whole time:

It starts early in the morning, and it finishes – well, sometimes there are some speakers from outside, or singers from outside, then the ceremony is slightly longer. But I think it finishes by about 2 o'clock.

I asked his 10-year-old son, Sundeep, if he enjoyed going to the Gurdwara. He said, 'Yes – it's a bit dull sometimes. But they serve free food and free sweets at the end of the festival'; which seemed a good, healthy attitude; and his brother Mandeep agreed. The older Sikhs go primarily to be fed and instructed from the Holy Book, as Surinder Singh Hyare told me: 'We gather there and read the Holy Book. And the Holy Book is all prayers, praise to God and his nature. So we sing there, we recite the holy words, and it's a sort of poetry, you see, fine poetry.' But equally, Sikhs go because it creates their own community and draws them together as friends. 'It socialises you along with other Sikhs,' said Amritpal Singh Hunjan: 'You are in a crowd of Sikhs and it makes you proud of being a Sikh.' Even so, some young Sikhs are finding that the temple has too much socialising and too little praying. Parmjot Singh Hyare spoke for them when he said:

One reason I don't go to our temple is because they tend nowadays to be like social clubs. I know it's the wrong thing to say, but it's true. People there, they just go to talk to each other, a lot of them don't go to pray or anything. Well, I know that if you want to pray, you can pray at home, as long as you've got the Guru Granth Sahib here, which most Indian families have. But I'd like to see people going there for praying purposes, and not for meeting purposes and talking about all of their problems.

For Christians also there is a strong pull towards weekly attendance at church, but no absolute obligation. For those who do go, almost all are now attending the commemoration or re-enactment of the Last Supper, when Jesus is reported to have taken bread and said, 'This is my body', and of wine, 'This is my blood'. But what does that mean? At one extreme, some Christians see the Last Supper, and the bread and the wine, as reminders of what Jesus did. This is how Mrs Lynch, a Pentecostal Christian, describes what it means to her:

> As we eat the bread, we say, The Lord's body; and when we drink the wine, This is his blood. It reminds us what Jesus did, because this was the last thing he did, I think, with his disciples. And we are showing forth his death: it is reminding us what he has suffered for us. And he said, 'as often as we do this, we do it until he comes again' – this is something that is very important in the Church – very important. And the minister always stresses that whenever we do this, we should examine ourselves, to see if we are at fault or at grievance with anybody. So we should examine ourselves, pray, seek the Lord's guidance, and so forth, so that we don't build up trouble upon ourselves. I think this is very important: we don't do it just for the sake of doing it, or as a joke. It's very meaningful.

Another young Pentecostal Christian, Michael Stevenson, also emphasised that the Lord's Supper is just as much looking forward as it is looking back:

> We observe the Lord's Supper, we do it because we remember that Jesus Christ died, that he was buried and that he rose again; and I think the most important part of the Lord's Supper is that Jesus Christ rose again. So we do it looking forward to his coming again, you see, and that's why we observe the Lord's Supper.

At the other extreme there are those who believe that the bread and wine become the real body and blood of Christ, though they stress there cannot be any explanation for this – it can only be accepted as a mystery by faith, as a Roman Catholic husband and wife made clear:

> She: His Spirit is present, yes: he said that he would come into us when we received Holy Communion – he would come into us and we could talk to him more closely.

He: You see, to try and put across that that host is the body of Christ, and the wine is Christ's blood, people would look at you daft, wouldn't they? It's just a wafer-thin piece of bread, and the wine still tastes the same even after it's been blessed. So they'd say it's a load of rubbish. But we have the gift of faith, and we believe that it is the body of Christ, and Christ's blood.

We've already heard another young Roman Catholic talking briefly about the Body of Christ (p. 56). I asked him what the Real Presence actually means:

To be honest, I don't know: it's a belief. There's many things we don't know that we believe in. I don't know: it's a mystery really. I believe it. But when you do believe in it, you get a lot of feedback from it. But I can't put it into words.

With that emphasis on mystery, it's not surprising that for other Christians the issue of *how* something happens is less important than the promise of Jesus to be with his disciples and in their lives. It therefore becomes a focal way of keeping in touch with Jesus and with each other – and for Jacqueline Rapson it means even carrying others with her into this event:

I don't just go to Communion myself: I take people with me – not in person, but *with* me: like, anybody I know that wants help, or that I'm thinking a lot of at that time, I'm conscious of taking them with me; and when I receive the bread and the blood, I really feel that that is Jesus' bread and that it is his blood, and that what he says is true. And it just confirms it for me. I feel he *is* there. I mean, I always have a feeling when I'm really in tune with God, I feel a yellow glow around me. Sometimes it's not there, but more often than not it *is* there, you know; and I really feel that he is there.

So the re-enactment of the Last Supper creates both unity and a sense of holiness. For John Callaghan in Liverpool (who defined what was going on as 'celebrating our friendship with God'), the reality of Christ's presence in the bread and the wine is that it enables him also to be broken for the good of the world: that's what matters for him, and not the definition, in some abstract way, of the Real Presence:

The breaking of bread is not just something that happens on the altar: it's a commitment that I make that I will be prepared

> to be broken myself in the service of others because of my love of God. Because that is what I understand the Spirit of Christ to be calling me to do: it's the willingness to be broken continually for others, which is an inevitable part of life. I'm not being dramatic, I'm not talking about martyrdom, I'm talking about things like getting up in the night, you know, when the baby's sick instead of kicking your wife to get up – that sort of thing. Actually I'm not very good at that, I just sleep through, but that sort of thing, that's what it means to me. Now what goes on for me, in the Eucharist, is best described, I think, in terms of a renewal of that commitment. The bread and the wine are for me symbolic of the presence of Christ who is prepared to be broken for others. And my aim is to be like that. I'm not very good at being like that, but that's my aim. It's a renewal of my commitment, an experience of shared strength from other people in the breaking of bread – what could be more real than that? In asking about the Real Presence, are you asking me to concentrate on a morsel and a liquid and what's in them? Because if you are, then we are both missing the point: what we are concerned with are spiritual realities, and the spiritual reality that I'm trying to express very haltingly, is a renewal of my commitment, through a renewed realisation that God gives himself to me, and that this is symbolised in the breaking of bread.

Not surprisingly the focal Sunday Eucharist spills over into other meals and gives them a character where people learn to take up a little of the pain and passion of Christ, as Mrs Emmett told me in Basingstoke, with her large family of adopted and fostered children:

> I believe that I am receiving all that Jesus stood for. When Jesus was in the top room and he was having his last meal with the disciples, and they had the bread and they had the wine together, I think the whole meal represented his thirty-three years or so, and his few years of ministry, and I think it all came together in that room over that meal. And that's why I love our main meal in the evening, when we are all round the big table. It's a nice feel to it, and it's a very important meal to me in this family: I look forward to it, and we all get together: it's the togetherness with all the problems as well. Because Jesus had problems at the meal table: he had Judas who he knew was going to betray him. And so it's very much really like our meal times, with all the friendship of the day, and anything

perhaps that hasn't gone right for any of us – perhaps one of us is in a bit of a scratchy mood: it's all there at the table, you know. While we're having that meal, we are working through some nice family time together, and I think that's what Jesus and all the disciples were doing. Everything had come into the room that night: all the healing of the sick, all the rows that he'd had with the Pharisees, all the teaching that he'd tried to do with the disciples and perhaps they hadn't quite got it right. It was all there. And I think, finally he just broke the bread up, you know, as we do our bread rolls – I think of that meal when we have, say, the crusty rolls, and we break them, because that's about the best way to do it. His breaking of the bread, I think, was his broken body, which was broken because of all the suffering and the wrongdoing in the world; and I think that when I receive the symbol, I'm saying, 'Well, I hope that just by having this little bit, I can take away some of your pain; and by having a little sip of wine, that it will help to take away some of your pain.' And I think people are doing that right throughout the world. And perhaps, you know, for a bit, a lot of the pain does go; and that's perhaps what made it bearable for Jesus.

Year by Year: Annual Festivals and Holy Days

But the passion of Christ, with its overtones of Maundy Thursday and Good Friday – the days on which Christians commemorate the institution of the Last Supper and the Crucifixion – is a reminder that people live religiously, not only day by day and week by week, but also year by year. Each religion follows an annual cycle and marks that cycle by festivities.

For Christians

The Christian year follows the preparation for the coming of Christ, the birth, life, and death of Jesus, the Resurrection, and the revelation of the nature of God as in itself a revelation of love, a Trinity of Three being One. But Christians have their high-points in that cycle. For some, it is Christmas. But Ray Turner, when I asked him which was his favourite part of the Christian year, had some hesitations:

I could be sentimental and say Christmas: I love to go to midnight Mass, I still do, really; but since the kids have grown up, Christmas has lost a bit of its magic. So now, Easter is for me

> the highlight, because there isn't the fuss, there isn't the material side of it – perhaps that's not a good word, but the hullabaloo if you like: it's a quieter time. And it's a more prayerful time.

So I asked him what the Resurrection really *is* – what does it mean for him?

> Well, what happened at Easter sort of epitomises me as a person: I was brought up as a conservative Catholic, and my parish priest says, 'Good people are nice, but wouldn't it be good if they were happy?' So the most important thing at Easter for me, is that I can see that we are now the Easter people: we are the Resurrection people. We are the people who celebrate Christ's Resurrection. To me, Easter shows me how I've developed as a Christian, from believing that it was all very solemn – don't eat meat on a Friday, don't do this, don't do the other. I used to think that the only way to get to heaven was this wearing sackcloth and ashes, and we were always being told about the martyrs and John the Baptist eating locusts in the desert. There's no way I can do that. And I look again at my old parish priest, I've never seen him without a smile. To me that's Easter, it's the smile on Christianity's face.

Some Christians are by no means certain that Jesus rose literally and physically from the dead, yet even so the Resurrection is still the key-point:

> I can't accept the Resurrection just like that. I can't say it's impossible, I just find that it doesn't fit into the God that I understand. I don't believe God is a magician, or a magic man that would break all the laws of nature. He works within the laws that he has created, his own natural laws. I think I believe that Christ lives through us all: if we see something in his life and try and live that way ourselves, then that is Christ reborn and that is Christ living on. Whether he actually physically came alive again and suddenly vanished on a cloud, I can't accept that. I know it comes in the creed and I say it every Sunday, but there's a lot of doubt there: I can't see it happening like that. I believe the inspiration and the ideas and the vision that he had have been passed on, and that's how he lives. And he could die if everyone denied it. But it hasn't happened yet, and I don't believe it will happen.

One lone voice, that of Dave Phillips, reminded me of the great attachment the English have for harvest festivals: 'It's nice when harvest comes round,' he said, 'because you only sing harvest hymns at harvest time. But really it's nice when any of the particular seasons comes round.'

For Jews

And that's a voice that Jews would recognise, because Jews also have a cycle of festivals which commemorate what God has done in creating and redeeming his people; but some of those festivals are themselves rooted biblically in the celebration of new life year by year in creation. As Mr Levy put it, 'The Jewish festivals are interesting because they are a mixture of the celebration of the passing seasons (because most of them have got an agricultural element in them), plus history (for example, the Exodus), plus their religious significance.' I asked his wife if she had one favourite festival. She answered:

> Every Jewish festival has its place in the year, and everything is a continuum; so you can't really say 'the High Holy Days' or 'the New Year' or 'the Day of Atonement'. *All* the festivals of Judaism are part of a whole, and they are part of the year.

I asked Mr Levy whether *he* had a favourite festival, and he answered in the same way:

> No, actually, I like all of them, because apart from anything else, most of them are quite fun. It's easy to say which one likes least, I think, and that's the festival of Pentecost, *Shebuot*, because it very much lacks symbolism. You don't actually go into Tabernacles, you don't have family meals as you do at *Pesach* [Passover], you don't have the long periods in the synagogue that are associated with the High Holy Days. And yet in a sense, if any of them is more important than any others, I suppose it ought to be *Shebuot*.

So the main emphasis in the Jewish annual festivals is on the saving action of God in and through his people, which continues down to the present day. Passover or *Pesach* remembers the Exodus from Egypt; *Shebuot* or Pentecost commemorates the giving of Torah; *Sukkot* or Booths/Tabernacles remembers how the Jews lived in frail shelters in the wilderness. For Mr Jack Schild (with his long memories of all the catastrophes and changes that have happened to the Jews during his lifetime), it is *Sukkot* which is the most important:

> The festival of *Sukkot*, I would say, is very important, be-

> cause it teaches us that God is our protector. You see, we were dwelling in Booths through all those years in the wilderness, yet God protected us. So it also teaches you to remember God: you get some people, if they achieve a lot, they sort of believe in themselves – 'I'm clever, you know, I've made a lot of money, I've got my Ph.D., I did this, I did that.' But *Sukkot* teaches you that you've got to think of God. God is behind everything.

Two other festivals, which have not been described so far, are New Year (or *Rosh haShanah*) and the Day of Atonement (*Yom Kippur*). These recognise the faults of human beings, and the need to do something about those failures, and the need to make a new start. So there is, overall, a balance between festivals for joy and those for forgiveness. Stuart Dresner summarised the main festivals for me:

> The main festivals are *Pesach*, Passover; and *Shebuot*, which is the festival of weeks; and *Rosh haShanah* and *Yom Kippur*, the New Year and the Day of Atonement; and they are the main festivals. The first one is the *Pesach*, which commemorates the Israelites coming out of Egypt and coming from slavery into freedom, and this is commemorated each year by an eight-day festival at which we have very special food: we don't eat any bread or ordinary cake: we have what's known as unleavened bread or *Mazzah*; and before the festival we very rigorously clean the house out, and eat up, or get rid of, ordinary foods with starch in. And the first two nights, we have a special meal at home which has a service – it's called the Seder Service – where we recount the story of the Israelites coming out of Egypt. It gives some quotations from the Bible, and some commentaries made by the rabbis on these events; and so it's a way of keeping alive the tradition. This links onto the next festival, the festival of *Shebuot*, which comes seven weeks later. The whole point about the coming out of Egypt was not just simply a going from slavery to freedom, but freedom in order to receive the Torah, the Law, and this is what *Shebuot* commemorates. It doesn't have so much work involved, because we eat normal food on *Shebuot*, although it's a custom to eat dairy foods; but that's not of strong religious importance. The main thing is that we remember that the Law was given, and that's its main purpose. They are happy festivals. Then, by contrast, we have *Rosh haShanah* and *Yom Kippur*. Both these are festivals in which we ask God for for-

giveness for our sins, and ask him for a year of peace and happiness and prosperity and good health, for the year ahead. But these have a slightly more solemn character – particularly *Yom Kippur*, which is a fast day; so we don't eat for twenty-five hours, from nightfall to nightfall, on *Yom Kippur.*

So the point really is, as Mr Klein put it, that *each* festival is the favourite one as it comes round in turn, because each brings something different to Jewish life:

> Every time a Jewish festival comes round (and certainly my children who I teach in school will agree), every time the festivals come around, they say, 'This is my favourite festival'; or, 'I'm so looking forward to *Sukkot* – *Sukkot* is the best festival of the year'. And when Passover comes round, they say, 'Oh, there's nothing better than the Seder night: it's my best festival of the year.' In fact, there's a lot of truth in this, because the way God has given us the festivals is not without reason. Each festival comes in order to add a different dimension to our soul.

For Buddhists

Buddhists are more like Christians in celebrating each year the important events of the Buddha's life, his birth, his Enlightenment and his entry to *nirvana*, but they do not spread those events *into* the year in the elaborate way in which Christians do. The one important festival is *Vesak* or *Vesaki*, which we've already heard described (p. 16). Again one must remember that this festival may be a matter of indifference to a Buddhist, because he is not involved in the historical events of the Buddha's life, as Christians are involved in the body of Christ which is derived from particular events. A Buddhist in the end must transcend and leave behind even the teachings of the Buddha – so attending *Vesak*, like attending to books, may really be a sign of ignorance, a sign of needing instruction and elementary support, as Dr Fernando explained to me:

> *Vesak* is all right: it's a day which commemorates the births, the Enlightenment, and the passing away of the Buddha. But why make extra effort for one particular day? For the feeble-minded, perhaps a day like that would be of much benefit. But to me, every day should be a day of effort – should be such a day. Why just one particular day?

For Sikhs

For the Sikhs, festivals cannot be so incidental. Their annual festivals celebrate the birthdays of the Gurus (and their death days), and the birth of the *Khalsa*; and although the festivals are not compulsory, it is usual to attend at least part of the long celebrations – which mainly involve continuous readings from the Guru Granth Sahib:

> We celebrate Guru Nanak Dev Ji's birthday, Guru Gobind Singh Ji's birthday – there's ten actually altogether. And each festival we do forty-eight-hour *akhand path*, as we call it, which goes on for forty-eight hours in the temples. At the end of the forty-eight hours, then we do *kirtan*, singing hymns; and we have lectures in the temples, and everybody joins in – and also anybody could take a part on his birthday. And then we have *langar* as well in the temples: *langar* is food: anybody can come up and eat food.

But Sikhism incorporates the practices of other religions as well; so Sikhs also celebrate *Vesaki* as a New Year Festival, as well as the Hindu festivals of *Divali* and *Holi*. Mrs Balbir Sohal told me something of this variety:

> We have *Divali* which we celebrate – though that's also a Hindu festival. Then we have *Vesaki*, which is the New Year, then the Sikh New Year in April; and then to some extent we have *Holi*. Then there's the Gurus' birthdays which we celebrate as well. Sikhism is a branch of Hinduism originally, and that's why we have *Divali* and *Holi* – and many of our wedding traditions overlap. For these, we'd probably go to the temple; and at *Divali* you'd light a candle at the temple, perhaps have some sweetmeats, and have a blessing for good fortune for the rest of the year. When I was younger, my mother would make a *deva* out of flour and water, and put a wick in and light it, and we'd have all the lights out in the house and just have candles and these *devas* burning all night; and she would tell us the story of Rama and Sita – and that was every *Divali*. For *Vesaki*, we usually have new clothes, or a new suit, and we go to the temple, and it's just a festival of spring, really, or the coming of the New Year. And when it's a Guru's birthday, we go to the Temple and pray.

For Hindus

Hindus have many different paths leading to the final Goal, and many different devotions to particular gods or goddesses, so they may well celebrate many different festivals. Mrs Kalia told me something of the festivals that she and her family celebrate in Coventry:

> We celebrate the *Navatri*, which come every six months – the nine nights and nine days. The nine days in September are leading up to the festival *Divali*, and the nine days in the spring are leading up to *Holi*. People observe it in different ways. Some people eat nothing, no cereal, nothing like that, only fruit or milk. Then two times, in the morning and in the evening, we have to pray. And then we grow some green plant – some corn or some barley – in the house, because green is a sign of prosperity. We also celebrate Lord Krishna's birthday; and *Dessara*, which is on the last day of the *Navatris* in September or October, when they come. It signifies the return of the victorious Rama from killing Ravana; and all sisters want their brothers to return victorious, and that is what they pray for at that time; because if the brothers are warriors, the females in the family have no outside worries – they have their protection always. It symbolises on that day that the brothers would always look after their sisters.

While I was in Coventry, Mr Ladd told me something more of the way some of these festivals are celebrated:

> The first one is *Ramanomi*: that is the birth of Rama. We celebrate at midday. The second one is *Holi*: that is done with a bonfire in the evening time, and people worship the fire at that time. The next one is *Janmashtami*: that is the birth of Lord Krishna, it is at midnight. The next one is *Navatri*, which is, I think, similar to harvest festival. It is enjoyed by our people, mostly the ladies, for nine days, and they sing songs to the goddess for nine nights. Then comes the *Divali*, which is the end of the year, and we celebrate our New Year on the next day.

Already we are building up a considerable list of festivals observed by most Hindus. Others may undertake a particular devotion – for example, a young Hindu schoolgirl keeps a regular fast in honour of Siva, the power of life and destruction in existence:

> I keep a twenty-four-hour fast every Monday. It starts from midnight and goes on till midnight, and I don't have any water,

> tea or anything until 4 pm on Monday evening, when I make the *prasad* and offer it to God first; then I have one third for myself, one third to the God Siva, and one third I give to my family as *prasada*. After that, I have a cup of tea and some water, until midnight, Monday midnight; after that I break my fast.

But for almost all Hindus *Holi* and *Divali* are the two most important festivals. *Holi* we've already encountered – a spring festival celebrating the exploits (sometimes mischievous) of Krishna; and, as Dr Gokal from Manchester told me, it's a very happy occasion: 'Religious festivals always conjure up tremendous happy moments, and one of the festivals that we celebrate is *Holi*, and that always entails throwing colours and having really great fun.' *Divali* is a new moon festival when all the household lamps are lit to celebrate the return of the sun which a malevolent water-spirit had hidden during the (Indian) rainy season. *Divali* is very much a family festival, and it begins, as Mr Kunvergi Dabasia told me in Coventry, with the children touching their parents' feet as a sign of respect. What else happens? Mr Mittal (president of the Hindu Cultural Society in Bradford, and therefore much concerned with the preservation of Indian tradition) told me how he celebrates *Divali*:

> At *Divali*, we decorate our temple, illuminate it with lights and candles, worship according to whatever way we worship. Some people worship goddess Lakshmi, for wealth; and some people worship Ganesha, some people worship different gods, Krishna, for example. But as for what I think, I won't worship the goddess or anything at all. I do go to temple, I sit there, I observe people worshipping, and I don't remember what does come in my heart, or whom I worship, or what kind of *mantras* at that time I recite.

I asked him what it means to worship Lakshmi for wealth. He replied:

> *Divali* is considered to be the calendar end of a new year for people of my caste, who are business people: they change their account books on that day, and they worship goddess Lakshmi, so that their next year will be prosperous and they will earn more wealth.

'But what,' I asked him, 'if next year is *not* prosperous: does that mean she's not doing her job very well?' He answered, 'I can't say, I can't say. But there is always something attached when they worship.'

For Muslims

For Muslims, both Sunni and Shia‘, there are two important occasions in the year, one to give thanks to God for giving them the strength to keep the fast of the month of Ramadan (the month when Muslims must fast during daylight hours). The other is the commemoration of Abraham's faith in being willing to sacrifice his son – who for Muslims was Ishmael, not Isaac. Mr Khan told me more about these occasions:

> There are no festivals as such, although there are occasions when the Muslim community meets at one particular place. Those occasions are, from the Sunnis' point of view (as also from the Shias' point of view), the *Id alFitr* and the *Id alAdha*. These are to appreciate and convey our thanks to Allah, for the fact that, in the first case (that is the *Id alFitr*) he enabled us to perform the fasting – that is to say we could fast for thirty days or twenty-nine days, and face this strain, and do it in a thankful way. This is not as an obligation, but as something which has been willingly accepted. The other is *Id alAdha*, which is to remind all of us about the sacrifice by Abraham of his son, so that in the cause of Allah, and in the cause of religion, we should not hesitate to offer any sacrifice at all.

The Shia‘ add the commemoration, not only of Muhammad's birthday, but also of the deaths (or in their view martyrdoms) of Ali, Hasan and Husayn, the nearest direct descendants of Muhammad. On those occasions, Shia‘ Muslims may physically participate in the suffering:

> We keep the Prophet Muhammad's date of birth; it's a day of great happiness, so we go to the mosque for that. It's like a party, and it's a happy occasion, not a sad one, like we have for the two months: in those months we remember that the Prophet Muhammad's family has been in very great difficulty and they have been very – how can I explain that? – brutally killed. Ali and his family were very saintly men, and they had a very rough and bad time. In these two months we remember and they are very sad days. So we go to the mosque: we listen to the priest, and at the end of the speech, we beat ourselves a bit – to share in the suffering.

So religions offer to believers stable landmarks, by which they can recognise that they are on the right road – or what they *take* to be the right road – as they journey into death. And so another part of the answer to my original question falls into place. I asked originally: what is there about religions which makes people so determined – determined, for example, to die rather than to give up their faith? The removal of familiar landmarks – whether the Euston Arch or the Book of Common Prayer – is always disturbing. The religious timetables of life, day by day, week by week, year by year, give to people a confidence by which to live and to journey through time. Maybe that confidence is misplaced; maybe the religious timetables, like pre-war Bradshaws, list unavailable journeys to non-existent stations. But that does not affect the *feelings* of those involved when the traditional 'markings of time' are threatened.

But faith will clearly always survive the iconoclasm of Oliver Cromwell's soldiers or revisers of ancient liturgies. *Far* more serious as a threat to faith is the reality of evil and the intransigent fact of suffering. So how do these religions account for the reality of evil and suffering? And how do they cope with it? Those are the questions we'll take up in the next chapter.

7
The Roaring Lion: Evil and Suffering

The Reality of Evil

An earlier chapter (God on a Bus: Experiences in Religion) ended with people describing the intense and memorable experience of pilgrimage. For one Sikh that experience of pilgrimage to the Golden Temple at Amritsar was about the only one she could remember as profoundly and genuinely religious (see p. 118). However, she immediately went on to say that when she made the pilgrimage a *second* time, she had exactly the *opposite* experience:

> It was partly frightening and partly very disappointing, I would say: when I went back five years later it was rather disastrous, because it didn't do anything to me at all. I don't know why, there was something in me that had died, and I wasn't able to feel it, to feel anything at all. I visited the temple deliberately, because I wanted to reassure myself that there was something still there; but there was nothing, I didn't feel a thing. It was just another building to me.

The two sides of that same event, that same pilgrimage, are a reminder that there are religious experiences of evil just as much as there are of ecstasy and of joy. So sharp is the reality of evil that it's frequently been personified: Satan in Judaism; Shaitan and Iblis in Islam; the Devil and all his works in Christianity; Mara in Buddhism.

Most complex is Hinduism, because in Hinduism gods and goddesses often combine within themselves the duality of good and evil. All things have a good and evil aspect, depending how you look at them: time goes slowly if you are waiting for a train, it goes very fast if you're running to catch it. The Hindu gods combine in themselves this truth of experience, that anything which from one point of view is good, from another point of view is evil. This is particularly obvious in the case of Siva, 'the erotic ascetic', as Wendy O'Flaherty described him. But it's equally dramatic in Kali: she's the goddess who symbolises the two aspects of time – bringing life, and yet equally taking it away. Devotion to Kali means coming to terms with this process and embracing it, but it's a very dangerous devotion, because traditionally it demands animal sacrifice. But what happens if she doesn't receive it? Mrs Chatterji told me:

> It is believed that if you do not offer in worship by sacrificing the animal, then she takes somebody from the family. Believe me or not, it has happened in two families. It has happened in my family: I lost a sister, and everybody told my father he should give up worshipping goddess Kali, and he didn't. He said, 'No. If Kali likes that, I wouldn't stop' – because he didn't sacrifice any animals. And it happened in one of our friend's family as well. She lives in Delhi, and she prayed to goddess Kali, and she lost her daughter not very long ago. And then she was told the same thing, that if you pray to goddess Kali, she wants sacrifice. If you don't give anything as a sacrifice then she takes somebody from the family.

I then asked her whether it is possible to offer a substitute for a living sacrifice, and she replied, 'No, it must be the animal sacrifice. Otherwise somebody goes. So I am very panicky about that.' And yet, despite that fear, her daughter *does* persist in the worship of Kali:

> I pray to Kali, MaKali. I don't 'not believe' in the other gods, but I don't necessarily pray to them at all. My Mum does say she's a bit worried about it, because of her reputation for wanting sacrifices and everything. But I believe that I sacrifice what I do every day to her. If that's not enough, well, I don't believe you have to sacrifice living animals and all that sort of guff.

Buddhists, or many Buddhists, have an equally strong belief that the atmosphere (and indeed all living things) of the universe are filled with spirits. One Tibetan Buddhist told me that he never moves a knife quickly in the kitchen in case he cuts a spirit in half in the air. So for a Buddhist, evil consequences can very easily be stirred up by disturbing the spiritual order, as Mr Poey told me, describing the death of his son:

> During the war I moved to the countryside and my son fell ill. At twelve o'clock sharp my sister happened to bring my son out from the house; and immediately afterwards he fell ill. He was one year old, so he could only call 'Papa', that's all; and I took him to bed to look after him and all that; and while I was

> looking after him, while I was lying beside him, my wife went to cook – suddenly she gave a yell, and that was it – finished. I couldn't get a doctor then; I raced and ran for a dresser – but of course he passed away. Then somebody told me, 'You happened to fell a very old tree, no leaves, no branches, which is two hundred years old; there was a very good spirit there – or whatever – there was a spirit there, and because of that, this thing happened.

Christians have identified the Devil as the agent and instrument of evil. Scripture warns the believer to beware of the Devil, that Roaring Lion which goes about seeking whom he may devour. I asked a young Christian, Michael Stevenson, whether the Devil had ever tried to devour him. He replied emphatically: 'Oh, every day, every day. It's a constant warfare. So you have to always, like the Scripture says, be vigilant, be watchful, because, you know, he comes in any form at all possible.' But the reality of evil can be a specific and definite threat, as he went on to say:

> A year or so ago I was going through the worst time I ever went through as a Christian, and I looked – I sat down and I looked in the mirror, and I said, 'God, why are you making me go through this? You know I cannot stand this sort of thing – I cannot really take it.' And I just couldn't. And I didn't get an immediate answer, but later on I was just sat there, and I looked at myself and I thought, 'You've come out of this, and you're a better person – you know?' And I thought, 'God, you're wonderful!'

God *may* be wonderful, but that doesn't stop the reality of evil occurring in the ordinary business of daily work. The testing moments of life do not necessarily announce their presence by drum and trumpet – but, as Cardozo continued, 'Some little, unassuming, unobtrusive choice presents itself before us, slyly and craftily, glib and insinuating, and frequently in the modest garb of innocence.' One man remembered what happened when it was announced that his factory was going to be closed down:

> Towards the end, before we closed down, there was a tremendous amount of evil. A situation was encouraged to develop, because, I'm convinced, the company wanted to close the place down. People no longer wanted to work; the management was corrupt and doing all sorts of malpractices, and both sides knew what was happening. I, like everybody else, was influenced by the environment in which we lived. In

> that situation where I found myself, I was being influenced. I didn't, you know, say 'Well, it's not my fault, it's all these other fellows.' I was part of it. I was becoming corrupt. Nobody bothered about what time you went in of a morning. The first guy in on the shift clocked everybody in. And management were selling all sorts of stuff to people for vast sums of money. And the stewards knew about that, and the management knew about what was happening on the shop floor, and neither one would stop the other one, because they were like two Chicago gangs, blackmailing one another. And to me, that was the most evil situation that I've ever found myself in.

Temptation and Sin

And yet for most people evil doesn't occur in such a dramatic or isolated way. It comes at them as a much more constant – indeed, never ending – test of faith and practice. That's how a Buddhist, originally from Sri Lanka, described the reality of evil to me:

> It's just temptation; it's just temptation. I mean, I see a figure of eight moving, then I might think, 'My God, she's my daughter's age!' And I feel ashamed that for that moment, I looked at her from a carnal point of view. I've not reached the state where I'm free of all these carnal desires – I will be a liar if I say so. We all have these temptations. That is where the saint differs from us. A saint never does anything where he has to think twice, to see whether what he's doing is harmful or beneficial – he doesn't have to. But you and I have to, that's why we are not saints as yet.

As yet: but 'making saints' is what Christianity is meant to be about. Yet obviously Christians who clearly believe that they have been saved do continue to sin: 'Oh yes, many times, several times,' said Mrs Lynch in Manchester. 'You see, it's something that we have to fight against, as a Christian, because the Devil always troubles us who try – the person who tries to be a Christian, the Devil seems to be at them most. So I wouldn't say we don't sin, because we live in a sinful world: I can just look at you and sin in my heart. So I can't say I'm not a sinner. But you don't go and commit sin just for the fun of it. You see, sometimes you can sin and you don't even realise that you sin. In your very thoughts, you can sin. And so that is why as Christians this is one of the things we have to do often, to pray; you always have to be praying to ask God to keep you, and to forgive.'

Sin and Forgiveness

So everybody at some time or other finds that the only way, as Oscar Wilde put it, to get rid of temptation is to give in to it; or as Mae West put it more recently 'Between two evils, I always pick the one I never tried before.' In other words, we all fall into doing things we know to be wrong. But if that happens, what do you do about it? Again it's very different in different religions. At one extreme, Mr Singh stressed, as a Hindu, that you cannot go *outside* yourself to ask God for forgiveness, because God is already inside you – your real self *is Brahman*:

> It doesn't matter if a person fails. The point is that his direction of life should be in the right direction. If a man keeps his eye just in the right direction, then there's nobody to ask forgiveness from, because the whole universe is the manifestation of that force of life which has framed the whole universe. There is no difference between the soul, between the life-force that is in man, that is in plants, that is in animals, that is manifest everywhere, and which we call the universal soul.

At the other extreme are religions in which there are recognised ways of seeking forgiveness. This is particularly obvious among the Sikhs because they have a special ceremony of admission into the *Khalsa*, or Brotherhood, which *can* be applied to lapsed Sikhs who wish to return to full observance [for a description, see p. 36f.].

But that ceremony applies when you've actually fallen out of the community, the *Khalsa*, or when you are coming into it for the first time. So I also asked a Sikh, Surinder Singh Hyare, what he would do to put right any lesser sins or offences. He answered:

> Go to the temple and pray there, and do whatsoever the congregation decides about it. They take it on them, and they decide on something that he has done wrong, you see, and that he should do this or that – say, a community work they might decide, like polishing all the shoes of the people. These are minor things. But in very, very wrong things even our own Maharajah (who is the king of our place, you see), he was given one hundred lashes for one thing which he did wrong;

> and he dare not say that nobody should touch him.

Christianity, as we've already begun to see, has a particularly strong sense of sin and of its forgiveness, because of the Christian belief that the death of Christ was intended by God to defeat the power and effect of sin. But what *is* this sin? One Christian said, 'Putting it basically, sin is anything that goes against the nature of God – anything that would insult God or hurt him. I guess that's the easiest way of describing sin. One thing, I think, would be by just ignoring the fact that he's there – hearing what God has to say and directly not doing anything about it. I think that's one of the things that would hurt God; and hurting God is sin.' Another Christian added: 'C. S. Lewis said "Sin is sin because 'I' is in the middle." And that's quite a good little phrase to remember. It really means, I think, a selfish act, something you do primarily because you hope to gain something out of it for yourself.'

So what do Christians, or would-be Christians, have to do about sin, and that offer of forgiveness in Christ? Simon Williams said:

> I suppose the basic words, which seem to crop up again and again, are to repent and to believe. To repent isn't a sort of grovelling in sackcloth and ashes. To repent seems to be saying, 'Well, I've come to a point in my life where I'm deciding to change.' And if there are things which you believe are completely incompatible with being a Christian, you don't promise to give them up, because it might be ludicrous to say, 'I'll never do it again'; but you say, 'Well, I acknowledge that these are wrong, and with your help, I'll stop doing them.'

Still, the fact remains that Christians do sin, even after they've accepted Jesus as Saviour and Lord, as Mrs Lynch said. So I asked her, 'What do Christians do then?' For her, it is a matter of bringing her life back into the way made possible by Christ:

> Well, since Jesus died for our sins, we have got a part to play. And the part that we have to play is to accept him as our personal Saviour – the fact that he died for our sins. He didn't just die and say, 'OK, I died for your sins, you can do as you like.' We have got a part to play as well. And the part that I believe we have got to play, is to not keep hurting, causing God to be angry, any more.

But important for many Christians in facing the fact of sin is sacramental confession; going to a priest who, they believe, has authority from Christ by virtue of his ordination to absolve. *How* they make their confession differs. But *some* form of confession is their way of taking seriously the reality of sin:

> I go to Confession. But it's not just a case of going to the priest and saying, 'I'm sorry for doing this, Father', and then it's all forgiven: I say my three Hail Marys, or whatever he gives me, and that's it, my penance. I believe, even though I'm genuinely sorry at the time and I've said the penance, that the slate isn't wiped clean. I'll still have to pay for what I've done, and this is what I term my turn in purgatory.

An Anglican saw the point of going to Confession as lying in the fact that sin has to be brought into the open: the very fact of talking about it helps to overcome self-deceit. But a young Roman Catholic teacher, Christopher Gajewski, was not so sure about the old style of Confession. He said:

> I'm not a representative sample of the Catholic Church on confession, I don't think – though perhaps I am of people of my own age. It's not so much going away from the confessional box – though that's ridiculous really, when you think about it: you go into this little box, this wooden-panelled box, with no inspiration on the walls or anything – nothing to focus your eyes on – and you just kneel there, and you have to say your sins through this metal grille; it has a curtain at the back, so you can't see a face, and you can't see a reaction of horror when you've told your sins – or delight when you haven't got many to tell! It's really off-putting. In fact when I went in, my mind just went totally blank – I could hardly remember my own name. But the move now is to just sit next to a priest and tell the priest what the things are that are worrying you – not just sins: I mean, 'sins' is a peculiar word. What is a sin? But just to tell him what you've done for the past fortnight, good and bad, and get encouragement from him; and he may discuss something with you, if there's anything worrying you. But obviously, that type of confession will take so much time. With a congregation of five thousand or whatever, it would be impossible to do that with three priests. So the other move is for a group confession. But I really don't think there's a need to tell a priest your sins. I think you should be able to go into a church and kneel down and just make a short sort of act of contrition, or whatever, in your own words, and tell God that you've done this or you've been mean to somebody, and say

> you're sorry, and try to make amends for the future. I think that is enough.

So in the end each individual has his or her own conscience – his or her relationship with God; and how that relationship is worked out and kept in good repair varies tremendously. As one Muslim put it:

> You could say we are *all* 'baddies', really. There are two types of sins. One is the one which you do with the people; and the other is the one which you do with God (like not praying, or not going to mosque). He is never going to forgive the first type of sin. He might forgive the second one, but there is no chance for the first one. So I suppose people like me, you see, whom you might call agnostic about what happens after death – people like me have taken it for granted that we'll go there and admit that we're bad, but at least we didn't do the first one, we'll say: you told us that it won't be forgiven.

So people in all these religions recognise the fragile nature of life – how easy it is to fall away and do things we know to be wrong, or even more to the point, fail to do things we know that we ought to have done. The power of religious belief is that it offers to people the strength and the encouragement to stay on course, even in the face of temptation, as a Christian, Mrs Emmett, told me: 'The first thing I say is, "Jesus help me, stay with me, put these thoughts out of my mind: I want you as my leader, and I love all that you did." And then I'm at peace. But it's a very fine line, you know. You can tip. I just about manage to stay on the fence. Well, yes, just: I don't kind of "fall off".' In Leeds, Pandit Chimanlal Pandya told me about the threefold Hindu defence against temptation:

> If a friend or a relative tells me to do anything wrong, then my heart, my conscience, bites me. It says, 'No, this is not good'; in the heart it says 'No, no, no.' He says once, twice and thrice, 'Don't do that, this is not good.' And that is why we say also sometimes to our friends and relatives, 'Though you are telling us to do this thing, it is not good, it is not good, it is not good.'

As a pandit, Mr Pandya is in control of many rituals, so I asked him whether people come to him to ask for protection against attacks from demons. He answered, 'They come, they come.' So I then asked, 'What do you do then?' He replied: 'I say, "No, this is all wrong, because according to religion, demons will not come to you, evil will not come to you, unless you do something wrong." So I say "Try to live a holy way of life, doing all the services and the social, and religious and cultural activities of the world. As for your intelligence, mouth and power of the body, no evil speak, or demons will come to you."'

And an Orthodox Jew, Jack Schild, agreed (looking back on more than seventy years of life) that his faith has kept him from doing things that he really knows are wrong:

> I haven't done any devilish things in my life. I've never done anything devilish; but one thing I will say, I'll be frank, and admit that it's my Jewishness and my belief in God that has helped me to walk along the moral path. You see, that I must say, being a human being, sometimes I might see a nice girl, I might admire her, you know. My Jewishness, and knowing that I *daven* and all that [Yiddish, literally, to go to and fro, a word for praying] has helped me, so that it hasn't gone any further than that. You see, you get some people who do immoral things – they have sex with women and all that kind of thing – even religious people: it's happened with even religious people doing it. But I haven't done anything like that, you see. And I would say it's because of my religion, because I believe in my religion, and that has helped me, you know.

So religions may themselves create great evils, as Pascal observed: 'Men never do evil so completely and cheerfully as when they do it from religious conviction.' Yet at the same time (and maybe for that reason as well), religions create a *seriousness* about evil: they create, if you like, an imagination of evil which does justice to its unmistakable existence in life and in experience. The people I listened to were all well aware of the power of evil to corrupt and destroy, not least in the fertile ground of faith: 'The Devil gets up to the belfry,' as Thomas Fuller observed, 'by the vicar's skirts.'

And yet religion, precisely because it *does* take evil seriously, also offers a corresponding power to resist. Above all, it seems to keep prodding people to remember the question *cui malo*? (though they would be asking it, not in Latin, but in Urdu, Punjabi, Arabic or whatever): to what evil may this action or this thought of mine be leading? To recognise that evil exists is already to have made a start in resisting it.

Suffering: Why?

So evil is one reality which threatens to corrupt or destroy religious faith. Suffering is another. In fact, suffering, in all its many grim and different forms, has come much closer to destroying the faith of many of those to whom I listened. It wasn't so much their *own* suffering as the suffering of others which tested faith – as Jacqueline Rapson remembered of the Italian earthquake: 'When the Italian earthquake happened I thought that was awful, I couldn't understand that happening. In fact, for about two weeks I felt a long way from God. I just didn't understand why that had to happen.' And a Hindu girl added: 'A lot of people say that either you have faith or you don't, but I don't believe that. When certain things happen – for instance, when two very, very close people died – I lost all faith completely for a long time; at least a year.' That was equally true for others: having to wait and watch while loved ones slowly die – often in great distress – raises very deep questions about the purposes and the power of God:

> I think the worst thing that happened to me – and it wasn't when I was very young – was when someone who was very, very close to me died, like a brother almost: my cousin, he was. I suppose it's death, really, and you're so afraid of it. But I was so bitter against God; because he was only thirteen when he died of cancer, and I remember he suffered a whole year, and I used to take him to the hospital for his transfusions and his pills and his treatments and everything. And I just watched him die, you know, within a year.

For others, their own suffering – especially depression – seemed to exile God from their experience entirely:

> I was ill after my youngest daughter was born. After about three months I had a depression. And I couldn't, I just couldn't get in touch with anybody; and I was really – I felt really far away. I didn't feel there was a God, I didn't feel there was anything. Not even a light at the end of the tunnel. I'd never experienced that. And when somebody said to me, you know, 'Can you see anything? Can you see any light at the end of the tunnel?' I said, 'No, I can't see, I can't think or feel anything.' I couldn't even pray for help to get over this depression.

Why, then, does suffering happen? Why is there so much suffering? Why do we live and die in such unequal ways? Buddhism, of course, the whole of Buddhism, is an answer to those questions. The Four Noble Truths lie at the very root of Buddhism, and they are the analysis of *dukkha*, suffering. The first truth simply says that *dukkha* is the truth that we have to deal with. The second is the truth of how *dukkha*, suffering, originates. The third is the truth of how it ceases. And the fourth describes the path leading to its cessation. Suffering only arises, according to the Buddha, if we try to cling on to something stable, something that is going to endure, in a world or in a universe where nothing is permanent. So the teaching of the Buddha simply points the way to breaking the bond of attachment to this world, or even to ourselves. All suffering will then cease, because then there is nothing left to be attached to. And many Buddhists have already described all this in earlier chapters (see especially pp. 28–31).

What arises from this analysis in Buddhism is a strong rejection of a God who has created all things. For how would any God dare, or even care, to produce a world like this? That at least is the question which Mr Poey asks:

> There is no Creator God, and that I believe myself. If there is God, God cannot pay special attention to this very, very small earth of ours, which is even smaller than, let us say, an atom in relation to the whole universal system. And if there is God, we must ask, 'Why is there suffering?' – like Bertrand Russell who said, 'Why did God take billions of years to form this earth, and end in Hitler and the hydrogen bomb?'

And another Buddhist added simply: 'When I saw the great and wide disparity that existed in the world, I couldn't accept the creation.'

But creation means different things in different religions, and to the Hindus, the way in which Buddhists reject a Creator God means that they are actually taking creation too seriously. For Hindus, creation is a kind of divine exuberance: it is *lila*, play, in which things are brought into appearance almost for the exhilaration of the creative act – the creator as an artist, with the failure and the success of the enterprise interwoven as a necessary condition of art – very much, in fact, as Picasso used to think of God: 'God is really another artist. He invented the giraffe, the elephant, the cat. He has no single style. He just goes on trying other things.' So also with the Hindus: the Source of all things brings all things into appearance. That appearance is known as *maya*, but there is nothing permanent or enduring *in the appearance.* It's the underlying reality, *Brahman*, the source and origin of all things, which endures. And it's *Brahman* which becomes manifest through all appearance. That reality cannot suffer or experience pain. It cannot kill or be killed. And because *Brahman* is in us, as *atman*, soul, this means for a Hindu that *we* – what we are essentially within – cannot suffer. So the practice of Hinduism is the realisation of the truth, *Brahman*, within us. What that involves is becoming detached from the present and superficial *maya*, appearance; and the many different forms of Hinduism are simply different ways of attempting that detachment. This is so fundamental to Hinduism that I asked a Hindu, Mr Chitra Pal Singh, to explain to me in more detail what *maya* really is, or appears to be:

> *Maya* means the creative force of God, if you will allow me to use the word 'God' for the life force; because I would like to be just abstract. *Maya* means the force of creation; the power behind the creation of this physical universe. This idea of *maya* is that everything that you see in this world is untrue. It's just like a dream. This is the interpretation given by Shankara. But even in the Vedas, *maya* is the force, which has brought all this world, this universe, into existence. So the point is this, that there is no suffering in reality in this world, there is nothing like suffering. Suffering occurs in the mind, in the attitude we have. That's why suffering is for men most of all, because they have got their mind, they think, and they interpret happenings into tortures. If suffering exists, where does it exist? It exists in the mind of man.

But none of that actually gets rid of the basic question: why then do particular instances of what at least *appears* to be suffering happen?

On this point Hindus and Buddhists, and also Sikhs, agree. Individual suffering is a consequence of *karma* – that law of reward and punishment which runs on from previous lives when we are reborn (p. 32). That can even apply to a deformed baby. The baby is born deformed, but the fact that it's born at all means that it must have had, not bad, but good *karma* in a previous life, otherwise it couldn't have been born as a human being. That was the point made by Mrs Kalia: 'It did something that was very good,' she said, 'that gave it the right to become born in a human form, but it certainly wasn't good enough, or perfect enough, for it to be a perfect baby.'

It follows that *karma* and rebirth supply the reason also why animals suffer. The point is that we may be reborn as animals if we are accumulating bad *karma* in the life we're living at this moment. 'Suffering of animals is caused by God,' said Mr Krishan Mittal, 'because he has sent that particular soul in that form to suffer, because that soul hadn't led the life previous to that form in the way God expected him to lead it.'

But Hindus have another reason also for saying why suffering happens, particularly at the present moment. The Hindu understanding of Time is that it goes round in cycles, in what are known as *yugas*: there's a cycle in the universe, beginning with birth, which leads to maturity, then to decline and finally to death. And after that it all begins again. The last stage of the cycle, before the new beginning, is known as the Kali Yuga, when evil dominates. Needless to say, we're in the Kali Yuga now. And that in itself is an answer to the question 'Why is there suffering?' as Mrs Chauhan told me very emphatically in Leeds: 'This is the Kali Yuga,' she said, 'which means that the time is evil. In the old times, long time ago, the prayer was very strong and powerful: it took a long, long time. Now, in this moment, people are never taking long, long time to pray.'

Sikhs also have a belief in rebirth, but they combine that with a much more unified belief in the activity of God working his purpose out, even if we don't understand it. Gurbachan Singh Sidhu told me:

> We believe that the suffering in this world is in fact created by God himself. What purpose he has in creating suffering and evil is something that we wouldn't be able to understand. It's his will that these things should be in the world side by side, just as we have day and night. No one can perhaps explain why God created day and night. Why wasn't there day all the time? So our belief is that whatever good and whatever bad there is, it has been created by him. And we are too small to understand his purpose behind it.

But the Buddhist question to the Sikh would still be, *Why* would God create a world like this? Sarbjot Singh Hyare, in answering the question, introduced a very basic theme, that this world is an arena – a vale of soul-making, as Keats called it in a different tradition: 'I believe,' he said, 'that this life is a test, and that everything you do, and the things that happen to you, are a test of your character, so the way you react is the way that you are perfecting yourself morally.' But what worried me when he said that was to understand how a baby (born, for example, with a genetic defect which leads to its almost immediate death) can be said to be being *tested.* He answered:

> This is my own personal belief: I believe that even through *that*, the child in his next life will learn something – that even if it's only a few seconds on this planet, it's all intended as a test. I believe that all living things have a part which is a part of God, so that God in his wisdom has planned intrinsically little, little things so that every living thing has contact with other living things, and it's all one huge web, and that animal suffering, like human suffering, is for their perfection.

Harbans Singh Sagoo added a further – and for a Sikh, vital – point, that through this network of suffering and rebirth, the grace of God is at work:

> What you reap here is not only the result of what you do now, but it could also be the result of something that you've done in your previous life for which you are repaying here. And if there is anything that I have done in my previous life, the fruit of which is still to come, I only hope that God in his graciousness will forgive me and not bring that thing up.

Rebirth and *karma* offer one account of why suffering happens. But clearly the Buddhist challenge, to the reconciliation between a creator God and a creation so full of suffering, is addressed much more to religions in which there is no rebirth, no long succession of lives working out rewards and punishments; and it's addressed also to religions in which the claim is made that God is loving and merciful. The traditional Christian answer, as Mrs Lynch expressed it, has been that creation was originally good: 'He created a good world, but, you see, what caused pain is sin. The world was made perfect; no sin was in the world until sin came into the world through disobedience.' And Mrs Williams reminded me (as we saw earlier in this chapter) that the reality of evil has its part to play, personified as the Devil:

> I don't think God created the suffering. Man created the suffering by going against God's will. I also believe that there is a Devil, and evil force in the world, whether the Devil brings disease, or the Devil gets into people to act in violent and hurtful ways.

But those answers require a context; and the context, in which the Christian response to suffering is held, is the manifestation of God as love in Christ. That love was apparently destroyed in crucified suffering on Good Friday. But on Easter Day it was seen, at least by Christians, to be the final and undying word – even though, as Ray Turner emphasised, it's not something that anyone can really comprehend: 'I can only say that in God's overall plan, he made his own son suffer: if you can understand that, or anybody can understand it, I don't know. I mean, it's beyond understanding. I just haven't got an answer for you, I just don't know.' This means that for Christians there is no particular answer to the specific problem of suffering. There can only be a holding fast to the *whole* reality of experience – not just the suffering but also the love, not only the pain, but also its transcendence. Suffering as the kiss of Christ is hard to discern or accept. But Christians can't do other than take the whole of the experience together. Mrs Emmett put it like this:

> I think that perhaps the whole of creation is a package, and we have to take the whole thing. I don't know why, though, the fox will chase a little rabbit and kill it, but it does. Perhaps we have to have the suffering in the animal kingdom as well as in the human kingdom.

Not answers, but allegiance to the fact of God as much as to the fact of suffering. Both are equally real – or seem to be equally real – to those who know them. Mrs Iles recalled how often she gets asked about this:

> I know, I have this at work, and we get questions like, 'Well, if there's a God up there, why has he had all this trouble in Poland? Why does he wreck lifeboats and houses and make earthquakes?' I feel terrible; how can I answer questions like that, when you get lecturers, archbishops – they can't answer it? But you have to say to them, 'Don't blame *everything* on God.' All right, they think they know he's up there, but that doesn't mean he's got a finger in every pie. But some good does come out of those things: you probably find that it's the poor people that give the most when anything goes wrong. Always.

For Muslims the challenge of suffering may seem similar, but in fact it's very different. Muslims don't associate Jesus *with* God *as* God. Nor can they think of God as Father. He is not: he is the omnipotent Creator, as Mr Mohammed Ali told me: 'The word a Christian says, "Father of children", we don't use that word. We say God is Supreme, he's the Creator. And we are his slaves.' The Creator, then, has created in this world a stage, an arena, in which men and women are tested by the works they do. If they don't pass the test, they are condemned to punishment; but if they do pass it, then they return to God forever to be rewarded in paradise. Muslims, therefore, accept suffering as part of that test, as Mrs Khan told me: 'Muslim people just take it as it comes. We have faith in it. Good, bad, whatever happens during our life, our everyday life, we just take it as a part of our life.'

But then, of course, the same question comes up again, of the baby born deformed: how can it be said that a suffering baby is being tested? Another Muslim, Mrs Qureshi said: 'That suffering is for the parents. I believe the child is innocent, he doesn't know what is happening. It's really for the parents.' Which seems a bit hard on the child. But even if we accept that men and women are being tested by the suffering they undergo, what about the animals? Why create a world where the animals destroy and attack one another? How do Muslims account for that? Mr Lakdawala said:

> Firstly, man is the crown of creation: everything in this world is created for man. Now in this world you can't forget that man has been created, and everything that exists is for man. So if the animal is consumed as food by man, I think that is not wasted.

But what about the animal that feeds on another animal? Is that wasted? Hajji Cassim Mohammad thought not, because the interlocking regularity of the universe requires this kind of balance, if there is to be any life at all. In other words, suffering of this kind can only be understood within an adequate understanding of creation:

> God has his laws: they're immutable, they aren't changeable; and presumably he has created the animal kingdom with the survival of the fittest, one has to live on the other. And if we study the animal life, we will see that one preys on the other: one provides itself as food for the other, and so the whole creation exists. Now with man it's different, because man has been created and given a free will. He has choice, he can choose, you see. So God has sent him guidance, and he has left him open to choose whichever direction he wants. Look at it from this point of view: what we don't understand now may not necessarily be wrong. If we have more time and we study the animal kingdom, we will find that it has to be like that, otherwise there will be too many of one. If we had a lot of

> gazelles and no lions to eat them – either gazelles or zebras, and no lions and tigers to kill them – we'll have too many; they'll eat all the trees down, you see. So something must happen to reduce them. And one has to prey on the other; one provides food for the other; and certain animals form food for human beings.

In the case of the Jews suffering is written into their own history and experience. Long before the rise of Hitler, George Eliot was writing, 'If there are ranks in suffering, Israel takes precedence of all the nations – if the duration of sorrows and the patience with which they are borne ennoble, the Jews are among the aristocracy of every land.' How, then, I asked Stuart Dresner, do Jews reconcile all that with a belief that God is the Creator, and that he is in control of what he has done? He replied:

> If we are to expect God to make a better job of it, that implies that God controls everything that goes on; and if God controls everything that goes on, then that means we would not have free will; and we believe that people do have free will to act as they want; and therefore, it's up to people to make something of the world for better or for worse.

His wife added:

> The Jewish view is that we're partners in God's creation, and that's very, very important. Yes, he could possibly have made a better job of it, as you say, but we ourselves have to make a better job out of what we are given: the raw materials are there: it's up to people to live in a civilised way. The point is that we are interdependent; the whole chain of life shows interdependency, and we are part of that; and if part of it seems cruel to us, then it's because it has to be cruel in order for the other part to continue. That is interdependency, and we can't put values on it.

And he, in turn, took that point further:

> People are superior; that is, humans have an intellect, and we have a right to use animals in a civilised way. Obviously, we can't be cruel to animals – and there are specific laws in the Torah about being kind to animals. But according to Torah, when man was created, he had a right to use animals for his own benefit.

That comment on animals goes right back to the story of creation in the book of Genesis, and that's a reminder that for Jews, as well as for Christians, Adam gets into the act. This is how Mr Klein put it:

> If Adam had not sinned, the world would have reached its culmination already in the first week of creation. Since the sin, there has been an imbalance in the universe, and therefore, there is suffering in the world. Some of the suffering which man goes through in the world is a form of punishment to cleanse him for his misdeeds, whether they be misdeeds in this incarnation or in a previous incarnation [in the Jewish sense of reincarnation: see p. 262]. However, it would be mistaken to see this punishment as a negative element. On the contrary, this punishment is a blessing if we receive it in this world rather than afterlife. Then suffering also sometimes comes to man as a test to see how deep is his belief in God. Everything that happens to a person is really for his good, and therefore it is a commandment to bless God for the suffering that one has, as much as for the good experiences which one has in one's life.

But how, I wondered, can you possibly bless God for the events of the Holocaust? Mrs Levy answered: 'That is the tricky point. That's where many people who've gone through the Holocaust have started to think, "Well, *is* there a God? Where is God?" The only answer we can give to that is that, if the Holocaust had *not* gone on, perhaps worse things would have happened in another way; and you have to console yourself with an optimistic philosophy, that all is for the good in the end, although it's hard to believe.' I talked to Jack Schild about this, who has many memories of these events. He said:

> When people ask me about the Holocaust – and even people here in the yard: one man says to me, 'I'm not going to *shul* any more, I'm not going to put on any *tefillin* any more, I'm not going to *daven* [pray] because of the Holocaust' – now what can I answer him? I can only say to him that I'm not going to give up the Jewish religion. I tell him, 'I know this is a serious question and it's very difficult – impossible to answer really.' I said, 'But if you want to take it that way,' I say, 'I can't give you a satisfactory answer for that.' Another chap told me that his nephew used to be an Orthodox young man, and now he eats bacon and ham and everything, eats on *Yom Kippur*, because he lost all his relatives in Poland, and he's the only one that

> survived; so he doesn't believe in anything. 'Well,' I said, 'what can I do about it?' I can't convince him. I can't convince him. I can only say that I lost all my relatives in Galicia, lost them all; and I don't think there were any survivors except those who left Poland before the war. They survived, but those who stayed on, they've all been – they were all destroyed. But I . . . I can't argue about that, you see, you can't argue.

That acceptance of the futility of argument did not seem to me (as I listened to him and others talking about it) to be an evasion of the facts. It sounded more like a recognition that the facts of life – and of experience – include *both* suffering *and* sovereignty: 'I, John, your brother, who share with you in the suffering and the sovereignty and the endurance which is ours in Jesus . . .', as the dream of the Apocalypse begins. The religious problem of suffering is how to avoid a kind of metaphysical schizophrenia: we all know what it is to wear what Whitman called 'the garments of agony' – 'Agonies are one of my changes of garments': pain, disaster, unbelievable cruelties are all part of human experience. But so too is God; and so too is *satori*, detachment, peace. The same woman, who told me about her depression (p. 174) and how it had destroyed her sense of God, went on: 'Gradually I got better, and then one day, in May, six years ago, for five days I had this feeling of happiness, of brimming over; and I couldn't keep this happiness down. And I knew that it was the love of God in me, showing me that I can be happy again. After about five days I came down again – not as bad as I was, but to an everyday level; but I shall always remember that feeling of happiness.'

So the truth, as people tried to tell it to me, seems to rest, not in attempting to reconcile the two sides of human experience, or in subordinating one to the other, but in accepting – even grasping – the reality of *both* without evasion; and perhaps also by affirming *in* life the ultimate victory *of* life. What that might mean we will see when we come to the chapter on death and on what these religions believe may lie beyond death. But before we get there, we have yet to see how these religions work out their faith in family life.

8
Families in Faith: Control or Freedom?

So far we have been concerned with a very wide range of human experiences – of prayer and meditation; of evil and suffering; of great happiness when, for example, people go on pilgrimage to places of religious importance. But none of these experiences take these people *out* of life: by definition we have been listening to people who have stayed involved in the ordinary daily life of the world: they have not become monks or nuns, gurus or sannyasins. *Their* religion, therefore, must begin at home – in the family. The strength or weakness of a religious faith is tested there, more than anywhere else – as one Buddhist put it: 'The most important thing in Buddhism is that there are a lot of practical things that we need to recognise and to do. Maybe eventually we go further and further, but at the moment, I think it is more important to establish peace and harmony in the world and in the family: it's in the family and among your friends that it's important.'

Family Centre: the Basic Importance of the Family

So however much living in a family has its moments for everyone of (as Martin Mull once put it) having a bowling alley installed in your brain, for almost all the people we listened to, the family is a great blessing, and very much the centre of their lives. As a Muslim, Mohammed Hassan, put it: 'The family is one of the stones of the whole building – indeed, it's the whole building: without these stones of family life, you can't build the house – the whole society.' For Jews the emphasis on family and children is equally strong, as a Jewish mother expressed it, with a different image: 'I see it as a chain: if one link breaks, the whole chain is not the same any more. We have to keep the chain whole and complete.'

In fact, as we shall see in the chapter on death, continuity in children is, for some Jews, the only kind of life beyond death which they can really envisage and be sure of. So for Jews, it is not really an issue that can be discussed: their children *must* remain Jews: 'Judaism can only continue if the younger generation goes on following the pattern, the tradition. Now I'm not saying survival is everything, but survival of Judaism is important. Judaism is a way of looking at the world and a way of living your life which we think is important. And if we think it's important, then it's important to us that it should be carried on.'

Birth and Belonging

This issue of keeping children in the faith – not by force but by their own consent when they come of age – is important for more religions than Judaism; and it raises, as we shall see, searching questions about the nature of education – about whether children should be separately educated if they are to stay in a particular tradition. One very important reason why this matters so much came through over and over again, from many of the people we listened to. When I asked, 'Why are you a Hindu, Buddhist, Sikh (or whatever their religion happened to be)?', by far the most common answer was, 'Because I was born into it.' Choices and decisions may have followed later: but the original context of birth is obviously critical, as these examples make clear:

> I was born like that. That's the original, basic reason. So the question shouldn't really be, 'Why am I a Jew?', but, 'Why have I remained an observant Jew to a certain extent?' I believe basically that the main reason why one remains religious is a very, very strong family background, where one is made very conscious of it. And it really becomes part of you. It's innate in you.
>
> I'm a Jew because primarily I was born into the religion. My parents and grandparents before them were Jewish, and therefore I automatically became Jewish, just through that.
>
> I am a Catholic because it is the tradition of Christianity into which I was born, but now at my stage in life it is a tradition which I have looked at very carefully. I gave a whole year of my married life away, not to check on it, but to explore it further; and it is a tradition which I think I should stay with; it's valuable, although I've got a lot of quarrels with it.
>
> I'm an Anglican because that's the faith I was brought up in –

partly; but partly because the Anglican church is the local church here. I mean, we didn't come here thinking we must join an Anglican church. We could equally well have joined another denomination; but for us we wanted to be *in* the church here, and therefore the Anglican church seemed the one to join.

It's because I have been brought up in a Muslim family, and my parents were Muslim, that's why.

It is because this was my way of life since birth and I have found it worth living in this Hindu faith and following it.

To begin with, I had a head-start: I was born a Buddhist so that I was able to study it. The influence is there all the time which made me think. And of course my parents did the right thing, which I have followed with my children. They made us study the Bible – the Old Testament and the New. They were not at all prejudiced. As they said, it's only by reading these books that you will one day be able to appreciate your own. And I find it's absolutely true.

The family is the basic thing from where a Sikh learns everything in this life, because how we learn all the morals, and charity, love, and all these things, they start from the family. They start from self-sacrifice: we are not for our own self, sometimes we do it for others. The family is the shortest way to move to that, you see.

With that kind of background and feeling, it is not surprising that there is a strong sense of urgency and demand to bring up one's own children securely in the faith. The next link in the chain must be firmly fixed, to go back to the image used by the Jews – who mark their male children *as* Jews with the sign of circumcision, as Mr and Mrs Levy described to me:

He: It isn't a very dramatic ceremony – though I suppose it's a bit dramatic for the child. A character called a *mo'el* carries out a ritual circumcision, which is quick and painless, using some instruments that were developed a long while ago. It seems to be anatomically highly successful and well proven – we've all survived it. It's an opportunity to thank God for the successful birth and to welcome this new male offspring into Jewish society.
She: That goes back even further than this. That goes back to Abraham.

Even so – even with that long tradition going back to Abraham – the effort to keep children as Jews stops well short of coercion. As one Jewish mother remembers:

> I can go back to the time of the publication of the Curtis Report, on the maltreatment of children (which was about 1944, I rather suspect), and I was at a tutorial college at the time; and I remember I was going on about it and getting worked up, and somebody said to me, 'Oh, you Jews do get so excited about these things.' And I said, 'Well, we Jews don't beat our bloody children.'

The Family That Stays Together Prays Together

But should children be forced to join in religious practices and observances? Should they, to take one specific example, be taken to church? Almost all the parents we listened to said there should be *some* discipline, so that children can learn at least something of what they will eventually have to decide about, but no overbearing compulsion:

> We think children are sent for a purpose, and we've been very lucky. We haven't had everything moneywise, but we have had six healthy children, and we reckon we have our wealth in those six children; and it's been hard at times; but we're just lucky. It's important to be a Christian – and fortunately we have the gift of faith. And there's no two ways about it: as far as we're concerned, it *is* a gift. People say,'Well, look, you were brought up with it.' Of course we were brought up with it. We have to learn by example. But as they get older, I've given the freedom to my children. When I'm getting ready to go to Mass, they're there, putting their shoes on, getting ready to go with me. And one or two of them, odd times, will say, 'Do I have to go?' And I say, 'No, you don't have to go; but if you can't give one hour out of a week to your Maker and you can live with that, fair enough.' They always go. And then they get the habit: habit-forming of going to church.

Certainly some of this hesitation about compulsory church-going comes from the experience of the parents who *don't* want to inflict the same thing on their children as happened to them – as Jacqueline Rapson remembers:

> My daughter comes to church with me when I go. She usually runs around at the back and makes a heck of a noise with the

rest of them, and yet she knows the pattern of the service. I feel that just by her being there she's gaining from it; because when I first went to church, we all went to church when we were younger, all the family, up until the age of about 14; we went to Sunday School: I dropped out then: I thought it rather weird – 'church', you know! I couldn't understand people being religious. It used to make me quite squirm. But having that basic 'going to church', and having that bit of knowledge about it, helped – it was something to grow on. You see, I went to a Presbyterian church, and the vicar always used to thump the pulpit – used to frighten the life out of me; and also my youngest brother used to drop the pennies on the floor, and I used to squirm with embarrassment, and he used to stand there and count the money, when it came to the collection, and it was awful really: I just didn't see any point in it at all. When I got to 14 I just couldn't stand the thought of having anything to do with religion – or classical music – or anything that was weird. But as I say, it was a foundation, even though I didn't know it then.

The Mother and Religious Upbringing

But if growing in the faith is going to be a matter of education in the home, not of compulsion, then the role of the mother becomes crucial – and that, as we will see in more detail in the next chapter, is a major reason why the role and the status of a mother are so strongly defined in most of these religions. What was equally apparent, as we listened to mothers reflecting on their relation with their children, was their strong sense of both privilege and responsibility. Here are mothers from three of these religions, Christian, Muslim, then Sikh, explaining how this responsibility rests on them, and how they understand it:

I think with all families, regardless of what religion, the important thing with children is to give them your time, and to listen, and to always talk to them, and let them talk to you. There is no greater gift that you can give your children than yourself: and that's your time.

I think that with mother you learn everything. So I have to teach the children about Islam. Sometimes I read books, or sometimes I tell them stories; and I have to ask them to do *namaz*, if they are not feeling very happy to do it. Usually they do it, because they know *I* do it every day. You see, Islam is a

> very simple religion; if you want to see, you can see everything.
>
> It's not as strong for us as for the Muslims – where the women stay at home and pray at home, and they more or less bring their daughters up, while the sons go to the mosque. But I think women do have a role naturally in caring for their children, telling them right from wrong. When they get older, most of the children start thinking for themselves anyway; and then either they say, 'Oh yes, my mother was right'; or they say, 'Well, no, there must be more to it; or maybe there is no God.'

The more open and hesitant note in that last account arises partly because of a correspondingly strong emphasis among Sikhs that the eventual and ultimate religious commitment *must* be voluntary – it must even be begged for, as Gurbachan Singh Sidhu made clear to me:

> I would very much love to see that my children remain Sikhs. But then there is no restriction, you know: I have no right to say anything about other religions, but in my religion, whenever you want to have a baptism, you have to beg for it. It's not just foisted upon you, you know, at the age of 3 or 4 years. You can get baptised at any age, 19, 20, even 70 years. Some people wouldn't get baptised at all. But they would still call themselves Sikhs. So in our case, it's a case of begging for it. And if my son is not prepared to beg for it, and is not convinced of the veracity of this religion, then we wouldn't ask him.

Marriages – Arranged and Otherwise

Of course, simply to recognise responsibility for bringing up children is not to say that it is easy to exercise it, nor is it to say that all compulsion has disappeared from the face of the religious earth. While we were making the programmes, a Sikh father was convicted and sentenced to imprisonment for kidnapping his daughter, when she defied his wishes over an arranged marriage and went off with a boyfriend of her own choice; which is a reminder also that marriage usually comes before children, in these religions. Premarital sex, contraception, children born out of wedlock are raising questions for all these religions, but traditionally the family is *so* important that marriage is not something to be left to chance. *That* is why in all these religions there has been the practice of arranged marriages – of families, as well as the two people immediately concerned, being involved in the making of the match.

Arranged marriages in a strong sense have virtually disappeared from Christianity, though some Roman Catholics still hope that their children will marry Catholics; and in marriages with non-Catholics, the Roman Catholic is still required – or as the Papal instruction puts it, 'gravely bound' – to promise to bring the children up as Roman Catholics. Similarly, in Judaism, arranged marriages in the strong sense are becoming less common – though we heard from a Hasidic Jew that *his* marriage would be arranged, or rather sanctioned, from across the Atlantic; and the meeting between a man and a woman would certainly be suggested or arranged by a third party, because otherwise (since young men and women are kept apart) there could scarcely be a meeting:

> When Hasidim get married – or maybe it would be better to say when *we* got married – this was done in the following way – and this is a common way of going about it. A third party, who is known as a *shadchan*, through his contact with people in Jewish society, would suggest to a boy and a girl, that he thinks that maybe they would be suitable married partners. Often the parents are first consulted, but not in every case. Sometimes the boy might be far away in another country, studying in Yeshiva, and therefore it might not be so easy to consult the parents first; and certainly even if the parents were consulted, they might not be able to meet the girl, because she might be three thousand miles away: it might not be possible. But the general rule is that a third party introduces the couple, because in the way of life that we live, there is no way really where a boy could meet a girl except through a third party introducing them. When we met, my wife and myself, the meeting was arranged as far as possible in complete secrecy; and nobody else, except the direct people who were involved in arranging it, would know about it. This is to avoid any upset which might occur, should the proposed union not take place. And nobody knows what happened, and nobody will go around saying, 'Well, so and so met so and so, and it didn't work.' This way we save embarrassment. There is no restriction to the number of times that the couple can meet, although a good *shadchan* will probably be able to judge whether really the couple are getting on well together, or not. And he will probably suggest if he can see that the couple are meeting too

often without making a decision, that maybe they should cease meeting each other. Because what one has to realise is, that this is not a case of a boy meeting a girl in a discotheque; this is a case of a boy who has decided he is ready to get married, and a girl, who has decided she is ready to get married; and she is ready to meet somebody with a view to marrying him. Therefore, already when these two people meet – and they already know a little bit about the other party because they are given information, they are allowed to ask for any information they require before they meet – so at this very first meeting they are already quite well advanced in their relationship, and therefore, it might only take at the most half a dozen meetings before the couple are quite sure whether they are suited or not.

The basic point of arranged marriages is that it brings collective wisdom and experience to bear – marriage, after all, has to last longer than the first immediate attraction. That's why those we listened to felt very strongly, that arranging marriages is far better than leaving it to the individuals. Marriage involves families, not just two people – indeed, it involves the whole society, as Mr Chitra Pal Singh, a Hindu, made clear:

Our people want to maintain this Vedic system of marriage. In this Vedic system of marriage, there are certain vows, there are certain promises that the bridegroom is supposed to make. But he does not make this promise to the girl. He makes the promises to the father of the girl. In our marriage ceremony, there is a ceremony that is very important, which is called *kunya dan*, the giving of the virgin, the giving away of the virgin. So it is not the girl who is choosing freely like that. It is the family, the father, who is offering the girl to the bridegroom. Now, in our Scriptures, this is a social thing: it's the duty of a man to offer a girl to the society. And it is considered to be one of the debts to keep the society going, because if there are no more girls, then there is no more society, the end. So it is considered to be one of the debts upon every person, that he gives one girl to society. He has got his son, he'll get a girl from somewhere else. Now in this country, the change is happening, but the point is still this, that the boys and the girls are not allowed to meet intimately. They can talk to each other when they are in the schools: they talk to each other, they like each other; and then the parents are always, if they have got a girl, they are always looking for boys. The point is this, that our girls are not allowed to be free, to do anything that they like, to choose anything they like. The whole point is that if our girl comes and says, 'Well, I am going to marry a Muhammadan', the whole point is that the whole social system is broken down, you see: our Hindu society is broken down. A girl which was supposed to go into a Hindu family is going out of it. So to a certain extent it does save, it does protect, Hindu society, because if the girls go out – well, there are certain things that our culture doesn't allow. And the first thing is this *kunya* that I told you about. *Kunya* means a virgin, a girl who has no sexual experience with another person before her marriage. This is the condition, you see. And there can be no Vedic marriage without it, because the father says to the bridegroom, 'Well, I am offering a virgin to you'; and this is one of the things that is the basis, the foundation, of our society. If the girl is conscious that she has been pure all her life, she has never desired another man, she can expect the same faith from the husband. And the husband promises there, at the time of marriage, that he will never abandon her during her whole life, whatever happens. She is there as his second self. She is the better part of him.

A Muslim wife, Mrs Khan, made the further claim that arranged marriages, because of the wider network of consultation, are more successful – at least in avoiding divorce:

In a country like England, where the people are free to marry after a long courtship, they are really very unsuccessful – eight or five or six out of ten marriages are ended in divorce. But in our country, our marriages, Muslim marriages, are usually successful. It's really very bad if we have divorce; we don't have divorce.

The point about arranged marriages that was made over and over again is that the parents are bound to be involved, because they want the best for their children, and they have the experience of life as well. This is how Hajji Cassim Mohammad put it:

Asian girls and Muslim girls, especially among the Muslim community, are not allowed to mix freely with the boys. So what chances have the boys to get to meet them, if you left it only on a meeting together to choose a husband, when they don't meet? Now, parents obviously would want the best for their children. There are very, very few who will just want to get rid of their children, get rid of the daughters and marry them to anyone. But the majority of families that I know would always like the best for their children. A father would like the best husband for his daughter and the same thing for his son. As for my daughters, it was difficult: I left it for them to choose and I told them whoever they choose must become a Muslim; because they must bring them to me. You see, my children grew up here. They attended Western schools, and there they met friends. And all their friends were English friends, European friends, because they couldn't mix with the Pakistani community, because we come from Trinidad. It was difficult, really very, very difficult.

So marriage is *not* between two individuals alone; it's between families; and for that reason an arranged marriage is stronger – or so those who practise it claim – than Western marriage. Mrs Dhesi is a social worker in Coventry who has a good deal of experience, therefore, of married and family life. She put the point very directly:

Your marriages are not successful. You can see how much a percentage ends in failure, in yours and in mine; and you say I've got to change *mine*! For what? Change for worse? I'm not ready to change for worse. If you prove to me your marriages are successful, I will. But our own way of marriage is better. I agree, I want to make it more flexible, adapt a few things. Take a case of a not fully arranged, a partly arranged marriage, which I think I agree to. But I don't want to entirely believe what other people are saying, because I want to see whether in practice it will be successful or not.

So how does arranged marriage actually work out in practice? Here are two descriptions of this experience. First, two Hindus:

He: My father, when he went to India, he sent me a nice photograph. I fell in love with the photograph, and that was this photograph.
She: I also saw a photograph; and we knew each other's families as well. My family knew his family, and his family knew mine, and both were convinced that we were competent enough for each other. He was very highly educated, and I was the only girl to be a graduate in that particular part of India we come from. My father thought that this was the best person for me.
He: After that, we had letter writing of a year's session, I think, and we discovered lots of things by writing these letters;

> and when I went there first to see her, my father said, 'Well, here we are, son, you must go and see her, and then approve or disapprove'; and that's what happened. Then we met for about four weeks, that's all. But we were not allowed to go out with each other, you know.
> She: But we knew each other through letters, we knew quite a lot, and we knew our families, you see.

And second, a Sikh wife describes her experience of arranged marriage:

> My parents knew my husband's parents many, many years ago, even before I was born. So it was a very close knit affair. When I first found out I was going to be married, I thought, 'Oh, I don't want to get married, I want to finish my studies, I want to finish my degree, please don't do this.' But my father was very ill, he had a heart attack, and since I was the oldest girl, and there was only my brother before me who had been married, and there were my younger sisters yet, and a brother, he thought that if he didn't get *me* married off he might have – it was a very, very serious attack. So because I really love my father, and I knew that he wouldn't do anything to harm me, whatever he thought was the best for me (although inside me there were so many conflicting emotions), I could never let my father down, no matter what happened. And I thought, 'All right, then, I'll go through with it;' and it's been such a – you know, I'm so happy. I never thought I'd be this happy. So all the tears before the marriage are well worth it, I think.

But did she manage to finish her degree?

> Yes. That's the thing: I thought, 'Well, they won't let me finish: they won't let me finish my degree, and they won't let me follow a career'; because at that time, that was very important to me. My career still *is* important to me; but my husband is far more important than my career, now. Yes, they let me finish my career and they let me work.

One Hindu (brought up in the West, and, as he put it, very loyal to this country) resisted an arranged marriage; but when he gave in to family pressure, he decided to go the whole way and *not* see his bride-to-be in advance – though in the end it didn't work out quite like that, as he and his wife make clear:

> He: My marriage was arranged through my maternal uncle. So in fact myself and my wife were from the same village. My

maternal uncle's family knew my wife's family very well, and it was suggested to me that in fact a marriage could be arranged.
She: You had a girl friend, so you didn't want to go ahead!
He: No, I don't think that's the entire reason – that's a bit flippant really. The point is that my parents put a great deal of pressure upon me, as being the eldest son in the family, and obviously the first one to get married, for the marriage to be arranged. And as I've said before, the pressure was on because I suppose our system is such that the marriage is arranged. Secondly, I wondered about the motives of our parents, as to *why* they should want us to have arranged marriage: is it entirely cultural, is it entirely religious, or are there other motives?
She: Does the financial come into it?
He: I'm sure it does. I'm sure it does. You see, the thing I think one has to appreciate is that in India we have a joint family system, where the financial aspects are very much tied up. Let me explain that: we have no welfare state, so really the family has to look after its own. One way of preserving this is to have a very close-knit family, in which we help each other. Now that, I think, is an admirable thing. But, of course, it does mean that, because we are financially interdependent, we cannot always practise our own wishes. So the wishes of the family are imposed upon us, for the good of the whole family, irrespective of what our individual feelings might be.

At this point, I commented that I could see the social reasons very clearly, as he was explaining them, but despite those reasons, did he, I asked him, have arguments in his own family about his own marriage being arranged?

Yes, I did. I think it would be untruthful to say that I did not have an argument. Let me explain again. My father had died, or he was very, very poorly, which meant that my mother really arranged the marriage for me. We did have an argument, but the argument, I think, was conducted predominantly within me, within myself, because I could see both sides of the story; whereas my mother could only see her own side. Obviously she had no inkling, she could not appreciate the fact that I had been brought up in a country where I had developed my own ideas, I'd had a good education, I have learnt to think for myself. So in one sense emotionally my mother is much more dependent upon me than I am upon her. So having realised that, I think any arguments that I had, although I might have

> had brief ones with my mother, on the whole they were arguments and turmoil within myself as to what I really wanted to do. I think my case is perhaps not unique, and I am sure there are many cases like this, that the arranged marriage *really* was seen as a security for my mother. Naturally – and this is perfectly true – if I have an English wife, my mother's position in the family as the head of the household would be very threatened – which it would have been. I'm not saying this is the *sole* reason why she wanted me to get married to an Indian girl. But I'm sure along the way, that to preserve the family unity, to preserve the figurehead of the family, as my mother wanted to do, it was essential that I should marry an Indian girl.

I asked his wife if she had had similar worries and arguments:

> No, I wanted to have an arranged marriage. My parents gave me permission, when I was in University, that if I like, I can choose a boy for myself. But I didn't want to do that, I just wanted to marry a boy which my parents suggested, because I thought that they can find a better boy than I can choose myself – because they can see the family, they can see the boy. I can only see the boy; and I knew that I was going to stay in a joint family: the mother-in-law would be there, the father-in-law and the brother-in-law; because mostly in India, all the joint family system is still there. So I was just thinking, if I choose a boy, I don't know what he will be like.

I asked them whether they had actually met before the marriage:

> She: Yes, we did see each other when he came to India: he came to see me and he gave me an engagement ring. But there were nearly fifteen other people with him as well.
> He: The point we're trying to make is that the *commitment* for me to get married to her was made prior to my leaving this country. So in fact there was no choice once I went to India as to which girl I was going to marry. Now, I took the thing to this ridiculous conclusion, really. I thought, well, if the marriage is going to be arranged for me, and if I'm going to have an arranged marriage, what's the point of seeing the girl? Because even if I meet her for half an hour or twenty-five minutes, or forty-five minutes as we saw in the television programme the other night, what's the point? The point is that within the confines of the system, it works: obviously the system has its own little set-ups, its own little rules, and it

> works quite admirably, really, in the sense that predominantly the marriages are arranged with girls because the families know each other.

All that helped me to understand why arranged marriages matter so much where the family is, so to speak, the social welfare system. But that kind of arranged marriage, in which the partners scarcely see each other before they are married, seems to be disappearing, certainly in this country. Harbans Singh Sagoo is a Sikh who recognises this, even though he also saw good reasons for the system of arranged marriages:

> Arranged marriages are things of the past. In the days past, arranged marriages existed in the true sense of the arranged marriage, where probably children of three or four years of age were involved, and the parents said, 'Right, my boy and your girl, when they grow up we'll get them married together'; and they would tie up their relations like that. But that sort of thing does not happen. I don't think this has happened in the last fifteen or twenty years that I have known. Marriages are arranged in the sense that all the footwork is done by the families concerned. But all this is done with all good intentions, because there is no parent that wants to see his boy or girl getting married and suffering as a result of that. They have all the best intentions for their boys and girls. But this is not really arranging a marriage, in the context of arranged marriages as we've known. But there is one thing, though, there is no courting. Our grown-up girls don't generally go to discos and parties and things. They may go to parties where the parents know where they are going, and how long they are going to be. But the parents feel, especially for girls, that that sort of freedom, to be able to go out with friends to discos etc., and late nights, is not on. I think there is good sense in that, and we try and educate our girls to accept this, because it is being done for their own good. Once again, although the majority of the girls accept this, there are some who rebel against the authority, and that is a fashion these days anyway. And they go away.

I asked a Hindu wife whether a young person could be compelled into a marriage:

> In the villages, but not in an urban society – it couldn't happen. I attended a marriage in April: I went to India when my youngest sister got married, and she had a lot of proposals (because it is an arranged marriage) from different people and

families; but she had her say, though. She is a graduate in microbiology and all these things, and my parents said it wouldn't be fair if they just push her to a family where she won't be able to do whatever she wants. So she could say no. Actually she rejected many, saying, 'No, I wouldn't like to be in that family, I think they're very orthodox and I wouldn't be able to go out,' things like that. In urban families, women do have a say, really.

So the main emphasis, despite the court case referred to earlier, is that there must not be compulsion, and that the young people concerned must agree – or more strongly, must make the final choice. But inevitably the early parental influence has its own strong part to play, as Gurbachan Singh Sidhu made clear:

What we would expect from our sons and daughters first of all, would be to become complete and good Sikhs. If they can do that, then many of the problems are solved. But supposing they are not as good Sikhs as we would suppose them to be, then of course they would have different opinions and different views. Our situation in that case would be to expect that they would at least have some vestige of Sikhism in them. For example, if my son is not prepared to marry a Sikh girl, and is thinking of marrying a Muslim girl, or let us say a Christian girl, then my attitude would be, first of all to dissuade him from doing this, if possible, and if he still doesn't take heed, then the next step would be asking him to see if his partner would accept Sikhism. And if that fails the last step would be to let him do what he likes. In the end it's his decision, and you can't interfere. Even if we do, even if we forced our feelings upon him, he would go away and say, I don't care. So what's the use of letting him go, by saying that and not accepting what he would like most?

But it's all very well listening to what parents expect of their children. What do the children think? What do young people make of this – those who have just got married or who are not yet married? There is certainly a recognition, among young people, of a drift away from arranged marriages to a more Western emphasis on individual choice. Parmjot Singh Hyare had got married just two months before I met him in Coventry. I asked him what he felt about arranged marriages:

I find that with my colleagues about my age, who are Sikhs, that they are worried about this problem of arranged marriages. They would prefer to use the Western approach, to pick out their own partner, and decide who to marry themselves. I've personally found that it's a form of guidance: through the family you tend to feel that it *is* the right decision, that others are guiding you for your good, that they are not trying to harm you in any way, that it's not being forced on you. It's a joint decision. It gives you that extra confidence that what you are doing is absolutely right, and it's a bit more binding, I feel.

And in fact, without exception, all the young people I talked to, who are likely to be involved in arranged marriages, regarded that system as a good way for them and for others. Nora Chatterji, a Hindu girl who has just taken her A levels, saw it that way:

With regard to arranged marriages, I don't see anything wrong with them – with certain changes: I think, for example, the boy and girl should be allowed to meet – I mean, it's just natural. That wouldn't be considered in villages, perhaps: you know, you don't see your husband. I can't see that. But I think arranged marriage is a good thing because the backgrounds are matched, and the incomes, so they will be able to pay for what you are used to being brought up in.

As a young Muslim put it:

Of course the families will be involved: I'll bring the girl and show her to the parents. They've got a lot more wisdom than me. If they say no, they can give their reasons, and I'm sure they will be right.

With that sense of obligation and dependence still wide-spread (even if declining), there is no question that arranged marriages, at least in the sense of strong family involvement and of 'footwork', will continue, as a Hindu teacher, Mr Ladd, made clear:

What we do nowadays – say, if I had a daughter and if she is about to marry, she's of that age, we see the boy. If he likes her, if I like the boy, and he is OK, then I say to the girl, 'Go, both of you, and talk to each other.' They talk to each other, and then they decide whether they are going to go further.

I asked him how long might that process be, when they meet?

It might be half an hour. But at that time we don't decide. If the girl says, OK, father, then we give them another chance to

> talk. So that is what we do nowadays.

In fact the real threat to this social system of marriage is coming, not yet from feelings of unease about the status and role of women in such a system, but from the sheer practical difficulties of finding suitable partners in communities which are small in number in this country. Hajji Cassim Mohammad has particular difficulties, because his family has been on the move so much:

> The real difficulty here is the environment, because (in our case especially) we found it extremely difficult, because we are Muslims from Trinidad, Asian Muslims from Trinidad. My father came originally from Hyderabad, India. We grew up in Trinidad, and the language of Trinidad is completely English, fully one hundred per cent Western. Now, coming from Trinidad to Leeds, there aren't any like that: I haven't found other Indians or Asian Muslims who are Trinidadians. So when it came to my children, when it's time for them to get married, we have problems. I spoke to my children, my daughters. I said, 'I would like you all to marry among your own people' – preferably, though Islam does not discriminate: we discriminate in religion only, not racially. And then my daughters turn around and asked me, 'Daddy, can you find us a husband who is a Trinidadian and an Indian?' And the only way I could have done that is to send them home to Trinidad.

This problem of equal match is even more acute for Hindus who have to find, not simply a general match of interests and background, but a *particular* match of caste, as we've already heard – and that is why there are Hindu marriage bureaux in this country, to link people of different castes who otherwise, because of the small numbers in this country, might never find a partner. Dr Gupta explained the difficulties to me when I talked to him in Bradford – and I couldn't help noticing that he, like Hajji Mohammad, could envisage a return to India as a last resort:

> First of all, we consider he must be an Indian, and a Hindu. Caste comes later on; and that too depends on the other credentials of the boy concerned. If he's physically handsome, attractive and works, it depends on its merits. Now in this country it's difficult, because we are few from our caste who have come to live here, because they are already far better off in India. I being a teacher in India, and of that caste, came here first for study, and found only a few families from our

> caste. The law has changed and she can't fetch a husband from India. So naturally we are in touch with the marriage bureau down in London which sends us some contacts: and then we go to visit those families and if something comes up, we will settle the marriage. If that doesn't come through our caste, then we will request the marriage bureau to send Hindu boys from other castes, and we'll consider them. Today we have got two other contacts through that marriage bureau, who are not from our caste. They are Hindus, and we are going to negotiate with them, and if they are suitable, we'll proceed with the other ceremonies. In India it's entirely different, because we have got a joint family system and we get contacts from relatives. In this country, and if I say in Bradford, I don't think there is another person of my caste.

I asked him how he actually went about meeting suitable candidates:

> Most of the cases that have been referred to us are from London, so it's a long drive and expensive, so we try that we should organise in such a way that she should ask to go there, and it should be one meeting. If some approval is there, we give some time to the boy and the girl to discuss mutual interests – half an hour, fifteen minutes, whatever time suits. Then we try to seek their opinion. Then again some other things may not be right – sometimes dowry, sometimes reluctance (on the part of our girl) could be from the parental side. So those things are considered and discussed later on when we are back. But we have got two or three families who have come over here as well. We have been to so many families, but it hasn't been settled. The point is that unless they are both happy, only then will we go ahead, otherwise not. If there is any danger of refusal or resentment from one, we are not going to press upon the boy to go ahead or the girl to go ahead.

I asked him: 'Even if the daughter gets older and older and is thirty-three, thirty-four, thirty-five?' He answered emphatically, 'No, no, not to that extent. I don't think so – we should not be so much pessimistic.' But still, I persisted, could it happen? 'No,' he said, 'I don't think so. My daughter is willing to go and live in India. If we are not able to find a boy in this country, she'll go there. She will find the right person. We have a saying, "Marriages are settled in heaven and celebrated on earth. The sacred unity of two souls is written by fate right from birth."'

The Caste System

In looking at the system of arranged marriages, it has already become obvious how important the caste system is for family life in Eastern religions – and not just in Hinduism: as we shall see, it affects Buddhism and Sikhism, even though they are supposed to have repudiated the caste (and outcaste) system.

Again, it is important to bear in mind the background in India. In origin, caste divisions were more social than religious, dividing up labour and responsibility into four classes. But through history, castes have multiplied into thousands of subdivisions; and no matter how difficult it has been to maintain the caste system in England, it still persists in marriage. Here is a Hindu explaining the origin of the caste system, regretting its rigidity as an evil, but recognising its persistence in marriage:

> The reason for this caste system has nothing to do with religion. It's a social development: wherever you find society, you find division of labour. During the Vedic times, the caste system was really the division of labour. Those people who did the intellectual role – did the writing of books, thinking of high thoughts, teaching students, making researches of mysteries, either of nature or of medicine or of astronomy, those people who were intellectuals, they were called, Brahmins. Those people who defended the country (these people were just voluntary, they were always ready, they were not the servants of anybody, they were soldiers to defend the country), they were called Kshatriya. Those people who carried on the trade and business and agriculture, they were called the Vaishyas. And those people who had no land, were called the Shudras. This has nothing to do with religion: this was a social thing: later on it became stiff. But during the Vedic times, the earlier times, they were not watertight compartments: people could change. We have got examples of Rishis who changed from Brahmin into Kshatriya, and Kshatriyas changing into Brahmins – and the Shudras all participating in what we call religion.

But, I asked him, what about now? Why has the caste system become so rigid and intolerant?

> This all happened because people became uneducated. During the Vedic times we have got a perfect educational system. But now the caste system has become a real menace: it has stopped all growth, all improvement, you see; so those

> people who are entitled, whether they belong to this caste, or that caste, they should get equal opportunity. There should be no hindrance if they want to marry a different caste. This hindrance is happening only in those who are uneducated. The whole basis is ignorance. The whole of this caste system is now based upon total ignorance. Those people who do not understand anything, they are not educated – they are the people who are the champions of the caste. There is another thing: the Brahmins, the priests, who support this system have got a vested interest in it. In the villages and in our families, there are so many ceremonies. Now these people, the Brahmins, they perform the ceremonies and they are paid for that in some way. They used to get golden bangles and cows and all the best of the things that the people had got. So they had got that vested interest. If there is no caste system, then what happens is that they lose their position.

But clearly the priests, the Brahmins, are not getting gold and cows in Leeds. So why, I asked him, does the caste system persist amongst Hindus in Leeds? He answered, 'The caste system does persist, because you can see it in the marriages. It is only in the marriages that you see it, because it's all based upon caste.' 'Is that a mistake?' I asked. He answered sharply: 'Yes, of course it is: why not? You see, the marriage in our Scriptures, the marriage is between a male and a female – it's not between a colour or a caste or profession or anything!'

But not all Hindus agree with him. Mrs Kalia is a school teacher who has lived in this country since 1953, so she has considerable experience of the changes in this country. In her view, the caste system will – and should – persist. She said:

> Yes, I think it is very important, because the caste system is not something that's evil, or something to be uprooted, or something to be got rid of. The caste system is a way of ordering society: you have classes in every society. Social structure wouldn't be possible if you didn't have different people doing different jobs – and no one is higher in status or lower in status because they are doing different jobs.

But the issue is whether the structure is *so* rigid that there cannot be social mobility: does the caste system, I asked her, allow the American dream of 'poor boy to President' to come true? She answered that it might – indeed it will, but not necessarily in this particular birth:

> If you believe in *dharma* and *karma*, then you believe that what

> you do [in this life] designates what your station in life will eventually become. Your *dharma* and *karma* is what you physically do, like kindness, being polite, by obedience, by helping others, by carrying out your work conscientiously, dutifully, faithfully, cheerfully, and honestly.

And Mr Mittal agreed with her: 'Yes,' he said, 'caste *is* important to some extent – to maintain the harmony and social structure of the society. But it's more social than religious.' So caste persists, and some Hindus support it. And even among Sikhs, who are supposed to have abolished the caste system, and who point to the teachings of the gurus criticising the injustices of the caste system, even among them caste persists in marriage. Amritpal Singh Hunjan is a young student who knows what is going on and doesn't like it:

> I am afraid I am very angry about it, because that is something I cannot forgive the Indian society for: that is the caste system. Being of a different caste doesn't mean that you are inferior, because God, as Guru Nanak, our first guru, said, All people are born equal; God does not say to some person, 'You are inferior and you are superior.' All people are born equal. Regarding the castes, it's the Hindus that created castes, and since we were originally Hindus in our castes, that unfortunately, even though that was criticised by our gurus, is still being practised among us, among the Sikhs – even though that was definitely criticised by the gurus, and they said, You must stop practising that.

That young student was not the only Sikh I met who protested against the persistence of caste. Mrs Balbir Sohal is equally clear about the gap between what Guru Nanak taught and how people live in their family arrangements:

> The only superior thing is, being with God; and everyone is equal; because that is the essence of Guru Nanak's teaching – that there is no caste system, although we do have it. That's a sort of hypocrisy, really: there is no caste system; and if they are true Sikhs there should be no caste system. But there is; there's the Jats, the Khans, there's so many. When it comes to marriage, you marry inside your caste. But now I think that marriage between castes, intercaste marriage, is becoming more frequent – there *is* intercaste marriage now, there's more of it now than there was twenty odd years ago, thirty years ago in my parents' time. I think caste might gradually die out. If

> you are a true Sikh you shouldn't believe there is a caste. But these intercaste marriages are mostly love marriages. It's usually a love marriage, if it's an intercaste marriage, not an arranged marriage.

So caste persists but it is undoubtedly breaking down in this country, even among Hindus, because some mixing in society at large is inevitable.

In fact there have frequently been teachers arising in Hinduism who have protested against the caste system – as Satya Sai Baba does at the present day. As one of his young followers summarised his teaching, 'There is only one religion, the religion of love; there is only one caste, the caste of humanity.' Still, even there the persistence of caste in marriage goes on, as another of his followers explained, when I asked her about her own attitude to marriage:

> Satya says there is only one religion, the religion of love. So, it does not tell me not to mix. If I did come across somebody of a different caste, I could introduce him at home, and he would be accepted on the basis that we had a lot in common. But all parents want to see you happily married off, and by selecting somebody of your own caste, it's making sure you have something in common.

So caste persists, not any longer because it organises society, but because it reinforces and strengthens marriage; and as one Hindu girl put it, *not* to be married is virtually unimaginable for a girl:

> Every Asian girl knows she has to get married, so her work is difficult: she can't rely on working at the same place, because once she gets married she may have to move to a different town; so she'd be lucky if she can get the same job. But for her parents, it is their duty to get us married, so every girl actually accepts it as part of her life.

Celebration of Marriage

With that stress on marriage and on the duty to get married, it is not surprising that the actual ceremonies of marriage are vivid and important. Among Hindus, the ceremonies may last for three days:

> The marriage ceremony takes at least three days, really, the

whole ceremony, and it is quite interesting, how it goes, every step: before you see the husband, before you meet the husband's family, there is a ceremony called *gaya hulud*: that means, you get all sorts of presents from the family. It is more family orientated than husband to wife. So it is mother-in-law bringing jewellery, father-in-law giving a present, brother-in-law saris, some giving *chapals* – different varieties of things come on a tray; so this is the beginning of the ceremony. A girl is very keen obviously to meet her husband, but she's not allowed to: you first make contact with the family and try to get on, and then you will have the man anyway: he will love you and she will love you. This sort of thing is taken for granted actually.

The central ceremonies for Hindus are described here by a Hindu mother and her daughter:

In the Hindu way, there is a different kind of party, and we ask a lot of families to come and pray to God. The ceremonies take three days. At the beginning of the three days, the girl is covered in yellow, and a few ladies come and sing wedding songs, and that goes on until the last day, when the girl's actually getting married. She has the yellow thing on again, and she has a bath – well, someone has to give her a bath and then dress her up; then in our way, the boy usually comes first, then the girl goes to get married; and the wedding usually lasts about an hour, two hours – it depends.

It depends how long the priest, the Brahmin, takes time for the marriage. Some priests take a half an hour, some priests take one and a half hours.

And then we go round the fire four times, and that just proves that you are married – and say the *mantra*. And during that time the priest will pray that you are successful in your married life.

So for a Hindu, there will have to be a civil registration *plus* the Hindu marriage – though a Hindu girl could be married in, for example, a church – but not a Hindu man, as Mr Chimanlal Pandya explains – who as the only full-time pandit in Yorkshire has to perform the marriage ceremony very frequently:

According to the Hindu way of life, the male is considered as the head of the family. So if the Hindu girl wants to marry an English man he or she can go to the church and can marry. That has happened. A friend of mine is an Englishman, he married with an Asian girl, a Punjabi, but not in this temple, because the male is considered as head of the family. So I told them to go to any church and get married. But if a Hindu boy wants to marry an English girl, or a Christian, or any other girl (except Muslim, because Islam is quite contrary to Hindus) so he can be married, he can come here in the Community Hall and I am doing it here.

Buddhists have a clear distinction between 'getting married' and Buddhism as a way to Enlightenment. Marriage is regarded as a social fact which has nothing essentially to do with *Buddhism*. So marriage – and for that matter divorce – take place in society; and if a monk comes in to bless a marriage, he does not come on the day of the marriage, because the *Vinaya* (the monk's code of practice in the Pali Canon) does not tell him to do so. Dr Fernando, a Theravadin Buddhist, talked about this:

Buddhism has got nothing to do with our civilian, with our civil, code. This is one thing which is very important to know. In Christianity the priest will bring the two of them, will unite the two of them. In Buddhism, the Buddhist monk has nothing to do with us, it's only a civil ceremony. The Buddhist monks don't come into it at all. They have no say in the matter. They may come and bless us; they may advise us, if we ask them for advice, but it just stops there. And in any case they would never come for a blessing on the day of the wedding. The Buddhist monks are not supposed to attend any sort of ceremony of that nature. But they may visit you later: if you are on intimate terms with them, they will come along. If they have known you, if they have known us since we were children, they would come and bless us.

I asked him why the Buddhist monks are not allowed to come to the wedding.

It's not according to the *Vinaya*, which is the code of conduct for the monks. They are excluded from taking part in these ceremonies, because the Buddhist monk is a person who has renounced worldly life. He is working on his own salvation, and he is in a monastery which has been provided.

With Jews also the *fact* of marriage is more important than a splendid ceremony – though a rabbi must be present; and with the strong Jewish emphasis on the family, it is certainly a happy occasion. Mr Oliver, an Orthodox Jew, described it for me:

With an ordinary Jewish family, the ceremony in the

> synagogue is, I suppose, just an ordinary ceremony, where the rabbi and the *chazan*, or the cantor, take part. The girl comes into the canopy, there is the sense of holiness about it, but it's not really looked upon as an absolute sacred ceremony; because this can take place in a room. It doesn't have to be a synagogue at all, it can be in your backyard, it can be round a hospital bed, which I know well has happened. But there does have to be a minister present, that's definite.

Jewish Scripture does not describe the marriage ceremonies in detail (though Mishnah and Talmud are more elaborate), so this has allowed many customs to grow up over the centuries, as a Sefardi Jew from Morocco remembers:

> There's a ceremony the night before, when the woman has to go to the *mikvah*, the ritual bath; and when the bride comes back, they have a little ceremony for her at home. That's a Sefardi custom, where the bride is dressed in a kind of kaftan, you know, the Sefardi dress, long dress; and they bring in trays: they bring a tray of perfumes, and a green substance, called henna, which they use on their hands and forehead; it's the sign of luck, I think, to take away the evil eye – to ward off evil spirits.

In the Muslim marriage ceremony, the Quran is obviously basic:

> A holy person comes and reads the Quran, and then two relatives of the bride come to the bride and they ask, 'Do you accept this person as your husband?' They ask three times, and you have to say, 'Yes.' And then the same thing happens to the boy, they go to the bridegroom and they ask him three times, and then you are married. Then after *nikah* [the contractual ceremony] we have got a big dinner party.

According to the Quran, a man may marry up to four wives. But Muslims are bound to accept the laws of any country in which they are a minority; and in any case, most Muslims argue that that permission was for exceptional circumstances:

> A Muslim man can have up to four wives, depending on the circumstances. The rule of the law of the Quran is one, the exception to the rule is four. When that rule came, when the Prophet received the revelation for that rule, there was war, and widows and orphans were left unprotected. The state could have provided food, clothing, but it could not have provided companionship for a wife, and a father for the children.

So the law came, since there were fewer men; women were asked to share their husbands. But the first wife must give consent. Again the rule is, the Quran says, 'Take unto yourselves one, two, three, four. But if he fears he cannot deal equitably among them, then have but one.' So the rule, as I said earlier, is one; the exception to the rule is four. If a man wanted to take on a situation like that, it doesn't arise now, because we have plenty more men.

Sikhs also have to separate the civil registration of the marriage from their own ceremonies. But it is the ceremonies which matter:

There is a small ceremony in the house, prayers and that, and people come and put a bangle, a *chura*, on you, and then some prayers again. Then there is a registry marriage a few weeks after that, and after the registry marriage, there is the Indian marriage. The Indian marriage again is just prayers. Firstly, you start off by meeting each other: our relations meet their relations, so they get to know each other; and then after that we go and sit in front of the Guru Granth Sahib, and various marriage prayers are said; and then we do four circles around the Guru Granth Sahib, during which the prayers are said as well, and then we are pronounced man and wife. That's it. Then we all have a party.

A good time had by all: that is the note which comes through all these different ceremonies and approaches to marriage. It is a time of happiness and blessing; and it is in the blessing that marriage is undergirded by religious belief and practice. A Jewish father spoke for more than himself alone, when he answered the question, 'Do you have any particularly happy moments that you remember in your religious life?', by saying, 'Seeing the happiness of our daughters when they got married':

I think my happiest memories are seeing my daughters married, seeing their apparent complete happiness at that point – seeing the ceremonies actually taking place, being under the canopy and seeing my daughters happy. I can't think of anything more pleasant in my religious life than seeing that.

9
Women and Children: First?

The strong emphasis, in all these religions, on the family as the cradle of faith has had its obvious implications for women as wives and mothers: the importance of the wife in creating a home, and of the mother in bringing up the children in the faith, has led, historically, to the role and status of women being clearly and strongly defined. These definitions of how women should behave have almost always removed women from public responsibility and activity, in order to set them free to create the home. This has resulted traditionally in what looks like a subordinate role for women – not inferior to men, but with a different role which leaves the husband with the final authority. That is indeed what has often happened – and, as we shall see, the wives concerned do not necessarily resent or dislike that relationship, since in their opinion it works effectively for the happiness of all concerned.

However, in the West, and in Christianity in particular, this traditional understanding of what a woman should be and do has been much eroded. As a result, the new norms of British society in general offer to women entirely different opportunities of relationship and/or career; and there is no doubt that this *can* create great strain for traditional patterns of life.

Status of Women: Sikhs

It is all the more important, therefore, to bear in mind what Harbans Singh Sagoo pointed out, that in dealing with the status of women, we are always mixing tradition and religion: the way a religion is lived is a mixture of what has grown up through the centuries and what that religion (in its texts or teachings) actually allows or commands:

> We're probably trying to mix a little bit of tradition with religion here. As far as religion is concerned, there is no dis-

crimination between the man and woman. They are held on a par, and they have exactly the same opportunity, whether in the house or in the religious sphere. So there is really no restriction, in the religious sense, on women going out to work, or anything else. But of course, traditionally speaking, in the Indian way of life, the woman has been the queen of the house, and she has looked after the house and the children, whereas the man has been the bread-winner, and he has been the backbone of the family as such. But that tradition has actually changed, in this country, because of the need to maintain a living standard, and therefore men *and* women have gone out working – even young boys and girls have gone out working. It has created some problems in some families, where boys and girls have become very liberal-minded and they have more or less taken upon themselves to decide their future, which is not in keeping with the Indian tradition. I think the views are changing in this sphere.

I asked him whether he himself welcomed such change:

If we go by the experience and the wisdom of our elderly people, I think the change is not a very welcome change, because in the wake of the change there have been problems; and we are experiencing the problems in the way of broken marriages, divorces and things like that. In the past, in the Indian society, the behaviour, the pattern of behaviour, had been what it was through many, many years of experience, devised by wise people, elderly people. But the youngsters are deviating from that set pattern, and naturally they are going to have to suffer the consequences. This is not happening wholesale, though. There are quite a number of families who are still sticking to the old pattern, and still enjoying the fruits of wisdom.

Another Sikh, Ranjit Arora, made the same point, that there is a distinction between what the religion says about equality, and the pattern of practice. I asked her if she found, as many claimed, that the Sikh religion is more liberal than some other traditions in its attitude to women:

I suppose it is. It's not holding women in a very rigid pattern, as many other religions are. I think that in comparison Sikh religion is fairly liberal towards women. In fact, as you probably know, all the religious sayings indicate that women are treated as equals and should be treated as equals; and I think

> Sikh families are perhaps more liberal. But in spite of that, yes, there is a pattern, in which they want women in particular to operate, which may not be very restrictive in terms of education and employment and social status, but it is certainly restrictive as far as a place within the family is concerned.

As she said, Sikhism has a strong emphasis on the religious equality of men and women – a point which was emphasised also by Mrs Balbir Sohal:

> Guru Nanak had a very strong belief for the mother and the woman, and they are not sort of shunned off, or anything. I mean, the women can read from the Scriptures, can read the Holy Guru Granth Sahib, can perform a service, etcetera. It's not just totally a man's world.

It has the same symbols and the same commitment for men and women, even though in the end, the man will still be the head of the household, as Mrs Dhesi accepted:

> Yes, oh yes. If he is not there, I've got to make a decision of my own, I've got to make it. But one thing I will tell you, in the family, if all try to make a decision, it won't work, so one's got to be head, to make a decision; so he's to consult the whole family, but he's got to say, 'Yes, it's the way we should do it.' So we all go along.

In that connection, one might well ask, what's in a name? Among Sikhs, as also among Hindus, it has traditionally been unusual for wives to call their husbands by name, but rather by the term of respect, Ji – as children do their parents (rather as some Victorian boys called their father, Sir). For one Sikh it is important that that continues:

> When the wife starts to address the husband with his first name, as opposed to addressing him in that respectable way, it's that detail, that respect, which is somewhere, deep down, beginning to disappear. And consequently other, smaller details will also disappear, and there will be none of this business of, you know, who is to be respected and how. Another major thing is that the children, picking up these things, are only going to learn in this way how their fathers and mothers behaved. And consequently when they get into their own environment of husband and wife, they are going to practise exactly what they have been taught in the house.

But in fact, this practice is already disappearing in this country among children – though it persists from wife to husband, as Ranjit Arora made clear:

> Yes, it is very much true of the Sikh wives, but I think it has changed considerably, in fact. I think it's more to do with generation difference than religion. I think both Hindu and Sikh wives, younger wives, do call their husbands by their names. It varies. My mother never called my father by his name. She used to call him Sardarji; others would just address their husband as Ji, or different patterns would take up. Sometimes I think it is also true of English wives as well. They used to address him as, Father.

I then asked her what Sikh children would call their parents. She said:

> Now that's again very different: Biji and Bauji used to be the traditional pattern. Most children these days called them Mum and Dad. It really differs. I remember when I was a child, we used to call our parents Biji and Bauji; but as we grew older, it was more or less Mummy and Daddy, no difference at all. It varied, it really did vary from family to family.

Hindus

The same naming practice persists also among Hindus, though a Hindu wife may well use her husband's name in company, because *that* is the dominant tradition in this country. That at least is what Mrs Pancholi does:

> I will, yes, when I'm talking to my friends, yes, I call him by his name. The role of women varies from family to family. Women are the transmitters of culture in Hindu tradition, and this role lies in the hands of women, and I don't think a man has time, or even the patience, to do that.

That point, about women as the transmitters of culture, seemed to me to be so fundamental, that I suggested to Mrs Pancholi that, in that case, women are really more important for the well-being of society than men. She responded:

> Women *are* more important; and throughout history, though we don't have time to discuss all this, I can give you hundreds of examples of what sort of significant part women have played in history. As you said, man is dominant, and I think

> that applies to all civilisations. In Western civilisations, man is the dominant one, he always plays the dominant part as well. But the role of the woman has never been low at all in Hindu religion, and I don't think it will ever be. Actually the status of women was very high in ancient religion, but as the time went on and foreign rule came – especially British rule and Muslim rule – the status of women had gone down. It was only for that time, but after that, the status has gone up. When Mahatma Gandhi started his movement, you would find that many Hindu women came out and supported him and they went to prison. And I believe India is the only country where women were *given* the chance to vote: they didn't have to fight for it. They just got it. So the status of women has always been high. In this country the women do come into contact with Western women. I wouldn't say that Hindu women want to be as dominant as Western women are, but at the same time, let me tell you that women don't want to lose their grace, their femininity; they may not be outspoken or blatant like Western women are; but they will let their opinion be known, they will let their colleagues know what they think.

In that sense, Mrs Chatterji, a school teacher, could say confidently that the pattern of married relationships among Hindus, especially the basic commitment and fidelity, will not change:

> The Hindu idea is of saying: however independent I am, I am emotionally dependent on somebody, and that somebody will be my husband. Once you are ingrained with this attitude, it is very difficult to change. We had an insurance man – my husband was doing some sort of policy – and he said, 'Would you like your wife – what will happen if your wife leaves you?' And my husband said, 'I don't think she will ever leave me: how could you say that?' This sort of thing, it just doesn't happen.

But although the fidelity and commitment remain, the patterns of role and status in marriage *are* changing. Some Hindus *are* trying to live as equals in their marriage – even though that upsets other Hindus, as this Hindu husband recognised:

> I think we've worked hard at that. I may have upset a lot of people by saying this to them – I've perhaps even upset my own family in some ways – but I think you mustn't get it wrong, you know. A lot of people have the idea that Indian girls are submissive, and they are meek, and they bow to every wish of their husband. It's not so. I think within, say, perhaps

> the Sikh system, or with the Muslim religion, maybe it's more true than with the more enlightened Hindu families. As my wife has already said, she's been to university, she's lived away from her home. She's obviously had a chance to develop her own ideas, and there's no way that I can force upon her what I think and I believe, without causing a lot of misery within the family. And of course, if she's miserable, then we're all miserable.

So there are many problems, particularly as girls go to colleges or universities, or pursue careers. But the controlling feeling is that one should never do anything to bring dishonour on the family. Mrs Chauhan told me in Leeds, 'There are many, many problems – many, many women are going the wrong way.' By 'wrong', she explained that she meant following their own careers. So I then asked her whether it was right, in her view, for girls to go to college or university:

> Yes: I've been to college, I was sent to college. But the trouble is life – you go to college, you go outside, anywhere as you like, but don't spoil your name; because you are a Hindu, your mother is of the Hindu people. She says, 'You don't spoil my name, you don't spoil yourself: you look after your life.'

But to hold a family together in that way means that a father will have to run a very tight ship even when, from a traditional point of view, he is being very liberal; and it becomes clear, from this Hindu father, that what is liberal in the context of one tradition may be extremely restrictive when looked at from outside that tradition. To begin with, he described his own – non-discriminatory – attitude: 'I don't discriminate, as some people do, that girls are different from boys. I treat them alike, and the same is with my wife; even to some extent we are more attached to our daughters than our boys.' So I then asked him whether this meant, in practice, that he would allow his daughters to stay out late at parties or discos. He answered:

> Yes, we do allow them. Not so often, but yes, they can: with our permission they are allowed; and they are sensible enough to know how many times they can go. So once in a year I say, Yes, in special cases: celebration of a birthday or special celebration in the college or university, they do go. They tell us the specific time, I go personally and bring them back.

I wondered whether there came an age when the daughters

would no longer have to ask permission. He said:

> In my case, there is no age at all: they are still asking me. My eldest asks me; because they feel that they are living with us, and they feel it a duty to ask permission. The home, you see, is like an entity which is to be administered in its proper way. So if we want to maintain the harmony of the family life, we should not give so much latitude to one person, and pressurise the other one. So we have to adopt a liberalised attitude, which can keep both parties happy. There should not be any strictness – or I should say, fanaticism – strictness to that extreme. No, they can't do this.

Muslims

In those circumstances, the authority of the father, as the place where 'the buck stops', becomes all the more important – as it does also in Islam, where tradition is very much a part of the religion, and where, as we have seen, the different roles of men and women are highlighted by the fact that it is an obligation for men to attend the Friday mosque; women *may* do so, but if they do, they will be in a separate space or place from the men; and in any case, their first responsibility is in the home, with the children. One Muslim made a sharp distinction between marriage and the mosque, arguing that the presence of women in the mosque would be a distraction and temptation:

> Men and women being separated means that the temptation is barred, from diverting them. A man in Islam manages so easy, if a woman wants to be with a man; it's just they need to say a few words, probably four or five words to each other, and it's finished, the marriage. As long as they want to be with each other, there's no restriction. They don't have even to have witnesses; but they shouldn't do it secretly. So why should we put these temptations? The mosque is not a club to arrange a meeting between a man and a woman. So in the mosque the woman is separate and the man is separate. There's no need to be intermixed. What's the point of mixing? I can't see it.

One reason for being together in the mosque (in the sense of standing and kneeling side by side) might be to reaffirm before God the unity of one's marriage, and to give thanks for it – or so I thought. But not so:

> Well, you'll be side by side when you get married: that's good

enough. Why do we have to reaffirm things which are already in you? It means you *need* to be reaffirming; it means you're not sure about it. You see, in Islam, mosque is for men mainly: women – in all school of thoughts as far as I know – it's better for them to be in their homes. But nobody should object to their coming. Women, they get a lot of trouble: as a female, they have their periods, they have their hormones, they have their emotions. So she feels happier at home. Mind you, she could come, there's a special part for women. It's split into half, putting curtains in between – this is male, this is female. They could hear the same thing, they could see the same thing, but they don't have to have their – what do they call it in English? – the Western mixed life, like churches – I don't know how in the synagogue they do it. But this is the reason. If you come into a mosque, you come in for the worship of God, a particular type of worship of God. You are not intending to reaffirm your marriages, or your relationship with a woman or a man. After all, you worship God when you kiss your wife: this is worship of God; you're fulfilling a purpose. You should give everything its share; if it is a wife, or a child, or a job, or a slave, or anything. You see, in Islam there's everything: God caters for everything.

That view is not held in Islam by men alone. Many Muslim women see the division of responsibility as necessary and desirable – and even as an illustration of the generosity of God. That is how Mrs Qureshi put it:

I don't go to the mosque, because Muslim women don't have to go to the mosque. They *can*; there is a separate room for the women, so they can if they want to. But they don't have to; it's not their duty to go to mosque to pray. The point is that God is not cruel, he is a God of love, and he is very kind to us. He knows how much a mother with children has to suffer and work hard, so he doesn't impose unnecessary sufferings on a mother. She has much more to do in the house to bring up children successfully.

But again, Muslims stress that it is important not to confuse the division of responsibility with the subordination of women. I asked Mr Ashraf Khan whether opportunities for women have been restricted in Islam. He answered firmly:

It is a complete illusion, because you have suggested several things: one is about the social status of the woman, and the other is that the woman has been put in bondage, and Islam has not done anything about it. Basically, when Islam came to this world, that is about 1400 years ago, woman was in a very bad state. Islam gave her the importance, and made the world realise that a woman is equal to a man, and Islam told them that heaven lies under the feet of the mother. So all those facts were emphasised, and woman was given a very important position. Now, when we talk about this thing – that woman is suffering in the Muslim countries – I personally don't agree with you. The reason is, that when we say that she is suffering, it is *my* opinion, it is *our* opinion; but is it the opinion of the person who is suffering? If you give her the chance and ask her, 'Look, you can live as a free woman in the West, do you want to live here? or do you want to live there?', the answers, in ninety-nine per cent of the cases, will be, they don't want to go.

Nevertheless, the fact remains that some young Muslim girls in this country *do* feel that men are superior. Miss Lakdawala (who has just taken her A levels in Computer Studies) recognised the strength of the tradition:

I feel men are superior, because that's what you've been believing ever since you were a child, and that's my way of looking at it. I have no special reason for believing that he is superior, it's just you've been taught things like that, so you tend to take them as they come.

There is no doubt that education and the following of careers is breaking down that feeling. Mrs Qureshi, who described why she doesn't have to go to the mosque, went on to observe:

To me, my family is my priority. I go to work, I earn my living to be a support to my husband, to be a support to my children; but I don't want to ignore my family for the sake of my job. My priority is my children – and my home. Most of the Muslim women or Asian women are not educated. When a woman or a wife is not educated, she is not confident. When she is not confident, she can't reason things: and when she can't reason things, she is weak. She may look oppressed, you can say that; but I'm sure there are educated families who are enjoying quite a happy life. They have mutual understanding, and they go to work together, they come home and they have a happy home life. It depends on the families; it depends on the husband's understanding, really.

Jews

Even more is this process of change – or this tension – true of Judaism: we've already seen that the separation or non-separation of men and women in synagogue is an issue between traditional and non-traditional Jews. I asked Mrs Cowan (who had been a Reform Jew before the war in Berlin) whether she had ever been separated from her husband in synagogue. She replied, 'I've never gone through with that: I've always thought it was very queer.' 'But,' I said, 'why does it seem very queer to you if it's been a part of the tradition for so long?' She replied: 'Because I felt the togetherness was very important. The only time I went to a synagogue where the women were sitting apart together, I went with my grandmother – and that was good enough, because I knew her so I went with her.'

For traditional Jews, the responsibility and duties of wives are clearly defined – especially after children have been born; and there is also a basic obligation to be married, as Mr Klein explained to me:

> It is one of the most important commandments of the Jewish religion, for a man to marry a wife, as it is stated clearly in Genesis, 'Be fruitful and multiply'. And this implies that one should be married – it is a tradition, of course, that this is something which is done within the framework of marriage. So, therefore, if women were to pursue a career and not get married, then how could the Jewish society first of all grow, which is a very important need for our spiritual and physical security? That answers the question about whether a woman should get married at all: she should certainly get married. With respect to whether a woman should pursue her career after marriage, if she has one, I would say that once a woman is married, she has, as her first responsibility, to look after her children, and to make her home a Jewish home within the Orthodox term of the word. This does not mean that she cannot go out to work. But once this going out to work in any way fundamentally breaks her capacity to look after her children, and if the children suffer, then one has to seriously contemplate at least cutting down the amount of work she does outside of the home.

His wife accepts and reinforces that view:

> For a lot of women, the fact is that they see their fulfilment

outside. They think home is more a burden: they need to go out. But the first fulfilment of a woman should be at home. That should be the first. And if she has got a mind, she can use it, and if she wants, she can have her children too. I give an example: for Jewish people, we have a special commandment of having big families. In the beginning a woman can have a job – let's say if a woman is a lawyer: she can cope with it in the beginning of her marriage; or when she has one child, two children, three. But if a woman has, for example, seven children, as sometimes happens, she won't be able to have such a job. So it seems a waste of time to go to university, and have this career, and then she has to stop in any case. So a woman should think very carefully before she starts any studies.

The marriage commitment is *so* fundamental and *so* sacred as a command from God that young men and women, in strictly Orthodox communities, are kept well away from each other – which obviously creates problems if they pursue further education in the UK system – hence the importance of specifically Jewish secondary or further education:

You see, first of all the separation of male and female sexes is something very, very fundamental to Jewish Orthodox life. And, therefore, already when a Jew goes to university, he is faced with the problem of having contact with a female world – not only the Jewish female world, but also the non-Jewish female world, which of course is something very – I'd like to choose the right words: let's say, it's not Jewish. I mean, as people probably know, Jewish people are very worried about assimilation. And, therefore, one must try and avoid any dangers of assimilation at all costs. That is why many Jewish – or at least Orthodox Jewish – children, after they go to primary school, continue and go to a Jewish secondary school, or grammar school; and after this they go, sometimes as early as the age of thirteen or fourteen, into what is called a Yeshiva, in which they continue their studies until they are married. Girls do not go to a Yeshiva, they go usually to what is called a seminary. And they stay there in most cases until they are married. The Orthodox Jewish view of marriage is that it is a very sacred occasion; and that this is the first time in which there is any physical contact between a man and a woman. We believe that man is weak, and therefore, he has not always got the control over his nature, especially when he is put in difficult circumstances; and therefore, as far as possible, especially in domains such as those between man and woman, we try to keep the man and the woman as separate as possible.

We've already heard how, for a traditional Jew, the responsibilities in the home are extensive – particularly in taking care that the food laws are observed. But there are many other customs and laws which express the fundamental beliefs about the married relationship. This Jewish wife, for example, explains why she must wear a wig in public, when she is married:

> The hair of the woman is called 'her glory'. She has got to keep her glory for her husband, right? So other men should not see her hair. Beside that, it's just a commandment, like any other one, and we don't exactly understand all the reasons for it. Another uniform is that she has got to be dressed very modestly, long sleeves, certain length of skirt, and she has got to avoid very low necklines.

That may seem a relatively small detail. Cleansing, or *mikvah*, after childbirth and menstruation, is far more extensive – and sensitive. For some Jews it remains profoundly important, not least because it gives order and renewal to the deepest relations between husband and wife:

> There's a commandment that when the woman has her period, she has got to separate herself from her husband – a complete separation: not to have relationship at all, and not even to touch the husband or to give something to the husband in the hand. And when her period stops, she has to count seven days of purity. It means seven days when she's not going to see any stain or any blood at all. And then when she has finished this seven days of purification, she has to go to the *mikvah*, to the ritual bath, to immerse herself, and she says a blessing after immersing herself. And then she is allowed to resume intercourse with her husband.

I asked what the reasons are for these practices:

> First of all, it is a commandment clearly stated in the Torah – in the Law – so that is the first and most important reason; because even if we did not understand any logic for keeping the laws of family purity, we would be obliged to keep them, because that is the law as it has been handed down. There is, however, a rationale to this law. In the whole of nature one can see a certain pattern, which with us is called advance and

retreat. In other words, if one looks at the ocean, one sees the waves go into the shore, and then they return to the sea. In a similar way, for any relationship to stay strong, there has to be a period of retreat. It speaks for itself. And, therefore, when a man and his wife separate themselves for a period of two weeks, when they come together again afterwards, it is almost like a new marriage.

But for other Jews, cleansing suggests that there *is* something unclean about these things – and that seems equally wrong – as it does to Mr Levy:

Mikvah is associated with the whole business of the menstrual cycle, and that's not something that makes much sense to us in a modern context. Certainly the idea, when *mikvah* was developed (and it goes back a long way: there are in fact a couple of *mikvahs* – that's the ritual bath – up on the mountain in Masada – so that's the Roman period, and it obviously goes back a long way), the idea was closely associated with the idea that women are unclean. We've learnt a bit since then, medically. So *mikvah* is not something that is a normal part of Reform Judaism. The distaste – and I think that's what it is – to *mikvah* associated with the menstrual cycle, is the very idea that women are somehow or other unclean for some period. They just happen to be going through a menstrual cycle, you know. They are clean all the time, if they're clean.

The point at which, to the outsider, Judaism seems to make the strongest distinction between men and women is in the different blessings said by a man and a woman in the Prayer Book, in the Morning Service. The man says: 'Blessed are you, O Lord our God, King of the Universe, who has not made me a woman.' And the woman says: 'Blessed are you, O Lord our God, King of the Universe, who has made me according to your will.' But for Jews themselves this does not mean that one is *inferior* to the other, but that each is thankful for the *particular* commandments that they alone have to obey. That is how Mrs Klein expressed it:

I don't feel in the least that I am second class citizen because I am a woman. I know I've got some commandments to do, and they are plenty for me, they are just enough. Some commandments I can do and my husband can't do them. For example, I've got to go to the ritual bath, right? and I have to maintain the purity of the family, right? It's my responsibility, and my husband can't do anything about it. He can't come and check

> if I have kept all the laws of family purity. That's my responsibility.

Even so, there is an increasing sensitivity here, especially among women, that they do *not* want to be assigned a particular role – they want to live a whole life. I pursued this further with Mrs Levy:

> Can we talk a little bit about the place of women? Because I think one of the things that I personally found within the Reform movement was something which I actually wasn't looking for, but something which made me increasingly involved with Judaism, and that was the acceptance of women as – I'm not going to say, men's equals, because I think 'equal' is a wrong word – but let's say, equivalent. It is a question of being a whole person, not in a particular role, but as a person – complete.

Combined with all that is an increasing resentment about the inequality of divorce – that it is much more in the man's control and initiative than the woman's: certainly Mr Oliver was sensitive to the injustice:

> If there is a break-up of the marriage, the only way a woman can get a divorce – from the Orthodox side – is for the husband to give her a divorce, otherwise she can never get married again. This is one of the things that people have been battling against for years and years. She has to get a civil divorce first, because it's the law of the land. And then if he wants to give her a [religiously recognised] divorce, he gives it to her, but it cannot be forced, because nobody can force him – we're living under English law. But in Israel, he can be forced. They can make his life very uncomfortable, you know, they can put pressure on him, by the job that he's at: the ruling Beth Din in Israel can get in touch with his employers and say, 'Look, a certain gentleman, he should give his wife a divorce, he's a blaggard, and he doesn't want to': they'll put pressure on him. It has been known: a year or so ago, they put a man in gaol. So there can be pressure in Israel. But you can't pressurise a man here.

I then asked him whether he thought there should be a change in the unequal provision for divorce:

> Oh, yes, no doubt about it. No doubt about it. Some people have an idea, they say that it should be put in to the marriage

> laws (which is what we call a *Ketubah*, which is the marriage lines) that in the event of a divorce, the husband shouldn't have to give her a *get* – shouldn't have to give her a bill of divorce. Well, I think it's terrible to have to insert this in your vows of marriage. So that's out. But I think, no, I definitely think – there are worse things than that – the question of a woman whose husband is missing – she can never get married. That's terrible. I know a lady in the East End, who would never get married, because her husband went to Russia to fight for the Russians in the 1914 war, he never came back. She had two children.

Christians

Christianity has had equally strong traditional attitudes about the authority of men over women, even if they are no longer enshrined in law – and those traditional attitudes still linger on, particularly in parts of the Church which have authoritarian structures of control – Roman Catholics at one extreme, and those who put strong emphasis on the unchanging authority of Scripture at the other. As one Roman Catholic father put it, man *is* the head of the family:

> The head of the household is always the man. I could be wrong in that – we do work as a team, we have to work as a team to survive, really – it'd be utter chaos. But it's man's sole responsibility to be the breadwinner, that's all. It bothers me that discipline has gone through the window. You take children in school today: there's no punishment. They try and talk to a child – *I* talk to my children, my daughters will tell you. They often say, Jingo, hitting a girl. But I'll tell my children three times, even from when they were babies to the ages they are now. I'll tell my child why it mustn't do something. If it persists in doing it, I'll tell it again. But the third time, it gets something that it knows what's going to happen to it if it does it, and it gets a smack, a sharp tap. I was on the other day, on about the fire, with the children. You can tell that child that if you put your finger in that fire it'll burn. But every child has to get burnt before it keeps away from that fire.

Could such a Christian envisage the ordination of women?

> No, I disagree with that one. I mean look at the way the country is – the state it's in now, through a woman. All right,

I'm sorry Margaret, but no. Can I be chauvinistic and say, I still think it's a man's world? I don't believe in women priests.

But his wife was not so sure:

I don't see any reason why not, apart from the tradition – that it's so traditional for men; whereas it would be so strange, I think, for everyone to see a woman ordained; and it would probably be quite hard to accept, even for another woman.

But I then asked her whether women priests might not bring into the Church insight which is missing at the moment?

That's a good point, yes, I think they probably could. I think a woman, if she had been married and she was a widow perhaps, and she's brought up a family, and then she became ordained, she would have a wealth of experience to help people. Yes, I think in that respect it would be a good thing. I think anyone with experience is always good: someone that's experienced the same thing can help another person much more easily, when they've been through it themselves.

Two young Roman Catholic girls (still at school) are equally uncertain:

I don't think it really matters. I mean, it's a tradition that priests have been male. The idea of a priestess sounds – I just don't like the sound of it. You hear that in all these demonologists' kind of thing. You get the priestess, the high priestess, I don't think it sounds right in a Catholic, you know. But still, it's happened, hasn't it? The first one has been ordained – that was in America, I think. I don't think it really matters whether it's male or female: doing God's will, that's all.

I then asked her sister whether she agreed. She answered: 'No, because women, I think, are much more emotional than men, on a lot of levels. Perhaps it's being old-fashioned, but I wouldn't want to give my confession to a woman, to a woman priest. I think it should stay men.' So I then suggested that it might also work the other way: some women, for example, prefer to go to women doctors. Might it not be the same with Confession?

It might be, but I think it's up to the priest to cultivate a friendlier atmosphere, perhaps, or a more understanding atmosphere towards women. Perhaps they are being treated badly by a male, and so they've got a thing about it, a stigma about it.

And even an Anglican, Simon Williams, is worried (even though in parts of the Anglican communion women *are* ordained), because changes in *authority* are different from more trivial issues – such as whether women should wear hats in Church, as Paul appears to have recommended:

> Well, personally, I've followed this whole debate about women, and it seems that the reason a lot of people give why they can't be ordained, that they can't administer communion, the sacraments, that leaves me cold. I can see no reason at all why women can't administer sacraments, and I think that's very ritualistic – apart from anything else, it sort of ascribes to the priesthood a power which I don't think the priesthood can or should possess. So I'm not concerned about that at all. But Scripturally you come back to this: the Apostles didn't seem to think it a wonderful idea that women should teach and have authority; and I'm not sure why. It's just that Scripture is there to be reckoned with. Personally, I can see no reason against them being ordained as priest, if you call 'priest' someone who administers Communion, and has these kind of powers to give absolution. None of that bothers me in any way whatsoever. But I still think – my own feeling at the end of the day is – that it seems to have been laid down in the Scripture, for some reason, that men should have authority in the Church.

It seemed to me, though, that men had authority everywhere in those days. So I asked him whether that authority of men in the early Church was just an accident of time, or whether it was an act of Providence?

> It's something I wrestle with. My own feeling now is that I can see nothing against women being ordained. But it's still a niggle, a niggle I have, it's there and I think about it. Obviously there are some things, like women wearing hats or having their heads covered, which I don't think they should do just because it's there in the Bible. So one doesn't say that everything that was there then, must apply now. But as I say, it seems to be a general principle, not just culturally related, but a general principle; and I know it's extremely unfashionable now for that to exist (and I don't like the fact that it is unfashionable; it would be much easier if it was in accordance with modern thinking) but it's there, so it's something that I just have to bear in mind.

Buddhists

Buddhism is equally unspecific about how, in detail, marriage should be organised and run: we have already seen that marriage in itself does not belong intrinsically to Buddhism, but that rather, Buddhism, especially the fundamental Five Precepts, are brought *to* marriage; and even *in* marriage, mental cultivation towards Enlightenment remains paramount:

> First, I resolve not to indulge in excessive sensual pleasure – not just adultery: in excessive sensual pleasures. In some books it *has* been described as adultery. But adultery is a man-made code; and it has usually been enunciated by men who are frightened that their wives would be unfaithful to them. And that's how I interpret this adultery, you know, whatever the penal code is. Suppose you are in Christianity, where an adulterer was stoned, and Jesus said, 'Let him without fault cast the first stone' – see the sweet teachings of Christ, again. If you take the teachings of Christ, they are very sweet. He said, 'Let him who is free of sin cast the first stone.' So anyway, the Buddha's enunciation, the Buddha's third precept, was, 'I resolve not to indulge in excessive sensual pleasure', so that even where sexual behaviour is concerned, indulging in excessive sexual pleasure with one's own wife is not conducive to mental culture. The whole point in Buddhist life is not to do anything to excess. Now the Polynesians, their chiefs have about a hundred wives. It's acceptable to the *society*, but the point is, where is the time for him to develop his mental culture? He has to keep all his hundred wives happy. He won't have time. I suppose his punishment is that he has a hundred mothers-in-law. That is a punishment in itself.

Therefore the status of a wife depends a good deal on the culture or society in which one lives, not exclusively on Buddhism – though in fact, for many Buddhists the wife is as much the light of the home as she is in Judaism, as Dr Fernando, a dentist in North London, told me:

> Marriage is not *Buddhist* marriage. What happens is traditional, more to do with racial characteristics. It's got nothing to do with Buddhism. But Buddhism does come in: in one of the Sutras, one of the discourses of the Buddha, where he discusses the highest blessings, he mentions this: when one of the dialectians asked him, 'Can you please tell me what are the highest blessings?', he enumerated a few. One is, 'Despise

> the friendship of fools, cultivate the friendship of the wise.' Then he says, 'Honour those who are worthy of honour.' This is one of the highest blessings. So this is how you should look after your spouse. The wife has always been regarded as the light of the home – the Jews have it too: on a Friday, the lady of the house will light the Sabbath lamp.

A Tibetan Buddhist gives exactly the same emphasis to the importance of the wife and mother in the home:

> Well, man is always the one who goes out, that is true; and woman stays at home. In decision-making in Tibet, the woman is very strong. Especially after marriage and children, she gains great confidence, and husbands always discuss with the wife and the whole family, because the children turn to the mother – they say, We must ask the mother. So the mother becomes the centre of the family; and she takes a lot of power. But in business, she doesn't go outside the village – she doesn't often go. So a man knows when he has to go out, and there he takes most of the initiatives.

Sex and Contraception

But we are not living in Tibet. And no religion in this country can escape the enormous (though deeply resisted) changes in opportunity and freedom for women which are occurring. Religions *may* be a part of the resistance. But equally they may provide the stamina to live and work for change, precisely because the underlying beliefs are so strong. Equally, no religion can avoid the changes in the meaning and opportunities for sex which widely available contraception has brought about.

Here the conflict may be much more overt, because of specific religious rulings or advice. For Roman Catholics, the papal Encyclical, *Humanae Vitae*, offered the moral advice that artificial contraception should be avoided. Some of the Roman Catholics I talked to, like this teenage girl, accept that advice. She said: 'The Church says that you shouldn't use any form of contraception. If, due to health reasons, you have to do that, I think that should be allowed: you shouldn't endanger somebody's health, just because it's against the Church to use that.' 'But doesn't contraception,' I asked her, 'mean that sex can also become a means in itself of drawing husband and wife closer together?' She answered:

> I don't agree with it unless there is a very good reason for

using it. Health reasons, I think, would be the only one. I think you should leave it up to God. Like my parents say, what happens will happen. If God wants you to have a child, you'll have one.

But other Roman Catholics – and they were certainly the majority of those I met – rejected the view that contraception is wrong in all circumstances, and some put the point very vigorously:

I am convinced, and was in 1968, convinced intellectually, that the Church – well, the Pope – had made a mistake over contraception. I can understand how the mistake came about. I am not unsympathetic to the values – in fact, I'm very sympathetic to the values that he tried to uphold. But I do think that a lot of unnecessary worry has been made over contraception.

Far more serious is the point Ray Turner emphasised, that trying to stick to *Humanae Vitae* may damage the very marriage and relationship which children most need if they are to grow up in security and love:

One of the biggest regrets in my life was trying to obey one of the Church's rules to the letter, and that was birth control; and I mustn't be on my own here: there must be millions of people that have gone through the same. The number of times that I've failed to go to Communion to be with Christ because I hadn't followed the letter of the law of the Church, is one of the biggest regrets of my life. It not only upset my relationship with God, it upset my relationship with my wife. She is not a traditional Catholic, I am; and I thought, 'That's the Church's teaching, we'll stick to it.' The Church's teaching it might be, but it's an ideal, it's an ideal teaching; and we don't live in an ideal world. We live with the people next door, and the people next door that way, and the television, and these are the things that we've got to live with. We're not shut up in a Vatican, where we can shut ourselves off from the world. We've got to live in it. And we can only be Christians in the world, and we've got to put up with the pressures that the world puts upon us. And, therefore, to answer your question, I don't feel in any way subjected to what the authority of the Church tells me. I accept what they say as being what they believe, and I take their advice – I listen to their advice; I don't always take it.

But contraception is not a problem for Roman Catholics alone. Judaism has had an equally strong command to 'be fruitful and multiply' (Ber./Gen. i.28). Is there a conflict for Jews? I asked this question of an Orthodox Jew and his wife:

> She: Yes, definitely, it is a conflict. Judaism says you ought to multiply as soon as you get married, and I suppose as long as there are no health problems or terrible financial problems, or something, one ought to have one's children. That is where we don't comply, really. It *is* conflicting with religion, definitely.
> He: Yes, I think that the problem is there, the conflict is there. But our view (at least my view) is that I don't particularly want to bring children into this world thinking, Well, we're going to have to scrimp and save all the time – not being able to give them as much as one can. OK, I'm not going to wait until I'm a millionaire to be able to have them, otherwise I'd have to wait another century. But try and bring them into a world where you feel you can do the most for them.

On the other hand, some Jews trust the whole outcome to God, much as the Pope would commend:

> We believe that God provides for everybody. We're not worried about that. And we don't believe in contraception of course, because we believe that everything comes from God. And we have the belief that if he brings a child into the world, he can provide for the child too.

Birth and Belief

Why *is* the issue of contraception so important? It comes round in full circle to children – to children as a trust from God in creation – to children as the only real wealth which matters – to the miracle and incredible delight of conception and of birth, even through pain. Not surprisingly all religions have their ceremonies surrounding birth – circumcision for Jews, as we've heard already, christening or baptism for Christians – except for those who believe it must be reserved for adult and conscious decision. Muslims have simple ceremonies, but they have the important custom of whispering the basic words of faith into a new-born baby's ear:

> The first thing we do is the *adhan* in the ear of the baby who is born. The *adhan* you may have heard in the mosque. It's to

call the people for prayer: *Allahu akbar, Allahu akbar* – you must have heard it many times: God is great, God is great. By that way, the baby knows that he is born to a Muslim family. So that is the first ceremony. And then the second one, within seven days (or one month or two months), you have to cut the hair of the baby, and sacrifice a goat: if it is a girl, one goat, if it is a boy, then two goats.

Hindus also have their ceremonies, as Mrs Chatterji described to me:

You have one ceremony when you are expecting a baby, called *Sadh* Ceremony, and that means the wife will have a new sari, and nice food, and things like that. When the child is born, we obviously take the child to the temple, and then in the temple, we have a little bit of *prasad*, from Goddess Kali, or whoever you believe in. And afterwards, when the child starts having solid food, we have a weaning ceremony, known as *Mukhe-bhaat*, when the child is learning to stand up, and entering the world, big world, you may call it. And that's a big ceremony, when you pray to different gods and goddesses, and ask for their blessing, and you have all the relatives and friends, and entertain them.

And Sikhs have theirs – particularly the naming of the child, as Mrs Bhupinder Dhesi told me:

The main ceremony is the naming ceremony. After the initial family gathering, the friends, relatives, everyone gathers; and we consult the Holy Book. The way the name is chosen is that the book is opened randomly, and the first letter on the beginning of the page is chosen as the first letter of the name. Of course, there are prayers that are spoken before this occurs. It's not done straight off. So in that way, through the Book, you are consulting God. You are asking him what the name should be – you say, 'Could you guide?'; and it's done in that way.

Bringing up Children

But life does not end at birth. Then begins the long process of nurturing the child in the faith – and that may not be easy in a Western society, with open schools and with many other young children following very different – and sometimes very undisciplined – patterns of life. I asked a Muslim father whether he regarded the responsibilities of bringing up his children as important:

> It is absolutely vital. I believe that the children are a trust to us from God, and in the other world, I shall be judged also in respect of how my children have behaved as a result of my training. If they have grown up good Muslims, if they have grown up good citizens, Allah will appreciate it. If I have developed them into bad citizens, into bad Muslims, I will suffer for it as well.

I asked him, as I asked all the parents I met, whether there are difficulties in bringing up children in their own particular faith in this country. Many more than half the parents said, 'Yes, there are difficulties.' In particular, they specified the very different and often conflicting values expressed through TV, newspapers and advertisements; and they were also worried about the absence, in many places, of cultural or recreational outlets except for pubs or discos.

But not *all* parents answered that way. Some said, No, there hadn't been real difficulties: provided that the foundations were well laid, they felt they could trust their children. A Christian mother spoke for them when she said:

> I think my family respond to love, and I think they feel that to be loving and caring is a nice way to live, and they try to be like that. And so I think that with the love side of life uppermost in their minds, the receiving and the giving of it, the rest of life seems to fall into pattern – falls into place. So it doesn't really seem difficult.

Education and Religion

But of course the deeply underlying issue here, for parents, is how they can immerse their children in the atmosphere of their own religion in a country where Christianity is historically dominant. Much can be done at home. But does it also require separate schools? After all, there are separate Christian schools – even separate denominational schools, not least in Northern Ireland. Given how important it is for some Jews and Muslims, as well as Hindus and Sikhs, to keep girls and boys separate until marriage, does that supply an additional reason for separate schools for Jews and Muslims – or for any other religion?

On this, we found very different opinions. In general, the

religions which believe in rebirth are far more relaxed about this – perhaps because the long road to enlightenment or release may mean going to many different schools in many different lifetimes. A Buddhist (Mr Wickramaratne) wanted children to learn about all religions. 'I'm all in favour,' he said, 'of teaching children all religions, so that rather than being born into a religion, he can understand other religions: decide for yourself, maybe later, what is good for yourself.'

In a similar way, Sikhs want their children to be *educated*: the religion will come, in life and at home. This is how Mrs Sohal put it:

> Sikh parents really do support their children in education, and many of them have come from India or Africa, in the hope that here is almost like a Utopia: the education that they never received, they hope that their children will get here, and that it will be a better education. And usually it's the parents who would like their son or daughter to be – well, the classic is a doctor; but a doctor, a teacher or something that's sensible, something that *they* would say is sensible. Anything like modelling, or something like that, is frowned upon.

What certainly is important for these parents is that their children should have a fair and sufficient opportunity to learn their own religious traditions and history. Certainly they resent any bias or prejudice in the teaching, which Mr Mittal, himself a teacher, felt that he could detect: he said: 'In the schools there is partiality. They are not treated as they should be treated. I, being a teacher, I find differentiation between different children of different nations or backgrounds – not only, I should say, Asians, but also West Indians and Greeks; and in some respects, there is differentiation between local children as well. It is sad. But this is the way of life.' But does that mean that each religion ought to have control over its own teaching, in its own 'denominational' schools? For Hindus, the answer was, emphatically, No – and here one Hindu contrasts that response with the Muslims:

> We don't want to be separate from the English people. We don't want to be separate from the Christianity. Sideways, we don't want to leave our own culture – you understand me? With Islam, they say, No; we should have our own school, our own language, and this and that. I talked only three or four years ago to the Education Authority in Leeds, to give one day one class; and I am the first man to come to teach that for half

> an hour or one hour, and I explain to them, in their language, what is the religion, in the ritual way.

And that contrast is correct. Almost all the Muslims who answered this question said they would like separate Muslim schools, because of the extreme difference between Muslim and Western ways of life. This is how Mohammed Hassan, the knowledgeable caretaker of a mosque in Manchester, put it:

> It's a very good idea; it should be done that way. But if you can't, you don't have to. Sometimes, if the school is so bad, you don't have to send your girls or boys to that school. There's dangers for boys, more than girls, in this society; how to be educated, how to bring them up. The Toxteth riots, Moss Side riots, it's all boys more than girls causing this trouble, because of the background, the society they live in, the schools they go to, how they think, how they fight. Really it's not the women's side of it. It's just that you need sometimes to educate men as men, educate women as women.

I asked another Muslim, Hajji Cassim Mohammad, whether he would like separate Muslim schools: he said, 'Yes, I certainly would.' So I went on to ask him why. He replied:

> The outlook on life is completely different from a Muslim parent's point of view, and a Western parent's point of view. We know, once upon a time, a Christian thought differently, but today he thinks differently again. Parents don't really like their daughters to practise permissiveness, but they do, they are forced into it, and they can't do otherwise. That's the situation we're going to be faced with. For the Muslim community, the Asian community, in the next few years, things will start changing, because there is that freedom, what they call freedom. If a child isn't properly trained, grounded in their religion, and made to realise that it's wrong to have illicit sexual intercourse, unless he has a sound religious background, he is going to fall to that temptation.

But since the schools *are* mixed, the Muslims make the same plea that their children should have time and opportunity in school to learn their own tradition. A Shiite Muslim mother said:

> Whatever religion they are, they should be taught whatever religion they are in. I don't mind whether it's separate schools or the same, but if they are Muslim they should be able to learn what Islam is.

Mrs Qureshi, a Sunni Muslim, saw the real issue as not losing one's Islamic identity: if the foundations are secure, one can be more open in learning from others:

> In education there is no harm in learning, but they should not lose their identity. They should learn their own religion first, and their foundation should be built. If the basis is there, they would not be lost – at least they have a pattern of life in front of them then. They can follow it. In any religion, we have got some good and some bad points. There's no harm in picking up the good points. We can share with Christians and Hindus and Sikhs; we can all learn from each other.

For Christians the issue is slightly different, since the Christian and the denominational schools are already in being. The issue is whether they should continue. And it's not an easy question, as Mr John Callaghan, who works in a Roman Catholic Sixth-form College in Liverpool, makes clear:

> That's a rather difficult one, for someone from the North-West, to pontificate about, because the Liverpool Archdiocese in particular has so many Catholic schools that it's difficult to imagine life without them. My working life has been in Liverpool and Manchester, and it's been in Catholic schools. If I can just take an aspect of that and say what I would feel about denominational schools for the sixteen to nineteen year olds (because that's been my experience for the last eight years), I'm not sure that it's a good thing. That is a bit of a heresy, I suppose, because Catholics value their education very highly. I'm not challenging the need for religious education for sixteen to nineteen year olds, but I don't know that school is the best way to do it. In fact, I'd go a bit further than that. I am fairly sure that if you have a transition, from an eleven to sixteen school to a sixteen to nineteen college, then it's not a good idea for it to be denominational.

And that was the almost unanimous response from those I talked to – that religion will come much more at home, not through divided schools. As one Catholic father put it, 'Regarding schooling, no, it doesn't matter to me which type of school they go to, because they'll get the Catholic education, at home, by example.'

Jews also have their existing separate schools, and for some – the Orthodox – it is urgently important that they continue:

> I believe very strongly that there should be Jewish schools, not

only Jewish primary schools, but Jewish secondary schools; and really the traditional Hasidic view is that a child should not go to university, certainly not to a non-Jewish university, because this will inevitably cause him problems. We have to be sure that the children do not read about information which is inconsistent with Jewish tradition; and also, we have to avoid them being exposed to morals, and particularly immodesty, which are the antithesis of the Jewish tradition. This does not mean that we do not train our children to understand about the world outside. We do not intend in any way to cloister them so that they will be ignorant of what is going on in the world outside. But particularly young children have to be, at first, sheltered a little bit from these influences until they are ready to understand them.

Other Jews made very similar points. I talked to a teacher in an all-Jewish primary school, and I asked her if she thought that was a good thing:

I think it is of value, because I don't think it in any way prevents them from the widening experience that can come later in life. But at the same time I think it provides them with a more solid base within their own religion and their own culture from which they can then go forward. And also they are learning Hebrew: part of the curriculum involves Hebrew. So having said this about Jewish children, it would be most unfair if I were to promote Jewish schools, and say that other religions and other denominations should not have their own schools. I feel that they certainly should, yes.

At this point I asked about Northern Ireland and the possibility (some would say certainty) that separate schooling reinforces hostility and violence:

Everything depends on the quality of the teachers, always, wherever teaching takes place; and I think that if you are going to have any system in which it's possible to indoctrinate children, then of course you are laying yourself open to this criticism. But I feel that a sectarian education in itself doesn't necessarily need to be an indoctrination. It could simply be education.

But is this even remotely realistic? Listening to Jewish and Muslim parents, one can understand what they hope for; but could it – or should it – be achieved? I asked a Jewish father if he had some sort of dream that one day there would be Hindu schools, Muslim schools, Sikh schools, and so on:

> What I really dream of is the sort of school (perhaps it would have to be fairly big), but a school where you would have all denominations – it might be a totally silly dream, but have all the denominations, and all those denominations be able to have religious classes, so that all the children themselves will be able to feel strongly in their religions, but at the same time have the very important thing of mixing with other children.

Their Children's Voice

But it's all very well asking the parents. What do the children think? Do *they* think there should be separate schools for each religion or denomination? Here is part of my conversation with a young Roman Catholic girl, still at school: I asked her whether she thought that there should be separate schools for Catholics:

> 'No, I don't think so really, because at school a lot of my friends aren't Catholics, and we can talk about religion without actually reverting to, Protestant is one thing and Catholic is another. I mean, we are all Christians, and I think it's good that we should have mixed schools, so that you can tell each other your point of view and just not argue about it, but discuss it.'
>
> '*Are* we all Christians?'
>
> 'I'd like to think the majority of us are.'
>
> 'But there was a time when the Church used to say, "Outside the Church there is no salvation."'
>
> 'No, I don't believe in that, no. I don't think that's right. That's not looking at it very realistically, because a lot of people aren't necessarily Catholic, but they are very good people.'
>
> 'Does that apply to all religions?'
>
> 'Yes, I think so, in my opinion it does.'
>
> 'So you wouldn't want to try to convert a Buddhist or a Hindu?'
>
> 'No, I think everybody should have their own beliefs and form their own opinions about life. What you believe is your own affair. Obviously, I'm guided by my parents' beliefs. I like being a Christian, I wouldn't want to change my religion. So I wouldn't want anybody else to change theirs. I wouldn't like to force it on them.'

That was the virtually unanimous voice: the children I talked to did *not* want separate schools for their own religion. So also was the verdict on arranged marriages from those girls for whom marriage was going to happen in that way – not one expressed any doubt or hesitation about it. In general, all the young people or children we talked to seemed glad to have had a disciplined home life. But, I asked them, did they feel that they had missed something, in not going to late-night parties and discos? Here are some of the answers – with a brief indication of the tradition they're speaking from:

Christian girl:
At my age, you know, I'd like to do that, but my faith does stop me from getting carried away. I'm glad I've been brought up the way I have been, because a lot of girls ruin their lives at an early age, because they go off and do silly things. My faith stops me from doing that.
Muslim girl:
I've been brought up in this country – I was born here. I've met all my friends here. I know that they go out at night and everything, but I've been taught that what you don't have you don't miss anyway. So I've never been out, so I don't really miss it.
Muslim girl:
You do feel it that way, but somehow, I don't give it a lot of importance at all, because I am satisfied with the way I've been brought up, and I feel that that is my way of life; and somehow that other way of life doesn't influence me at all. I'm quite content with what I've got.
Hindu girl:
I have work to do at home, and I am quite happy with the work I am doing now. Cooking the dinner for eight children, and with the family and all that, it's quite a lot of work to do. I do think about it; but then again, I think about my parents' reputation and respect, because it's really hard for an Asian girl to go out with friends; because according to other people, they might think she's a bad girl, mixing with other castes and other colours. They'll think, She goes out with boys, and she doesn't think about her parents.

Of course, there may be tensions on the way, as this Hindu girl remembers, but a happy outcome:

Yes, there was a conflict, but not with my friends: it was really with my family, because my friends used to advise me about how they were carrying on in the Western world, and I used to come home and say, 'Can't I do the same?' And they said, 'No, we're not supposed to do this, give me the reasons'; and I couldn't understand the reasons at the time, because all my friends were really just enjoying themselves in the Westernised way. And now, looking at them, they are really left behind, because some have broken marriages, some have left home. And they have no life at all, whereas I am still respected – and I'm still loved by my parents; and I haven't lost anything actually by those strict ways, which I couldn't understand at the time, but now I'm grateful for.

Of course we need to remember again that we were not listening, in making these programmes, to the children who *have* left home, or to those who *have* abandoned their tradition, or who *do* resent the discipline. That would be a different, though equally important, exercise. We were meeting those who have tried to stay in their faith and in their family. And for them, there is no doubt that they do see their life as a different and serious undertaking. I asked a young Muslim if he experienced any difficulties in growing up in this country and keeping his faith. Here is that part of our conversation:

'The only difficulty is that you can't do all your prayers, and I particularly miss the fact that I can't do the *jumna* prayer in the mosque, because I've got classes. I think that's the main problem really.'

'Is there no difficulty in the things you might see on TV?'

'TV is very corrupt. You can't watch TV without committing sin.'

'So you avoid watching television?'

'Yes, I watch extremely little.'

'What sorts of things are *not* sinful on television?'

'News, nature programmes, medical programmes. And even if I do watch a film, you can always take your eyes off the screen. I take my eyes off the screen when there's a bad scene.'

'What about books?'

'I never take the book which is bad. It's up to me, if I want a bad book; and I don't want them.'

'How do you know in advance of reading them which are bad and which are good?'

'It's on the cover. You can tell a bad book from the cover.'

'But you could put something like Shakespeare's *Hamlet* into lurid covers, with plenty of sex and violence. How can you tell then?'

'Oh, no that would not be a bad book. If you're reading it for the purposes of literature, it's OK.'

I asked a young Christian the same question, about the difficulties of keeping the faith while growing up:

'To be honest, there are difficulties, yes, there are a lot of difficulties, because for a start, as a Christian, you are different. You cannot do everything an unsaved, or non-Christian, person does. Like, somebody would swear when they really want to express themselves. I cannot do that. There are certain things, you know, I cannot do.'

'What about watching television?'

'I watch television, but you have to be very careful of what you watch, because it is there, it's being pumped into your front-room every night. You have to be careful of what you watch.'

'It's difficult to know in advance, though, isn't it?'

'Yes, it is, very difficult. You see, that's what I mean, you're always bound to sort of get trapped, as a Christian, as a human being, because you are human, and that is the area of error. But that's one good thing: Christ is always there, making intercession for you. You see, the moment you fall, Jesus Christ is there saying, "Father, forgive him."'

So then: among the children, as much as among the parents, there is a deep commitment to the stability of the family. There is a certain irony in that. The Conservative Party has seemed, in recent years, to be running two policies, one of limiting immigration, the other of strengthening family life and discipline in the community. If they really wished to achieve those aims, to judge from what we heard and saw as we went around this country, they should deport the English and encourage a massive immigration of Jews, Sikhs, Muslims and Hindus, for whom the family is the vigorous and self-supporting foundation of life and happiness. Many certainly do 'opt out', and we were only meeting those who have not done so. Still, the family is clearly not 'a bowling alley in the head' for all people. But whether family life is happy or unhappy, it does not go on for ever. Sooner or later we all die. What do these religions believe about death? Why does it happen? What, if anything, is going to happen to us beyond death? These are the questions we will be looking at next.

10
The Long Journey: Death and Beyond

'All I know,' wrote Pascal, 'is that I must soon die, but what I know least is this very death which I cannot escape.' But about what we know least, we can speculate most. And it is in their explanation of death and of what lies through or beyond death that these religions give the most varied accounts. We've already seen, in a very broad way, how Hindus, Buddhists and Sikhs agree that there are rebirths – reincarnations (many millions of them); but whereas Hindus and Sikhs believe that there is something – some self or soul – which is reborn, Buddhists do not. Jews, Christians and Muslims believe, in general, that this life is the only life we have on this earth (though there are some traces of reincarnation, particularly in some forms of Judaism), and that beyond this life lies the judgement of God – exercised in very different ways – on what will be our ultimate and final state.

Dealing with the Dead – Hindus

But before we reach the speculation and the belief, there is the plain fact of death and of the necessity to dispose of the dead body. The different beliefs show up very clearly in the different customs which surround and accompany death. Because of their belief in rebirth, Hindus do not have a long period of mourning – because the person essentially has not died; but the discarded body must be cremated and the ashes mingled with the sacred waters of the River Ganges – directly if possible, but indirectly in any river or sea, because sooner or later that water will itself mingle with the Ganges. Mrs Chatterji explained this to me, when I met her in Coventry:

> At death we believe that the soul goes, and we shouldn't disturb the soul by crying a lot. So we have a ceremony, called *shraddh* ceremony, where we invite people and entertain them, and ask them to pray for the soul. And also we must put the ash in the River Ganges and have *tarpan* ceremony: after

putting the ash in the River Ganges, we will do this ceremony.

But, I asked her, how do you put the ash in the River Ganges when you live in Coventry? She answered:

I can tell you what happened in my family: my sister was married to my brother-in-law and he was an accountant in India, and then they went on a three-year contract to Zambia. And she died in a car accident – she was only twenty-six with a little boy; and he took the ash back to India and put it in the River Ganges; he made a special journey where the River Ganges has got three branches, that is the holy place. So if anything happens to me or my husband or anybody, I can carry the ash with me and take it there. In fact also we should have water from the River Ganges in the home – we used to have it: I don't know whether we have it now. Suppose I'm dying of cancer, and if my husband comes to know, the first thing he will have to do is give me this drop of water before I die.

So the dead, among the Hindus, are sent away on their long journey; and as they die, it is important that their last thoughts are fixed on the form of God to which they have been devoted – Rama, for example, or Krishna – because the last thoughts of a Hindu affect the next rebirth – just as the last thoughts of a Buddhist affect the next form of appearance. And as Mr Ladd told me, the *atman* (soul) of the dead person is equipped for the journey:

When a Hindu dies we have some religious formalities at home. You know, this is the last journey, this is the journey. So when we go on our long journey we take everything with us. So we give everything to him, to the dead person. We say, 'These are your things to be used on the way.' We give everything, money, food, everything, everything; and it is cremated with the body. And then with the ashes, those who can afford it send the ashes to India. If not, they just put them here in the River Thames or any other big river.

I asked him what he believes happens to a person when he or she dies. He said:

What we believe is that the soul inside, the *atman,* never dies. Just as – I give you an example: when my clothes become old, I bring new ones and put on new ones instead of the old ones. The same happens to the *atman*: it just changes the body; it goes from one person to the other person.

Could it, I wondered, go into the body of an animal?

Yes, yes, it could: it depends upon what he was thinking at the end of his life. So that is why, when we know that he is about to go, about to finish, we say 'Ram, Ram,' in the ears, so that he can concentrate on that word.

If possible, a pandit should conduct the ceremonies for Hindus, so when I met Pandit Chimanlal Pandya in Leeds, I asked him to tell me how he deals with the ashes:

We Hindus believe the River Ganges, the River Jumna, are the religious rivers and they mix finally with the sea. So whatever we are doing, or disposing of, in a ritual way it must go into the sea, because the sea is the most ritual place of water. When it came to the ashes of the dead, I used to go with the community men to Scarborough, Blackpool, Southport, Bridlington, many places around the coast – but probably to Scarborough, because at Scarborough I can get this launch. We never throw the ashes away near the shore; we dispose of them about a mile away, going out to sea with the launch. The boatman takes out the launch and then he also stands up, like us, in that way. There we do the ceremony to the ashes: we worship with the milk, then we anoint, then we take rice, and then some flowers; and like that, we then drop the ashes – but it's not the ashes, it's the *man's* ashes we are dropping in that way. And then, finally, in a bucket or some vessel – we don't throw it even, we put it in, so that the ashes will go away with the water into the sea; and finally we bow down ourselves and then come back. Every time, we're doing it that way.

I went on to ask him what death means to him:

Death? Death is final. So what I have been learning is to live in this way: when we came on this earth, we came crying – the small baby cries but the parents and everybody laugh because they've got a son. But we should live in such a way of life that when we die, *we* should smile and call out to death: 'Oh, any time you can come down and take me – I'm ready for you'. So we should leave this world laughing, and let the people we've left behind us weep and cry. So my last prayer is, 'Sri Krishna, Lord Krishna, take me with you.' That is the last prayer. And when any person's death is come close, within a couple of minutes or something like that, that's the chanting we are

> doing – 'O Lord, take me with you'; because whatever we speak finally, at the end, will be the next birth.

Sikhs

For the Sikhs, there is a longer formal period of mourning, as Jagat Singh Nagra told me:

> Death is a very sad thing for the family, and for many days people will come – relations and friends – to the family and say sympathies to the family and pray to God that the family will be able to bear the loss of the dead person. And some Sikhs – I think most of them – have a special *sadharan path* ceremony. They can do it at their home: they bring Guru Granth Sahib, the Holy Book, to their home and read it. There are two ways they can do it, either an *akhand path* – that's forty-eight hours continuously – or it can take many days, to read through the whole book. And when it finishes it's called *bhog* in Punjabi; and then all the friends and relations sit, and that's the end of the ceremony – I mean, that's the end, in the sense that they pray on that day that the departed soul should have peace.

But after that period, there should be no further remembrance – again because of rebirth: the departed person *is* still alive, a point which Gurbachan Singh Sidhu emphasised:

> When a Sikh dies then they have a small prayer: they would read that prayer, then wash the body, then take it to the crematorium. Having finished with the body, they would then either come direct to a Sikh temple or they would come to the home of the deceased, where the Holy Book will be read for the next ten days. Sometimes this period is extended to two or three days more, making it thirteen days, but normally it's read for ten days. On the tenth day all the relatives and friends will join together and then that would be the end of it: the dead man would no longer be remembered, the way Christians or other people are remembered by erecting a mausoleum, or by putting a stone anywhere – though in fact some people *do* remember the dead every year, but that's a tradition that we've borrowed from Hinduism – it has nothing to do with Sikhism. In fact we are not supposed to remember the dead ones, we are to concentrate all our love for the living ones. The dead are dead and gone, there's nothing we can do about them. But, as I say, there is a tradition among some of our people,

> not very well versed in Sikhism, who would on a particular day ask some of the Sikhs to take dinner at their home. It's not a bad practice, though, because having taken their dinner or lunch or whatever it is, they will then say the prayer to benefit the dead soul. Whether this has anything to do with the dead soul, I don't know.

I asked him what Sikhs do with the ashes:

> The ashes, back in the Punjab, are normally taken to Amritsar, which is a holy place of the Sikhs, and they are thrown in the river. Here the tradition is not as strong as it was back in the Punjab. Some people tried to throw the ashes in the River Thames around London, but there were some problems. Some people have scattered the ashes in the field, some have buried them underground, some have thrown them in the flowing water, some have done nothing.

Buddhists

Buddhists also cremate bodies and believe that tears should not be shed – if they *are*, it is for the failings of the deceased person in this life, or for one's *own* failings in one's association or friendship with the dead person. Buddhists also see a distinction, between cultural traditions in dealing with the dead, and Buddhist teaching: the purpose of Buddhist teaching is to come to a true understanding of transience (of which death is simply one example) in such a way that transience cannot arouse any feeling of attachment in us; so mourning, as a sign of attachment to what has died, is in itself a failure, as Dr Fernando made clear:

> Of course we do have the monks to come and comfort us – comfort us in this sense, to bring hope to us, to remind us that nothing is permanent in this world, and that we've got to accept it – that this is only a temporary sojourn in one's long journey. So when we cremate the body, according to one's financial resources, the Buddhist monks will come there and preach to us and discuss impermanence, so that it will be easier to take the blow. And if you analyse it very carefully, you'll find that sometimes tears are an indication of remorse. People who cry and cry and cry are people who have failed to do something for the dead – for the person who is dead – when he was alive; and now they find that time has cheated them and that they have been cheated. So that is why they cry, I

personally feel. There is no need to cry if one has done what one should have done.

Jews

But if we turn to Judaism, we find the exact opposite, because for some Jews – and for large parts of Jewish Scripture – 'being remembered' after death is perhaps the only kind of life beyond death that there is. Buddhists believe in continuity through death, even though there is no 'me' being reborn. But for Jews there is only what God as creator wills. If he wills to create a new life for the dead, so be it. But in any event, whatever happens beyond death, the continuity in the people, from generation to generation, is in itself important. So the emphasis in Jewish burial customs (and it should be burial in Jewish ground so that if there *is* a day of new, resurrected creation, the faithful can be gathered easily) – the emphasis is on supporting and helping the survivors. Where the actual burial is concerned, there is a great democracy in Jewish death. This is how Mr Levy described it:

> The rites of passage to do with death are much more to do with the survivors than the dead. The traditional way of being buried as a Jew is in fact to be buried rather than any other way of dealing with the body. Cremation isn't the normative way of doing it, the theory being that if you're a pile of ashes, and the Messiah comes, it's a bit difficult to get up again. So what one tries to do at death (and obviously I don't have much experience of it) is to create a situation where the survivors adapt in a sensible way. And so we don't hurry through the process of mourning, we actually encourage, as part of normal mourning practice, a period of seven days when the family sit in formal mourning and are visited, and there are prayers in their homes – and it's perfectly normal to talk about the deceased, to give the close relations of the deceased the opportunity to come to terms with the reality that somebody they love isn't there any more. And the mourning period goes on beyond that, so that people don't go to festive occasions; and life is subdued for quite a considerable period after that. The actual funeral service is fairly simple: prayers are said in a chapel; the body's interred, and each of the people attending the funeral plays a role in covering the coffin. The preparation for burial is more complicated: it involves washing the body, and generally making the deceased look reasonable and wrap-

ping it in a shroud. Certainly embalming is out, or any of that sort of thing.

And his wife added:

It's very important in Judaism that death is an equal thing – that's why embalming is out, and rich coffins are out. All Jews are buried in the same kind of shroud and all Jews are buried in the same kind of simple coffin.

Muslims

For Muslims, death is returning someone to God:

The soul, what we call the soul, is the *ruh*, spirit from God, which will return to him. When someone dies we say: 'From God we are, to him shall we return.' And we do return, but the next life is a different stage. So we look at death like a door, an entrance. Once we go through that door there is no coming back. You go on to the next phase.

If possible, the burial should take place without delay, although, as Mrs Khan pointed out, that may be difficult in this country:

When someone dies we are very sad, very sad. As soon as the person dies we have to clean the mouth, close the eyes, and straighten the limbs of the body. Then a person comes to give the dead person a bath, and within eight hours we bury the person. In this country, though, it takes time: they don't release the body from the hospital, often for five or six days. And then, anyway, many people send the bodies to Pakistan – and I have told my husband and my children that if I die here, send me to Pakistan.

Mr Abdul Rahman put the same emphasis on the speed of burial:

When the Muslim person, the woman or man, dies, it is immediate that we should hide him. We should hide him: that means, we should send him into the grave as soon as possible. So, once the soul is away from the body, we bring the body home. In our country when the person dies quickly we try to make arrangements to wash him and then take him to the *salat aljinaza* which is the last prayer; and as many Muslims as can get together, they try to get together for his *jinaza*. And then we say the last prayer and bury him in the grave with the face facing Mecca. The imam must be the person to lead the prayers of the *jinaza*, but if there isn't any imam at the time, anybody can stand.

Like the Sikhs with the Guru Granth Sahib, Muslims read the Quran during the mourning period – which may continue for some time:

> There are prayers and there are ceremonies as well. People get together and they have a certain period of mourning; and especially the closest people to the person who's died will mourn for a month or so. Where it's a wife, the immediate family would mourn for at least forty days. Then they have prayer, they read the Holy Quran and everything, and that's how the ceremonies are performed; and after that they usually have meals. In your dress, it means that you can't come dressed up, but there isn't any particular colour. Usually you find that women would dress up in white, but that's not necessarily so – it just depends from person to person.

Muslims are again similar to the Buddhists in stressing (though for different reasons) that one ought not to cry:

> When Muslims die, we mustn't cry. People can't help it, crying, because it's something you can't control. But we mustn't cry, because if we do – well, the person to *us* is dead, but to Allah he is *not* dead. So we try to bury the person quickly, because in a way it's torturing him: he can hear the people crying for him. So we try to bury him quickly for his own good.

What Goes On?

All these different customs reflect the different beliefs in each religion about what a human person *is*, and what may happen to that person or personality beyond death. So what are these beliefs? What, in the Eastern religions, does rebirth mean? *What* is reborn? And where is it eventually leading?

Hindus

For Hindus the essential point is that *what* is immortal (in us or any other living form) *is Brahman* – the Absolute all-pervading power which many Hindus call God. It is that soul, or *atman*, which projects itself into time as *jiva*, and which is reborn many, many times, until it realises its identity with God. This is not an easy idea to grasp, so I asked Mr Chitra Pal Singh (who has stayed on in this country, in very difficult circumstances, to encourage a deeper understanding of Hinduism) to explain this to me in more detail:

> Our Scriptures say that the realisation of the soul is in our own self: you understand that there is something in you, and that 'something' doesn't change. When I was born, I was just a little child; now I am grown up. My body has changed, my mind has changed and developed. I have learnt different languages, but there is something which has not changed, and that is my identity. It's not peculiar to man: it is the same with all living things; they maintain their identity throughout their existence. As long as their body is there, they live as an individual, and they have this identity, the same all the time. Every little tree which grows is the same, from the beginning to the end. That unity, which is behind there, is due to the force of life: and that force is called 'soul'. It is not in any way different in a man, or an animal, or a plant, or in any living thing, there is no difference. The principle is the same. The whole universe is the manifestation of this force of life, which has framed the whole universe. There is no difference between the soul – the life-force – that is in man, that is in plants, that is in animals, that is manifest everywhere, which we call the Universal Soul or God.

With that 'background belief', what happens to the *atman*, or soul, when a body dies?

> That principle of life never dies: that force of life is always there: when a man dies, his soul leaves the body. What our Scriptures say is this, that the ideas guide the soul into a body where those desires that have not been fulfilled, can be fulfilled – far away. If a man has got the desires of becoming more powerful or more rich, then those ideas, at the time of death, go with the soul and divert the soul into a family, into a life, where he can get fulfilment of those. So if you wish to stop being born again and again, our Scriptures say, there is only one way, and that is to become selfless: nothing for yourself, no desire even for the least for yourself, and in the end desire nothing; because as long as there is any desire left, that desire will lead the soul into some kind of body, where it will see its fulfilment.

So rebirth depends on desire, and the form it takes is determined by *karma* – that strict account of good and evil deeds, which can be modified by the help of God, and by the efforts we make in this life. But the system remains one of reward and punishment, as Mrs Chauhan made clear:

> As our religion says, death will be the end of my physical life. But we believe in rebirth, so my soul can go on in some other form. It depends on Almighty God where he sends my soul – and I might come in other shape. If you believe, as the Hindus do, that there is one God, and every human being is a part of that God, then being part of God is being part of one great family; and just as, in a family, if you have children who are naughty, you have to punish them – and if they have been good and they have adapted to what you want them to do, then you reward them – life is like that.

Not surprisingly, the thought of *karma* affects how Hindus live, as a young Hindu wife made clear:

> *Karma* encourages me: when I think that we are going to come back, then I want to do good things, and I want to do my prayers so that God doesn't punish me. He won't punish me if I do good things. I'm always scared if I do anything bad; if I lie, or if I do anything wrong to my husband, if I do anything wrong to my mother-in-law, then God might punish me for doing wrong things. So I always have these things in my mind when I do something wrong, I always go to that photograph of Ram, and do apologise; I say, 'Please forgive me for that and guide me.' I think God is there, and he's always watching us, what we are doing, wrong or right. Every time I start doing something wrong, I always get an instinct that I am doing wrong – I shouldn't do this. It's always God who stops me doing that. I'm not scared of my husband or of anyone else. Whenever somebody stops me, it's always God. I feel that thing in my mind, that God is watching me, and if I'm doing anything wrong, he will definitely punish me. When I die, he'll punish me.

That may sound like religion born of fear. But in fact it is closer to justice – that our deeds *will* get their reward. And in that context, perfect justice casts out fear, because detachment – getting rid of any desire for anything – rules out the possibility of wrong deeds; and in any case, God is close at hand to help. Mr Singh (who explained the relation between *atman* and Brahman) went on to say:

> The purpose of existence is this: when this universe comes

into being, this is the purpose, that there should be this uplifting of everything from the physical into the spiritual region. The *Gita* says, 'Whenever there is an imbalance between the power of good and the power of evil, then I, Krishna, appear in a form to balance them up, to cut down the evil and increase the good.'

Sikhs

Sikhs also believe in *karma* and rebirth, and Amritpal Singh Hunjan summarised it in this way:

> What you get after death depends on your *karma* – the *karma* means, your past deeds. If you have been a good boy, right, you're supposed to go to heaven; and if you have been a bad boy, you are reincarnated back to earth, or sent to hell. Then you have 225,000 lives before you become a man again; and then you have to become a *good* man to go to *heaven*.

For Sikhs, as for Hindus, it is *karma* (the account being worked out from previous lives) which explains the inequalities of this life, as Gurcharan Singh Kundi told me when I talked to him in Leeds:

> There is always a connection from your previous life, because if that connection from your previous life is not there, how come a child is born at 0900 hours in a rich family, and a child is born in a poor family at the same hour where there is no bread? Those two kids, those two babies, haven't done any sin as far as we are concerned in this universe, they haven't.

I asked him whether it might just be an accident. He replied very firmly:

> No, oh no; there are no mistakes or accidents in the book of God. Oh no; he will never ever make a mistake. We people can make mistakes, but not him.

But *karma* is not absolutely automatic or inevitable in its effects: it can be modified by the help, or the grace, of the Guru, a point which Harbans Singh Sagoo emphasised:

> According to the Sikh belief, there is life after death; but it's not a mechanical formula – it's not a formula that just says, if you've been good, then after death you will be so and so, and if you've not been good, you'll be so and so. It's not like that.

> The important element to remember in the Sikh teachings is that the grace of Guru plays a very important part; and all *I* hope is that the Guru is gracious. When the time comes, if he is gracious, then there can be either a rebirth or *moksha*. But a true Sikh never works towards *moksha* because that prayer or devotion has an *aim*, and you are not really searching for Guru's grace. My devotion is to abide by the Guru's command and hope the Guru will be gracious. And I hope that if he is gracious, then that *moksha* will be available; if not, then it's entirely in God's will whatever else he wants to do.

But if a soul *is* reborn, it will certainly bear the mark or impression of all that it has initiated and experienced in its previous forms of birth, as Gurbachan Singh Sidhu made clear:

> We have a belief that the soul never dies – that the soul persists even when the body is gone. And we also believe that whatever good or bad I did in this life, it leaves a sort of impression on my soul: whatever good or bad I do in this life is imprinted, as it were, on the soul, and this lasts with the soul. The soul will have the same tendency to steal if I'm a thief in this life; and it will have a tendency to accumulate wealth if I'm doing it now. When I take the next birth, all these tendencies will still persist.

Buddhists

For Buddhists, it is misleading to talk of rebirth, because that suggests that there is a 'something' – a self or soul – to be reborn. Buddhists believe that there is a continuous process or sequence of change, but no self or soul travelling through the process. Human beings are a flowing together of different energies and materials, which constitute them in such a way that they can think and feel and move and meditate. But life is nothing more than the accumulation of five *khandhas,* five constituents of human appearance. Through death, that process moves on into new forms of appearance, on any one of six levels of being – from hell to heaven – until the process is brought to an end through Enlightenment, which is *nirvana* – the ceasing of *dukkha* or transience. But there is no self or soul which goes on through the process. This again is not easy to understand. So I asked Mr Poey, originally a Chinese Buddhist from Malaysia, to explain it to me:

> The Buddha has taught there's no such thing as a soul in one

unit. The flame of life goes on, just like the flame of a candle which can be lighted to another candle – the next candle may be either short or long, red or white, and so on – it goes on. So there is no such thing therefore as rebirth. Now, Buddha has taught that we have to do good; refrain from doing evil and purify our minds.

And the reason for his saying those things is because he said that to be born is to suffer. To be born is to suffer; to live is to suffer; to be sick is to suffer; to grow old is to suffer; and to die is to suffer. And, therefore, he says, I have come to teach you to cease all sufferings.

But the obvious question, at least for the outsider, is this: how can *I* reappear if there is no self or soul going from one life to another? He answered:

Yes, the Buddhists, as I said, do not believe in a soul, but they do believe that death is the dissolution of the five aggregates, which they call the *khandhas*. The five aggregates are perception, sensation, mental formations, consciousness, and incorporating of matter, material aggregates. These are the things that go, from life to life. Therefore, Buddha says, we have to stop rebirth if we are to stop our suffering; and his teaching is based on suffering. Sooner or later the holding together of the aggregates weakens, and as we grow old it passes off and goes to attach to any material form, such as in the womb of another human being, and we are reborn again; but in the meanwhile, it could also be in the form of spirits, depending on what we have done in this present stage of our existence.

So there are identifiable appearances but no persistent, continuing identity, as Rohantha Fernando put it:

The fault, I think, of Christians is that they think of themselves as John Smith all their lives, and when they die, the idea of being born as somebody else is something totally alien. But as a Buddhist – and to myself as a scientist – you are not John Smith: you are molecules in a body being changed every fraction of a second. Every few years, every cell in your body has been replaced, so even while we are talking, you are changing all the time. And I suppose I would think of death as a discontinuity: the change is always happening. It's not that I'm me this time and somebody else next time. I'm simply a being that is changing.

This means of course that a Buddhist is actually being 'reborn' – moving into the next stage of appearance – every single second, not just at death, as Mr Wickramaratne told me: 'In a way,' he said, 'your body, your mind, your personality changes, it's a continuous process: so in one way you will be born again every few minutes, maybe.' But I still wanted to know what the 'you' is that is being born again. He answered:

> In Buddhism, it's not like in the Hindu religion or various other religions, where they talk about a soul going from them. We don't believe in a soul. It's a consciousness, something like that: just as the consciousness ends, so it begins again.

But in fact many Buddhists themselves see a real question here: if there is no soul or other substantial reality being reborn, what sort of process or connection is there between one life and the next? Mr Twewang Topgyal, a Tibetan Buddhist, saw the problem:

> Well, you know, if we build up on this assumption that rebirth does take place, then the connection obviously cannot be physical, in terms of a molecular connection – that is out of the question. Also, I don't think it is commonly accepted as being a conscious connection either, otherwise most of us would be able to remember whether we had been a monkey, or fish, or whatever we have been in our past life. So I think the connection must be a very, very subtle connection. Of course, there *are* instances where people do seem to remember, or they do seem to have, momentary glimpses of certain events which have taken place in the past. But I don't think most of them are rooted in any sense, and I don't know whether it is possible to prove it or not.

For many Buddhists (including Dr Fernando here) the experience of instant recognition of places and people is important support for their belief that something does go on from one life to another:

> When the body disintegrates, it's like the movement of a leech; before he lets go of his previous position he's already got a grasp of the other. You know how the leech moves? The Buddha once compared it to the movement of the leech: before you leave this life you've already got a grasp of the other. And it seems to me that there must have been some connection in a previous birth. Why do we sometimes have this magnetism that exists or is sparked off when we meet

someone? Why, with a total stranger, do you seem to like the personality of that individual?

I asked him if he had had that experience himself. He said:

Yes; when I first went to Australia, I met this young man. It was my first year, and just my second day in Perth. I went to see this cricket match at the university campus, and there he was all padded-up. I was very lonesome because I didn't know anyone at all. And I was just watching the cricket, feeling a bit homesick, when he walked up to me, smiled, introduced himself, shook my hand and we became the best of friends – so much so that, in my second year, he went to Ceylon, stayed with my parents, and he made me stay at his fiancée's place. Today he is one of the leading political figures in Australia.

What *is* the Soul?

But if Buddhists have problems in *that* direction – about how there can be a connection between one life and the next in the absence of any obvious connection – Hindus and Sikhs have problems in the *opposite* direction. As the Buddha himself pointed out, it's all very well claiming that the soul or *atman* is reborn, but what *is* that soul which no one has ever seen or identified? What *is* reborn? In their attempts to answer that question, we can hear an uncertainty among Hindus and Sikhs very comparable to the Buddhist uncertainty about how the connection between one life and the next actually occurs. I asked a young Hindu girl how she knows that she has this soul which is going to be reborn. She replied simply, 'I don't.' Her mother then came in:

Soul means *atman*. I believe it's the particle of the big universe, and it sort of goes back into the cosmos, as they say; but how and why we don't know, but we still believe in it. It's a sort of fate probably. You can never see it; but people say sometimes – some elderly people say – that it's the voice from within that is your soul. Because there are many who *can* hear the voice – and that is the soul. You don't know, there is a lot of controversy about it.

Some Sikhs also tried to answer that question: since we cannot see or produce the soul as an object for examination, how do we know that it's there? For some, it is simply a matter of belief:

Well, I exactly don't know, but many people believe – and I do

> as well – that there is a soul in every human being which is immortal, and it's your deeds which make you better in your future life. If you do good deeds in this life, then in your future life you may be better off. Now there are many living beings, like ants, animals, human beings. Human being is considered a much better life than animals. What I believe, along with some others, is that if you don't lead a very good life or you are harmful to other people, then you may be born as an animal or something, not better than you are now.

For others, it's a matter of authority and tradition which they then test:

> Well, we don't necessarily believe the things that we see; and we also believe certain things that we can't see. You can't see electricity, can you? You can see the effect of electricity. You can see the effect of the wind, but you can't see the wind itself. You can't see what is ahead in the future, you can't see goodness, you can't see so many other things; you can't see God, for example. If you have a belief in God, that is simply because somebody before you said that there exists something like that. Or you infer, from certain unexplained or inexplicable happenings, that there must be something of that sort. The point is that we try to understand the inexplicable or the things that we don't know through two different channels: firstly through the word of the Guru, which to us is true all the time and shall always be true – whatever he says we must accept it. And secondly we ourselves try to experience and to find out, to substantiate what he has already said. We can't go against it. But we are always on the lookout to find out something that would substantiate it so that we are fully convinced.

'Soul', then, is the means of our connection with God. I asked a young Hindu, Asha Pancholi, what the *atman*, or soul, is. She said: 'It is God within me: it's part of my heart, it lives in me, actually, the soul.' So I asked her: 'In other words, the soul isn't something you have, like toes or a nose?' She answered:

> No, it is just a spiritual thing, it's got no shape, no size, nobody can see it, it is extremely tiny. You can only get this through meditation, I think, or through your good deeds. But I don't think you can get *moksha*, to be with God, completely in one life; it needs thousands of lives, I think – millions of lives, I should think – before you can reach that sort of stage.

Traditionally, as she said, there are 84,000,000 rebirths. I wondered whether you can tell whether you've reached 83,999,999, and that this birth is the last one. Her father came in and said:

> It is your environment which will tell you that. If you just stay where you are connected with the spiritual things all the time, and leave a lot more time to meditate and to be with God, then you know, I think, that you are nearing. This, anyway, is my belief, that as you are nearing God, he will give you opportunities when you retire or something to go near to him and forget all the materialistic idea. But at the moment, for myself, my duty is to look after my family, to build myself a good living, a good standard of living, and to help my people under me and people above me.

That, of course, is an echo of the four *ashramas* (pp. 14, 148). But it still left me wondering how a Hindu identifies the soul. So I asked Dr Raman Gokal, a consultant at the Manchester Royal Infirmary, whether he, as a doctor, with much knowledge of the human body, could help me to find the soul. He said:

> The soul is a very difficult thing. The soul is usually associated with the heart, and I guess that's where it is. I think in all Hindu Scriptures, once your heart stops beating, that is it: your soul has vanished, although patients can be kept alive and ticking over without perhaps any life present there – they may not be brain-dead.

That sounded to me more like the living attachment which has traditionally been called *jiva*, as opposed to *atman*, which is eternal and unchanging. When I put that to him, he replied:

> But that is the same thing: your *jiva* or your *atman*, whatever that particular entity is, is the same thing. And I think that that is a part of God himself. There is a God in everybody. What you have in you, what we call *atman, jiva,* whatever you like, is a bit of God.

So the soul is the animation of what would otherwise be a lifeless clay or stone; as it enters into different forms of matter to animate them, so it can leave them, as a Sikh, Harbans Singh Sagoo believes:

> We know from the religious teachings that there is this thing that leaves the body, and that causes this body of five elements to die and become useless. There must be something that

leaves the body when death comes for the body to be rendered useless. That is the only one point which brings us to the point of believing that there is something in the body – not just in the human body, but in whatever type of body one is in, which is the soul.

A Hindu, Mr Krishan Mittal, agrees with him:

Science has developed everything – let's say they can create a human body – from artificial fibre or material; but they won't be able to infuse life in it. I have seen an exhibition in India. There was a model of a cow. It was fibre-glass outside, inside every system, muscular system, everything was perfectly working by means of some electrical device, everything. But it was lifeless. Who infuses life in you? When you find he or she is dead, and the soul departs which keeps our body functioning, everything is dead when it goes out, flies out, you are dead. That is the soul, I believe, and that soul goes to God after death, and it's up to him what happens – and, as I believe, it depends on my actions and deeds in this life. If I have been leading a virtuous and good life, a gentle life I should say, according to God's judgement then he might say, 'All right, this soul has done his duty, it can remain'; or if I have been leading a sinful life which is immoral, against my belief, he can send my soul to suffer, to be in some such as an insect or some other creature which could be a beast, and so I have to suffer till I come back again after my death in that very form.

Contact with the Dead

But if dead people have gone on to another life in some other form, is it possible to stay in contact with them, or find out where they have gone? I found that among Hindus and Buddhists especially, there was widespread belief that you can. Mrs Chatterji told me in Coventry:

According to Hindu philosophy, yes, we can. We had two deaths in our family, people of whom I was very fond, and it was told that they visit you in dreams. That's where I came in contact with them. And again there is another Hindu custom which I didn't know of then, because I hadn't heard this part. I dreamed of a dead person, who was my husband's cousin – a young chap who committed suicide here – a doctor. He was very fond of our family, so I told my husband that I often see him in dreams, coming and asking for food. Then later I told one of my friends, and she said, 'Then you must go to the temple and give whatever food he wants – because that's a very bad thing: when he comes and asks for food, it means some other soul will go.' And actually that happened, because I didn't know about that thing at that time.

So dreams are important, but there also seems to be some other kind of communication as well, as Mr Mittal, the President of the Hindu Cultural Society in Bradford, told me, when I asked him whether it is possible to be in contact with those who have died:

Yes. For example, my mother has died. She died in 1970, at Christmas time. Before her death, I felt suddenly as if we are so close, and I knew it was an imminent sensation, just like a wireless, [to say] that she is suffering; and I was so much upset at college that I was at the point of going straight away back to India. Then some people said, 'Well, why don't you just send a telegram?' So I sent a reply-paid telegram, and I got back the reply that she had died. Then after her death, sometimes I think about her and I see her in my dreams, and we talk to each other. So I don't know what kind of contact, what kind of connection, is there, but it is.

Buddhists are equally certain that the connection, with those who have died and gone on, can be made; and it is entirely natural for a Buddhist like Mr Poey to go to the temple to find out what has happened to his father – though he himself, as he emphasised, remains open-minded about what is happening, when I asked him whether it is possible to find out what has happened to someone who has died. He said:

That's a very good question! In the Far East, in my own country of Malaysia, even today you could go to a temple, and somebody will go into a trance: you give your date of birth, and then they will go into a trance, and then they say, 'Well, now, that's your father coming to see you'; and his voice will be about the same, and he will talk probably in my language, or in Indian language, or whatever it is. And I myself have been there once – not to consult for myself, because I was told by my parents that it's not a good thing to contact the dead, because if you try to contact the dead, you are causing them some suffering. When I went, I accompanied somebody else. He contacted his mother – and I knew his mother, because he was a cousin of mine. When the man went into a trance, I heard him coughing, and the voice was that of his mother, and she could say how many children she had and this and that – so many things she could say that were true, because I knew the mother. But I have an open mind – because by that time I had already studied psychology, and I was a lecturer in practical psychology. And therefore I had an open mind.

Other Buddhists do not hold back from what they take to be the evidence before them, and Mr Wickramaratne told me, when I met him in North London, how his parents had set about helping his dead brother – though he stressed that he did not believe it himself.

When my brother was killed in the accident, my parents went round all over the place to see if they could contact the dead, and they said that through some medium they contacted him, but I don't believe in those things. But they said he talked to them – and the things he told them were unbelievable: he was able to tell them a particular mark on the shoe that he was wearing; and when they came home to look at it, it was torn in the particular place where he said it was. He also said that he was being punished by some *deva*, for something that he had done, and can they help him by doing some good deeds? And he made mention of a particular temple, and said, could they go there and make offering of flowers, or give something to the poor people there, the beggars, and pass on the merit of those good deeds? Of course when they went to the medium – it was my mother and father, two brothers and young sister, five of them – they didn't say to the medium, 'We've come for this particular purpose, and I want to know this particular thing.' All you do is stay in the crowd, and suddenly the medium, if his thoughts and your thoughts connect, he just suddenly comes forward and sits there. You don't speak a word. And then suddenly he says, 'You have come to ask about your dead son.' This really shocked my parents, because nobody there could have told him why they had come or who they were, even: because they had taken a lot of precautions, going to this place, not to go in the family car, even, in case somebody recognised them. Then he said things like, 'Yes, your son had this tragic accident, but don't worry, be happy because he's all right now.' Then my father wanted to speak, and the medium suddenly takes on the voice of my dead brother: he asked if anybody wants to ask a question. My father wanted to come forward, but he said, 'I don't want to talk to you, I want to talk to my sister.' Now my sister was very close to him, so she said, 'I'd like to know how you are.' He said, 'I'm perfectly all right: I want to give the suit I was wearing to' – he mentioned the name of a particular place where some poor children lived. 'You should give my clothes to those people,' he said. Then he said about being punished by the *deva* and about doing those good things for the merits to be passed on. And actually the day was given when they could go to the temple and put some flowers. They went to the place, just as he said; and then they came back two weeks later, and he wanted to know why they had come again. He said, 'Why are you disturbing me? Why are you calling me from my work?' And they said, 'Well, we just wanted to know that you are all right.' He said, 'Of course I'm all right.' And he even told them about a stranger who gave them matches when they went to the temple to light lamps for him.

Where 'off' Earth are we Going? Hindus, Sikhs and Buddhists

Where, then, is rebirth leading in the end? For a Hindu, it is leading back to God – or to the reality which is already present in us, and which releases itself from its entanglement in this or any other world in order to recover its unity with what really is. This is *moksha,* release:

> When I die, I hope I'll attain *moksha. Moksha* is becoming free of the cycle of birth and death. I don't want to be born again. This is my last journey in the world; I don't want to come back: I want to be one with God. And I have that positive thinking, that I'm sure he would want me to be with him – he would never send me back now: there is far more happiness with him, and I hope I will attain that.

What is the final goal for Sikhs?

> I hope that with God's help my life will be the end, that I will reach a unity with God: I hope that I will join the God-company.
>
> It will be peace, and the end, and reaching God. Reaching God means that you are out of the cycle of rebirth and you are attached to God.

For a Buddhist, union with God *is* possible in the next form of appearance, but that cannot be the final state, because all things, *including* God, are caught up in the process of change. The final state of *nirvana* is completely beyond description, as we've already heard Dr Fernando explain (p. 30).

But however indescribable *nirvana* is, Mahayana Buddhists believe that some forms of continuity on the very edge of *nirvana* can turn back in order to help those still on the way. These forms of reappearance are known as *bodhisattvas*; and I asked a Zen Buddhist, 'What is a *bodhisattva*?' He answered:

> I see it not as any abstract sort of phrase in books, I see it as a quality in so many people, many different kinds of people. It's a kind of serenity, an acceptance of things as they are – a contact with love. In all its dimensions, and all its variety, I see it so many times. It brings tears to my eyes when I see it, a quality in someone – and often surprisingly in the last place that you're looking for it. You see more *boddhisattva* activities, more holy activities, more signs of that in supermarkets than in churches or temples.

Jews, Christians and Muslims

Rebirth and reincarnation have certainly appeared as beliefs in the West – indeed, it still appears among some Jews, in the sense that the soul, or the living principle which turns clay and dust into life, comes from God and may be put back into another life on earth by God – either for more training or for leadership. Mrs Benaim (an Orthodox Jew from Gibraltar, now living in London) told me about this:

> Yes, I feel that reincarnation exists; yes, I feel it does. It's said – though I can't exactly say where – that the soul can return to earth a maximum of seven times. Each time, if it hasn't fulfilled enough things in one stretch of life, it can then come back again and fulfil another set of conditions.

But in general in the West, the belief is that through death the self or the soul or the resurrected body (or some combination of all three) enters into a final relation with God – or, perhaps, *fails* to do so, as Michael Stevenson, a Pentecostal Christian, reminded me:

> It depends on what side of the fence you're standing, if I can use that term. A Christian looks forward to death, because death for him means being absent – not being in this body but

being present with God. That's what death means for a Christian. OK, for an unsaved person, I guess death means a life of eternal damnation. That sounds like a doom-preacher, and a lot of people just say 'doom merchants'; but it's no use covering up something when it's there. It's got to be said, and that's the way I look at it.

So death is a dividing of the ways, with the hope that one's real and essential self will be united with God, as a Roman Catholic made clear when he said: 'I believe that I have a spirit, which I'm calling my soul. And when I die my spirit will leave the body. The body's no longer required. My soul, my inner self, will go to God.' In that context, it is not surprising that this life is regarded as an arena in which our souls are tested and formed, as Muslims especially emphasise:

The reason for death is that everything has got a sort of a cycle to it: there is a beginning, there is an end to this life on this earth. The Muslims believe that man has been sent on this earth as a test. He is undergoing a test for which he will be rewarded, or he will be punished, in the other world. Therefore, death is nothing but the culmination of his worldly life, so that he can be judged according to his deeds in this world.

But for Jews, all that is, or may be, very much less clear-cut. Jewish Scripture says very little, in any detail, about life after death. It talks much more about creation; so that if there is to be anything beyond death, it can only be a consequence of a further deliberate act of God's creation. Therefore what I found among Jews was a reluctance to speculate; and that reluctance to speculate is itself very biblical:

I don't know what's going to happen to me when I die, but what I believe happens to people is that I believe in life after death. Unfortunately, I don't know very much about it. I would love to be able to know much more about it, because it fascinates me. There are basically the dimensions of hell and heaven; but I don't think hell is quite as it's depicted in the popular description of it.

Equally biblical is the strong emphasis (among many Jews I met) that the only continuity beyond death which we can be sure of is the continuity in our children and in their remembering of us. Mr Cowan, a Reform Jew, put it like this:

Well, the body perishes – ashes to ashes, dust to dust. What happens to the thing that we call the soul is again a very individual thought. My feeling is that it doesn't get lost. But I think it mainly goes through to the next generation. What I do, what I think, what they think about me (which I don't know a great deal about, to be quite honest), all that encompasses something which they carry on. It may be in their minds, it may be in their hearts. They will talk about Grandad to *their* children. Something of what I say, or what I believe in, I think will be passed on. And possibly that may be the main thing that happens. It may be that somewhere there is a world or a grouping where the people's spirit (whatever that is) is gathered together, and maybe it is something which feeds the future generation; but this is hidden from us. This is something which nobody can tell.

But that kind of belief is not confined to Reform Judaism. Stuart Dresner, in the Orthodox tradition, said something very similar:

Well in theory my spirit is supposed to be preserved in some way. It's a mystical sense, but I find that concept rather difficult to accept. I think the best that I can hope for is that we will have children who will carry on our genetic pattern, or whatever we have trained them to do – or our beliefs and ethical behaviour – and hope that they will carry on the best of whatever we can offer.

So continuity in children is not just a biblical emphasis, belonging to the past; it is still being expressed now – as here by Mrs Jacobs:

When I was about thirteen, I was at one of the many schools I attended in my childhood, and it was one of the happiest schools I attended. And I can remember in a discussion (which in itself was probably quite unusual in a class in 1939, as opposed to being taught in a class), I can remember my teacher saying, 'Heaven isn't a place, it's a state of mind'. This is one of the very few things I can remember so clearly of my school days, and it's something that I think about from time to time; and when we say when somebody has died, may her soul rest in peace, I think it means that that person should be spoken of and thought of and remembered by the people who were close to them while they were here in this life. And I suppose it's a sort of vanity that I have – and I admit freely – that having been blessed with four children, perhaps we'll have the blessing of grandchildren; and if they can remember us and

> tell their grandchildren, that's what will happen to me.

So for many Jews, the reality we have to deal with is death itself, not an imagined world which lies beyond death, as Mrs Jacobs went on to say:

> Although my father had been ill from December till the day that he died – the first day, in fact, in April – I knew that he was going to die. It was an extraordinary experience to know that this strong pillar of a man had gone out of my reach forever – and that I'd have to answer all my questions myself. But on the other hand, at the same time I had this feeling – or part of me had the feeling – that it was a temporary thing. But that was wishful thinking, and the other part of me knew that it was final, and that this was another side of God that I had to learn about. Because although my grandmother had died (but at the age of ninety-two), she was already a generation away. You see, when you lose a parent, you're a step nearer to death yourself. And when you have lost both your parents, there is nothing between you and death.

I asked Mr Oliver, an Orthodox Jew, 'What's going to happen to you, when you die?' He answered, 'Is that a religious question? If I was a scientist, a brilliant scientist, perhaps I could answer, but as an ordinary mortal, with just average intelligence, how could I?' 'But what,' I asked him, 'do you believe or hope?' He said:

> I shouldn't like to answer that question. I'm sorry, because there are too many doubts in my mind. Much too many doubts in my mind. We talk about – and lots of our prayers are about – the Messiah: the rabbis, at the time when the Jews were terribly oppressed, they came out with this idea of the *Mashiach ben David*, the Messiah, the son of David; but this was a time of persecution.

The Messianic Age

That agnosticism is deeply biblical. But what he mentioned there was the Messiah – and that is equally biblical. Also it is a reminder that in the Western religions, and especially in Judaism, the last things, the final goals, are anticipated in the events which happen now – and indeed, they *may* be fully realised and completed within our own history. The (Jewish) Bible says much more about the return of *haMashiach* (the anointed one in descent from David), than it does about life after death; and it is the Messiah who will inaugurate an age of peace and harmony, when each man will sit under his own vine, and the wolf will lie down with the lamb.

Some Jews believe that we are on the very edge of the coming of the Messiah and the Messianic age:

> We feel we are on the brink of the coming of the Messiah; and therefore there has to be (just like there was many thousands of years ago, before the coming out of Egypt) an army of God. So there has to also be an army of God now, because we expect the Messiah very soon; and in fact the Rebbe has popularised a song which has the words, 'We want the Messiah now', because he says that if a person really wants the Messiah to come, then he will come. And he says that one of the reasons why the Messiah has not come, is because people do not really want it to happen.

I asked him, 'What will the Messiah be like?' He answered:

> First of all it must be understood that the Messiah will be a normal man, born of man and woman, and nothing supernatural, in any sense of the word. The Rambam is the authority who writes perhaps most clearly about the time of the coming of the Messiah – the Rambam is Maimonides; and he explains that a man will arise, a descendant of King David, and he will bring the whole Jewish people back to the Orthodox way of life. The Baal Shem Tov once met the Messiah in one of his spiritual revelations, and he asked the Messiah, 'When are you going to come?' And the Messiah said: 'I will come when your teachings, the teachings of Hasidic philosophy, spread out into the world.' For that reason, we, the Lubavitch movement, feel the need to get through to every single Jewish soul and to bring a unity amongst the people.

One of the first consequences of the return of the Messiah will be the rebuilding of the Temple:

> Definitely, this is one of the basic, one of the most principal, changes which will happen when the Messiah will come. The Temple will be rebuilt and we will perform the sacrifices, as we did in the olden days. And that is one of the reasons why we at present have to study the Torah in such detail, because when the Temple will be rebuilt, one has to be ready to know what to do and how to live. It's too late then to start learning

the laws; the laws are so complex, that one has to be ready.

But not all Jews are so sure about this. Whether the Messiah *will* come as described, is one of those divisive issues between traditional and progressive Jews, as Mr Jacobs told me in Manchester:

> I think the conception of the Messiah is a difficult one for progressive Jews. I think it is more difficult than for a traditional Orthodox Jew. I find it very difficult to know what I mean by the Messiah. Do I mean, really (if that's the right word), a state of the world? Or do I mean the coming of some being? It's very difficult, a very difficult thing to answer, or even, in a way, to think too much about.

So will the Messiah come? That's what I asked Mr and Mrs Dresner, living in the Orthodox tradition, and this is how the conversation went on:

> 'If ever he were to come, I don't see it as something that would be in our lifetime, or the lifetime of our children. I do feel it would be at the end of time, rather than in the foreseeable future.'
>
> 'Why can't the end of time be in your lifetime?'
>
> 'I suppose for the same reason as you expect the sun to be there every day in the morning, simply because it always has; so you can't conceive of the end of time being in your lifetime, because it hasn't been in the lifetime of previous generations. Why should it be in yours?'
>
> 'So how do *you* feel about the coming of the Messiah? Will he come?'
>
> 'I'm a bit doubtful myself whether he'll ever come. I think it's a bit of a mysterious hope which we shall be looking forward to, but I find difficulty in imagining that one day he will come. Even though it's supposed to be one of the basic articles of faith, I find difficulty in accepting it. I mean, when the Messiah comes, there are supposed to be various things happening, all of which will be terribly complicated. First of all, there's supposed to be peace in the world, and there's no reason why all the conflicts that exist, over territory and ideology, will suddenly cease, just because the Messiah has come. Secondly, there's supposed to be a resurrection of the dead, which would raise all sorts of difficult problems, because, do they come back in a spiritual form, or with a body, and if so, where would they all be?'

Others see themselves as agents in the building of the Messianic age:

> I don't believe as we sing about or we talk about the Messiah, the son of David. But I find in a certain sentence in one of our prayers that it says: Do not call your children, Children, but call your children, Builders. And in that sentence, I feel, is the Messiah. Because we are builders of the future, and it's for the whole world: the Messiah is for the whole world, not just for the Jewish people.

So Jews *may* have strongly traditional beliefs about life after death, and of going to heaven where, as a Hasidic Jew, told me, they will study Torah in its pure, not physical form. And there may be a judgement, as Mr Jack Schild, an Orthodox Jew, told me, when I asked him, 'What will happen to you when you die?'

> What will happen to me? Well, I suppose I'll disintegrate bodily – bound to: but we believe that the soul leaves the body, and we believe that there's judgement after death – that you are called or summoned, to a court, a celestial court; and you are judged on all your doings throughout the years that you were alive, and you are either rewarded or punished accordingly. That's what the Jews believe.

The Resurrection

But by far the strongest voice among the Jews we listened to was the voice of cautious reticence and of refusal to speculate about the exact nature of life after death. Not so the Christians. For them, the belief in the resurrection of Jesus from the dead places death in an entirely different perspective.

Christians, by and large, expect or hope to get to heaven as God is – though perhaps with some further purifying or purgatory. A Roman Catholic said:

> I believe I will go to heaven, though perhaps I'll have to go to purgatory first. I hope I'll go to heaven: heaven to my mind is perfect peace – that's the only way I can describe it – for all eternity.

His daughter agreed:

> Yes, I'd like to think I'd get to heaven. Obviously there's a vast difference between heaven and hell, but I don't look at them as actually being places. I think heaven is more a state where you

> are just in complete happiness. I can't imagine what it's going to be like, only that I know I'm going to be contented.

The basic point for Christians is that 'heaven' is to be with the risen Lord:

> Well, I'm hoping. I trust the Lord that when I die, I'll live with him, I'll reign with him; because I am trying my best to live a Christian life, so that when I leave this world I know that I will find a place of rest.
>
> Now that I've accepted Jesus Christ, we look on death as a sleep – that's to say, a passing from death into life: and death is just a rest for a while, until Jesus Christ himself shall come back and claim his people: that's what we call the rapture.
>
> For me, for every Christian, for every born-again Christian, death is to be taken away, to be with God, to live with him, that's what death means – to be absent from life and to be present with God.

So whatever life with God beyond death may be, it is *not* of our creation: it can only be the acceptance of what God creates and offers, as Simon Williams makes clear:

> I believe that I shall be with God in some way. It sounds so amazingly arrogant. It's certainly not because I'm a good person or I deserve it. Or that I'm any better than millions of other people. But it's something that I accept by faith: it's an offer which I've taken up, and I know – and as the years go by I'm more and more aware that I'm not worthy of it and I don't deserve it. But it's still there, and so I can only accept it.

I asked him whether he felt that he could lose it. He said:

> I don't know – it's certainly baffled other people. I suppose I feel myself, that if you place yourself by faith, by saying to God 'Well, here I am, I'm yours, it's not because of anything I've done that I've earned it: I accept it'; I suppose in that case you can't do anything to lose it either. You didn't do anything to gain it, you can't do anything to lose it. But it still seems hard to actually equate that with saying, well, suppose in 30 years' time I totally renounce the whole thing, and I'll have nothing more to do with it and all the rest of it . . . I don't know, to be honest; I honestly don't know.

But if life with God beyond death is of such a quality, why not commit suicide and get on with it? Michael Stevenson, a Pentecostal Christian, replied vigorously:

> That is definitely wrong. You see, as a Christian you're here to help others, to point others to Christ. For me to go and commit suicide, you know, I don't think it's God's will for my life. I mean, God didn't say to me, 'Go and jump off the Empire State Building.'

The point here is that if eternal life means to be living in association with the risen life of Christ, then eternal life is not really 'life *after* death'; it begins *now*, in his company. That's how John Callaghan sees it:

> I find it boils down to a matter of understanding what you are actually saying. For example, most Christians talk glibly about eternal life, but actually when they use the term eternal life, what they are really meaning to say is life after death. Now 'eternal life' and 'life after death' are different things. So the practical problem of how you live your life now does alter if you know what you mean by eternal life: because we are not waiting for something that we haven't got. We've got something that we don't recognise, if it really is eternal life that we believe in.

There is, then, a basic assurance in the Christian approach to death. Some may be very uncertain about the detail – and share an almost Jewish agnosticism:

> I'm going to be remembered for a while, people will remember my personality. I'm not sure whether I want to be cremated or buried. But I think that whatever happens to my earthly remains, I don't think my personality will die, my memory will fade; but I don't know, I really don't know. I'll just have – I know I'm not afraid to die. I know that Jesus' body was all broken on the cross and he had a pretty awful ending. I know that men have died more horrifically since, men and women and children. But I think that what happened to Jesus' personality, the bit that I believe in, that I've got to cling hold of now, perhaps it'll be reborn in another way. I don't know, I don't know. I'm not frightened, definitely not frightened: I think everybody's personality will be with him, I think it goes to him – because I believe that God created us in the beginning and we all go back to him.

But others live with very literal pictures. I asked one Christian if there is a real garden 'up there'? She said:

> I'd like to think there is, because you're always told it's a pleasant place, far, far away. I can just imagine walking, where I don't have to garden for once and get rid of the weeds. It's going to be a happy place. And you always find that people love to go to gardens, like Kew Gardens, and all the big ones, St James's Park: people always look so nice and smiling when they're walking through there, don't they?

Muslims: Hope and Fear

But whether literal or not, the sense of following on, where Jesus has led through death, remains, for Christians, profound. For Muslims there is no question about the literal truth of the pictures of heaven as a beautiful garden, or of Jehannam, Gehenna, as a place of fire and torment, because that is how they are described in the Quran – and the Quran is, in a much stronger sense than in other religions, the absolute Word of God. At death, the angels of death come and take the soul, which will be restored to the body on the *yaum udDin*, the Day of Judgement, as Mr Khan told me:

> Well, when I die the first stage is when I will be buried. The angels will come and ask me the two questions about my religion, whether I believed in Allah, and whether I accept Muhammad as my prophet. If I give those answers correctly, that is to say, 'Yes, I believe in Allah, and that Muhammad is my prophet', the straightforward answers, then I will be required to wait until the Day of Judgement. But until the Day of Judgement there is a long time, so therefore, I will be told at that stage of my likely result on the Day of Judgement, whether I will be going to heaven or hell. So the result is that my punishment may begin, not directly, but indirectly, because of my knowledge of what I'm going to get. If I'm going to heaven obviously it will make me happy. If I'm going to hell then it will make me sad, because I expected to do good things and expected to be good, but I must have done something very bad. The Day of Judgement is nothing but a trial to show to each person – to convince him by evidence – why he is being sent to hell or heaven, because of his deeds. It's not because God has decided that you should be sent to heaven or hell, it's because your deeds are there, which will be identified and explained to you. And he himself will accept that this is

absolutely correct, because those are the words which cannot be denied.

I asked him whether, in the interval, his soul will still be with the body, or whether it will be in a separate place. He said, 'It's in a separate place.' Then I asked him where heaven and hell are – remembering that in the famous Night Journey, Muhammad was taken up – literally up – to heaven. So is heaven 'up there'? He said:

> Yes it is, heaven is up there, and the reason for that is that we have been told that it is up there. But again let's say for the sake of argument (and it is limited only to that), let us say that it is on this earth somewhere: then if this earth comes to an end, what will happen to heaven and hell?

I asked him, 'Does the punishment in hell go on for ever?' He replied:

> In some cases, yes, but in some cases, if it is of a limited duration, then once that duration is completed, that person will be entitled to go to heaven. Because, for example, if somebody did three years' imprisonment, he comes out after three years; but if somebody is given the life imprisonment, so that means he stays there for ever.

So the resurrection and the judgement will happen exactly and literally as they are described in the Quran, as Mrs Qureshi emphasised:

> When a person dies, obviously his soul goes back to heaven. All that is left is the bones in the grave. Muslims believe – and I strongly believe in it – that on the Day of Judgement all the bones are put together and as a body we are going to answer for our deeds. So we believe you should not be cremated. But again, even if you've been cremated, it doesn't mean to say that God can't put you together. That is what a Muslim believes: he can make the impossible possible; so there's no problem.

All this means that there is a strong emphasis in Islam on reward and punishment, as Mr Abdul Rahman told me:

> Islam says, and the prophet of Islam has said, and the Quran has said, once a person dies and reaches into the grave, all of a sudden two angels appear and wake him up. His soul returns to the body. The very first question which is asked of the

person, whether it's a man, woman or child, big or small, is: who is your God, what is your religion, who is your prophet? If the person has been good . . . what I have been told is this (because nobody has been into the grave; but we believe that what the prophet has said is true – every single word is true; and what the Quran has said is that because it is the Word of God, it's true): if the person has been good and has done the five prayers a day, once he opens his eyes in the grave, he would be looking at the sun as it is setting (because that's the time the two angels come), and he would think that somebody is just standing by. He wouldn't think that he is dead and he is in the grave. He'd say, 'Leave me alone.' You see, the time of the third prayer comes exactly when the sun is setting. So he would say, 'My prayer time is gone and I have overslept, so please let me pray.' And if he has said that by the help of God, I don't think that the angels would bother him any more – because he has answered every question. And if he hasn't done this, if he has been into the pubs and clubs and doing all the worldly things, and trying to snatch the things off anybody else, then the punishment would start from that very moment.

It follows that *after* death it is too late to make amends, as Mr Mohammed Ali pointed out:

According to the teachings of all the Muslims, and I think most Christians, they believe that all human beings, no matter who they are – whether Christian, Muslim, Jew, Hindu, black, white – we all stand in front of our creator, without any doubt. In this world there is injustice, there is a lot of unkindness, there's a lot of greedy people by nature: they want to bring down one person, they want to bring up another person. All these things that you see, there has to be a place for justification. There must be a place for justification because we can't do it for ourselves. When I go out and somebody insults me, I turn my face and sit down and say, 'Well, I can't do anything about it.' Because human beings are supposed to respect each other. We have a code of conduct, we have a law. God has given us sincerity, understanding and knowledge, so that we work and we think and we help each other. But there are a lot of people and nations which don't think that way, they don't follow their religion. But God will punish him for it, there is no doubt. If that wrong outweighs his good, then he will definitely be punished.

But What is the Soul?

But for these three religions, as for Hindus and Sikhs, the question obviously arises: what exactly *is* this soul which is making its journey to God? As one might expect, many Jews tend to be fairly agnostic:

> I feel there must be something after death. I can't believe that even if, in religion, everything is so abstract, the important things are abstract: this world is so material that you can really relate the one to the other completely; so without the person (or whatever part of that person there is) continuing, how can there be relationship?

But which part of the person is it? Mr Benaim told me:

> I think the closest Judaism says of the soul being manifested within a physical body is the blood; that's the closest one gets to it. And that is one of the reasons why Jews aren't allowed to eat blood. It's supposed to be the soul of the animal or whatever. I don't think any of the soul is abstract, but you can't really say it's a material part of the body. I think it's simply important to be able to think of a life after death.

And a Reform Jew, Mr Cowan, added:

> That's the very centre of what makes you the person you are; because without it we're all the same. We're the same chemistry – I believe it's about nineteen shillings' worth of chemicals and a lot of water. But otherwise there's something that makes us different people; and that's it.

Christians may have a stronger sense of continuity through death, as a consequence of the Resurrection, but they still have their questions about what actually continues – as Mrs Iles told me:

> I've wondered if you become whole, when you're there. As you can see, I wear spectacles – I've had them since I was a child. And I often think: will I be able to see properly when I get there? My own brother was mentally handicapped: if I saw him, would he be whole? I've never remembered him like that. Would I recognise him now?

Another Christian, Peter Thompson, recalled how difficult it is to explain the nature of the soul to a child:

> I tried to describe this to my son. I used the word brain, and

then I changed it halfway to soul, and this confused him. I don't know what the soul is – whether we actually die and are reborn again, then it's the resurrection; but I can't understand that.

In fact, here, as with Hindus and Sikhs, the language of 'soul' is clearly a language through which people try to express the reality of their existing relationship with God – and with others in a new style of living; and also their belief that those relationships will not be destroyed or go simply to oblivion. This is how Liz Williams, a Christian doctor, put it, when I asked her about the soul:

I don't know which molecules it is, or what I'll look like, or what I'll sound like. All I know is that God, whatever he or she is, is going to be there. It may be an entirely spiritual affair.

What do Muslims believe will continue through death? We've already seen descriptions of the *ruh*, the essential part of a person, which is kept in a safe place after death, until is it reunited with a body for the Day of Judgement (pp. 247, 271). Mr Lakdwalla told me that there are different opinions among Muslims about the nature of that resurrection:

Some consider it a spiritual revival, some consider it a physical revival as well. But if I look to the literal meaning of it, perhaps I would say, 'Yes, bodily as well.' But it's very difficult to explain, what is soul.

But that uncertainty does not indicate any fundamental doubt about the reality of the soul as the middle term between God and his creation in general – as Hajji Cassim Mohammad emphasised:

The reason we believe it is because God has said so, in the Holy Quran. Now God does not tell lies and we believe that the Holy Quran is his words, so we believe that whatever he has said is true. So there are a lot of things that we can't understand right now, but that does not necessarily mean that they are wrong. We can't feel the soul, we can't see it, but we can't see electricity either. But we know, because there is a bulb here, which tells us there's electricity running there.

But that last attempt brings us round in full circle: it sounds very much like Buddhists explaining the process of reappearance by energy, or Sikhs using exactly that same example of electricity to point to the powerful but unseen realities of life.

In the end, in these religions, it's far more important to live *as* a soul than to be able to define it – to live faithfully, as a responsible agent of one's life and relationships, on the long journey into truth. In this chapter, we've seen what many people believe will be the final nature of that truth.

But what we've also seen is a note of warning and of final judgement – an emphasis that we are indeed responsible, and therefore accountable, for what we do. So there may be punishments, as well as rewards, beyond death. In the final chapter, we'll see what that judgement may be; and we'll begin to raise the question of what people ought to do, in this life, in order to avoid a bad outcome in the next. *Are* there issues of truth, linked to salvation, between the religions?

II

Points of Departure: Issues of Truth and Salvation

Judgement and Punishment: Everlasting or Not?

In the last chapter, we heard mostly about what may be *hoped* for beyond death, and only a little, mainly from Christians and Muslims, about what we may need to fear. But in fact all these religions believe that men and women are responsible and accountable, and that there may be punishments beyond death as well as rewards. Some of those punishments, as we shall see, may last without end. This means that, where religions are concerned, the choices which people make in this life, and the things they do, have an *ultimate* significance: they may have eternal, or at least long-term, consequence. In Eastern religions, the very notion of *karma* depends on consequence (for good *and* for ill) running on from one life to another, as Pandit Pandya explained; and he emphasised that for Hindus there *is* a final judgement, very much as Christians and Muslims also believe:

> According to the Book – there are eighteen Puranas, seventeen of which show you what to do from birth to death; but there is one Purana in which it is explained from where we have come and to where we have to go. So according to that Book, I can explain to you, that God, at the same time as the baby is born, is giving life to the baby. The parents are not giving life. The God who is giving the life has given three things to a human, very important to me and to you, and to everybody: first, a nice intelligence to understand what is good and what is bad; then a nice mouth to speak what is good and what is bad; and nice power in the body – what work we should do and what not. Now God who is the Creator, God the Sustainer, and God the Destroyer, has given us these three things, through which we should do the best and the good. But because it is human life, we have done some things bad and some things good, and ultimately we will get the result: the result of the bad thing will be always bad, the result of the

good, always good. So finally, just as in Christianity, God will call everybody one day and ask what you have done. And Islam also says it, and the Hindu also says, that God will ask what you have done in the life: you are given nice intelligence, nice mouth, and nice power in the body. And whatever they did, we say that there is a person, man, God, power of God, who is maintaining the records of everybody individually, of what he is doing throughout the life, and then he gives the result to him after death. But what that result will be, that we don't say. We can't say.

We've already seen that rebirth *can* lead to terrifying outcomes – and even Buddhists have vivid pictures of torments and punishments in hell – though eventually one grows beyond the pictures, though not beyond the reality of pain and wrong choice:

A lot of these pictures are for the purpose of visualisation. I mean, presumably we want to have some sort of a concept of hell, and therefore one has to have some sort of ghastly picture of a physical environment. I think that portrays what hell is all about. I think there are two levels: if one is at a very elementary level, then one really needs to be frightened of doing something. And therefore, there must be some sort of penal restriction. But if one's ideas are slightly more developed, then I think hell itself is a creation of the mind. I would like to think that it really doesn't exist – it's a creation of one's own *karma*, or lack of understanding, or ignorance.

In a curious sense, there is a Buddhist harrowing of hell: the Buddha, like Jesus, penetrates to the worst despair and torment, and redeems it, as David Brandon described:

There's a beautiful Sutra about the Buddha going down into the Seventh Hell, which is the deepest hell of all: it's the hell where it's entirely silent, because everyone is not screaming any more, because they've given up hope. And the story is that the Buddha goes there and plays.

However, the point of rebirth is that punishment (even though it is completely just, according to *karma*) cannot last for ever. By acceptance of what has happened, and by living as one *should* live in whatever form or level of life one has arrived at, it is then possible to move upwards again. So can punishment last for ever? A Sikh, Surinder Singh Hyare, answered:

No. According to our religion punishment is only for a short

> time while a person accomplishes his teaching, you see. It's really a course in further teaching, where he gets the punishment. And if he takes it happily, then he will get rid of his ill easily.

But, I asked him, what if he *doesn't* take his further instruction happily? He said:

> Then it still goes, because that thing also comes in grace, that teaching. If one takes it in gracefully, seeing that it's all God's will, and if he takes it that way, then it starts helping him, uplifting him.

A Hindu, Mrs Chauhan, agreed: 'No, it won't go on for ever,' she said: 'When you take your next life, they say that if you do good things in that life, then when you come again after that you'll have a better life again.' Exactly the same point was made by a Buddhist, Ugyan Norbu: 'There is nothing permanent, not even punishment. There is nothing which never ends – except Enlightenment.'

But in the West, there has been a far stronger sense that salvation or its equivalent is an offer in this life, and that if we do not respond, or live as we should, by the time we die, we will be separated from God for ever – and that separation may take the form of unending torment. That picture is still particularly strong in Islam, because that is what the Quran says; and the Quran, as we've already seen repeatedly, is believed by Muslims to have been directly given or sent down by God – so what it says can scarcely be doubted. The one who denies God and his word is called a *kafir*; and the most disastrous offence in Islam is *shirk* – that is, making anything equal to, or in any way like, God – *that* sin *cannot* be forgiven. So if we ask a Muslim the same question, 'Does punishment last for ever?', the answer is both yes and no – for some punishments, yes, but not for all. Mr Khan – himself a lawyer and therefore perhaps sensitive to the preciseness of detail which law requires – made this distinction:

> In some cases, yes, the punishment goes on for ever. In some cases it may be of a limited duration, and if it is of limited duration, then in that case, once the duration is completed, that person will be entitled to go to heaven; because, for example, if a person deserved three years imprisonment, he comes out at the end of three years. But if someone is given life imprisonment, it means that he stays there for ever.

For what offences *does* it last for ever? Mrs Khan told me:

'Number one is *kufr* – you don't believe in Allah; number two is if you murder someone; and number three is suicide. Any of those Allah will never forgive it.' I asked another Muslim, Mr Lakdwalla, does the Fire last for ever? He answered: 'You are punished in proportion to your sins. Once your sins are purified, when you've been punished for your sins, then you get the reward.' 'So,' I asked him, 'does that mean that nobody will be in the Fire for ever?' He answered firmly: 'Except those who have committed *shirk* – and never repented. *Shirk* is considering someone to share the Oneness of God. God is One, and anyone who tries to make something part of the God is committing *shirk*.'

So *shirk* and *kufr* are unforgivable. So also is suicide, the destruction of God's gift and creation: 'If you commit suicide, you'll be doing it in hell for ever – until God wishes it otherwise,' as Mr Hassan put it briefly. But *shirk* (associating anything with God, or saying that anything is like God or *is* God) is *the* unforgivable offence. Do Christians come in that category? After all, they associate Jesus so closely with God that traditionally Christians have regarded him as God incarnate, manifest in human life. Or what about Hindus? We heard earlier that the pandit brings the idol or the representation of God to a liveliness beyond that of a dead image (p. 149). Can a Hindu or a Christian come into a secure relation with God beyond death, according to the Muslim picture? Mr Khan went on to answer that:

> The straight answer is no. The reason for this is that Allah has said in the Holy Quran again and again that he is not going to forgive the man who believes in more than one Allah. If we believe in more than one Allah, then we are the sinners in his eyes – that is to say, we don't accept him as the sovereign authority: we associate others in that. So, I'll give you a small example: if I say that I am a very good person, I work in the various voluntary organisations, I work in the hospital and serve the humanity, I distribute all my money in the charities, but I say that I don't accept the coin of this country, I am committing treason, for which capital punishment is still on the books. I am liable to be beheaded. And I say to them, 'Look, I am feeding twenty English families, I am looking after fifty Englishmen who are in the hospital, don't you look at my good deeds?' He says, 'Those good deeds are subject to your acceptance of my authority. I don't demand anything more

from you, you just accept me by name, that I am your king, then you do whatever you please, nobody's going to disturb you.' But I say, 'Look, I'm not going to accept you'. What can God do? But so long as a person believes in one Supreme authority, and he says, 'There must be one who created all this Universe', it is possible, or very likely, for him to go to Heaven if his deeds justify it. But if a man says, 'Oh no, there can be two Gods, there can be three Gods with supreme authority, or five or one million, it doesn't make any difference', once you leave the figure of One, you are out. As long as you believe in One, all is well. Now the problem is when people talk about Lord Jesus, as you have just said: in that case, people start associating Jesus as God. They make him God – in fact, more powerful than the God himself. That is to say, on the Day of Judgement, *he* is the Saviour, and not God to whom we do the right or wrong. God is not in a position to decide what is good or bad for you, or to punish you for this: the Saviour is Jesus. And if you don't believe in Jesus as a Saviour, you don't become a Christian. So that is where the distinction arises between the Muslims and the Christians.

But in fact, I pointed out to him, Christians stress that they *do* believe in One God; and Hindus believe that their gods and the goddesses are not each the One, the Absolute, but only manifestations, or ambassadors, of the One. Mr Khan agreed, but still insisted on the importance of the behaviour associated with the belief:

The Hindus say, 'Well, look, we don't believe in all these: we believe in one God, but when we say that this cow, or that particular thing, or this thing, is a God, we don't accept that *as* God, but we see the God through those things.' Now when you say it, that is fair enough. But this idea of seeing through one thing to another thing is very difficult. A very educated person, a highly intellectual person, can do it, but not the majority. The majority, when they go and worship a particular object, a particular idol, they are not going to think that this idol is only an idol, and has got no power, and that it is through him that I am thinking of the One who controls the Universe – and that this is needed because I cannot see him. Now that concept is not open to an ordinary individual. So let's take the example of the educated people. One friend of mine, a doctor, and she's a lady doctor in this city, said this – she gave me this very argument. She said, 'Look, I don't believe in it.' I said, 'You say you don't believe in it, fair enough. I will ask you one question: "Do you have an idol in your house?"' She says, 'Yes.' So I said, 'Well, you go and slap it. Don't throw it over there, just slap it gently.' She said, 'No, I won't do it.' I said, 'Why? That idol has attained some importance of its own. You are not seeing through it. Your sight is limited to that idol.' That is where the distinction arises. It's where you start giving importance to the idols, where you say, 'This one can give me a child,' or 'This one can give me the money, as Lakshmi can give me the money.' So now in Islam, we have got this black stone which people kiss. But when 'Umar, the second caliph, went to kiss it, he produced his sword and he said, 'Look, I know you are a stone and I can smash you to pieces. But I am kissing you, not because I have any respect for you, but because the Prophet kissed you; and to imitate his example, I am kissing you. If he had kissed another stone, I would have kissed that stone. I don't care who you are.'

Another Muslim, Mr Mohammed Ali, wouldn't comment on other religions, but stressed the indispensable fundamentals of belief:

I'm not going to speak about other religions. But those who don't believe in the Oneness of God, those are the ones who don't believe, as far as I am concerned. There are seven fundamentals of belief, and the second fundamental of the seven is the belief in the Oneness of God. The others are, belief in prophets, belief in the Book, belief in the angels, belief in bad and good (that is, the destiny), and belief in the Day of Judgement; also belief in life after death. These seven fundamentals a Muslim must believe. A person who wants to accept Islam must believe them, and those who don't believe in them have no share in the hereafter. Whether it is a Muslim, whether a Jew, or a Christian, or a Hindu, makes no difference.

A Shiite Muslim I talked to in Manchester believes that Hindus do commit *shirk*, but he still sees hope for at least some of them. I asked him whether Hindus can go to Heaven. He answered:

Basically, they can't go to Heaven. But some of them are good human beings. So they will be treated better than the others. Though they did not believe in God as we believe, still we believe that it is one of the virtues of God to do justly; so justice means they should be given the reward of their greatness, of their honesty, of their character, though they did not believe in God.

So the final judgement, in Islam, rests with God, and it depends on an exact balancing of the good and the evil one has done, as Miss Lakdawala put it: 'Where hell and heaven are concerned, it's all by the judgement of God, isn't it? And it's all according to your deeds. I wouldn't say that a Muslim definitely goes to heaven, and a non-Muslim does definitely go to hell. It just depends on the deeds that you have committed in this world: it's judged according to your deeds.'

But what a Muslim can and does know is that after death it is too late to repent: the acts are done and the balance is set. After death we move on, for better or for worse:

After death you can say nothing. Once you are dead, you will say you are sorry for this and that, but God is not going to listen to your speeches. That time is over, once you are dead. Now it is up to God to make decisions about your good deeds and bad deeds. I suppose he'll make us again like we are today, human beings, so we can understand what it is, and we can take the punishment, if it is there, and otherwise enjoy the heaven. If we are not like we are today, and we are in some other form, not a human form, we can't get any punishments, you see.

So Islam has very literal pictures of what happens after death, with a judgement depending absolutely on the balance of good and evil deeds; and the punishment (if punishment is deserved) *may* go on for ever. Christians have also had comparably literal pictures of heaven and hell – and some still do. I asked one Roman Catholic what will happen to me if I don't turn to Jesus as my Saviour before I die. He said:

Well, I'll put it bluntly, I think I'm sorry for you. All right, you get these people, these cynics, who say that when you go through the velvet curtains, you're just a pile of ash and you're finished. I can't believe that. I can't believe God put me on this earth and gave me what I've got so that when I die it's finished. No, I can't believe that at all. I think there is a heaven, and I think that's where we'll go.

But why, then, would he be sorry for me if I hadn't turned to God before I died? He said: 'For the simple reason that I don't think you'd go to heaven.' 'So where would I go?' I asked. 'Well, to put it bluntly,' he said, 'I think you'd go to hell.' 'And what is hell?' 'It's the Devil,' he said. 'You see, we're very simple type of people. It's either here, or there; there's no in-between: you either get there, or you go to the other place.' However, it was he who had told me about purgatory earlier on (p. 268). So I asked him further about that. 'I think I shall definitely go to purgatory for a start,' he said, 'because I've a lot to atone for – I think we all have. I believe that you have to have your soul purged before you get into heaven. So I shall definitely go to purgatory. In fact, I think everybody will go to purgatory. Because we've all got something to atone for, haven't we?'

But what *is* purgatory? I asked a teenage girl what purgatory meant to her:

> When I was younger, purgatory was a place where, when you died, you stayed there until you'd done enough penance to reach to heaven, to get to heaven: you weren't pure enough, you'd sinned and all that, so you weren't pure enough to go to heaven. But now I'm beginning to think that perhaps purgatory is your life on earth, and you have to make up and decide: you've got two roads to go down in your life, one's the good road and one's the bad road: you as a person, you've got freedom of choice, and you decide which of them you're going to travel. So I'm beginning to think that really how you lead your life decides what's going to happen to you when you die.

So purgatory is an intermediate stage on the way to heaven, a place of temporal as opposed to eternal punishment. But not all Christians believe that – and for others, the next life follows directly, with its consequences of reward or punishment. What is different here from the Muslims is the strong emphasis that we cannot *earn* rewards, by our good deeds exceeding our evil deeds: '*All* have sinned,' as Paul put it, 'and come short of the glory of God'; therefore, no one can be saved who does not accept the need of a personal Saviour. That at least is how Mrs Lynch, a Pentecostal Christian, put it:

> If we don't accept him as our personal Saviour, the fault will be ours because he will reject us; because we've got to remember that we live this life here, and certainly we know that when we pass away from this life, it's not the end. We have got another life to live. This is not the end, because death is not the end. The Scripture tells us that if Christ should come today, and those who remain and have not yet died and gone down into

> the grave, he will take them away and give them a body, and everybody will get a different body, because it won't be in the flesh any more at that time: it will be spiritual.

For Christians with a strong Scriptural belief of that kind, the consequence of punishment is as literal as it is for Muslims, and the pictures of torment are as vivid as those of the Buddhists:

> Jesus Christ put it like this. When he was talking about hell, he described it as a place where the fire is not quenched, and the worms die not. That's the way Jesus Christ put it: a place of agony, a place of torment; a place where you are not only suffering in the flesh, but you have the thought that you had a chance to know Jesus Christ in his perfect love as your personal Saviour, and missed out on that chance.

I asked him whether that condition goes on for ever. He answered: 'It goes on for ever, yes.' So the punishment is real; and as with the Muslims, there are many Christians who believe that *some* sins cannot be forgiven – suicide comes up again in this category – so do offences against children, because of the specific saying of Jesus, to which this mother alludes:

> God is merciful, very merciful. But there are certain instances, he's told us – for instance if we take our own life while the balance of our mind is clear and do it knowingly – then we are lost to him: there is nothing he can do. We are lost to him. He cannot save us. Also, if you harm children in any way, either by example or by deeds, then Jesus said at one point that they may as well tie a stone around their leg and throw themselves into the deepest river. So, therefore, they must be lost to him. There are certain ones, as I said before – very few – but there are certain ones that he cannot help. If there was any way he could help them, I think he would, and I think he tries to help them right up to the very end, to get them to change or to be how he wants us to be. But if he can't, then he's lost them.

I asked a doctor in Basingstoke what is so wrong about suicide – from a Christian point of view. She said, 'I suppose it's because God created you in his own image and you're deciding you don't like his work – you don't like anything about yourself, and you want to end it.'

So in the view of at least some Christians, there *are* sins which cannot be forgiven – even though the old distinction between mortal and venial sin seems to be disappearing. I asked a Roman

Catholic what a 'mortal sin' is. He replied:

> Well, a mortal sin would be if I took your life: that would be a mortal sin. It also happens to be a mortal sin if you miss Mass on Sunday. Now the difference between taking one's life and missing Mass. . . . Well, you just can't compare the two as a sin. But they are mortal sins. And if we die and we're not in a state of grace, we've been told that we cannot enter the Kingdom of Heaven.

So in the end, sin, for a Christian, is a fundamental choice against God, which reiterates the wrong choice of Adam and Eve:

> God created man in his own image, as an extension of his love, really, to manifest himself in different ways. But he also gave man free will, and so you have another force coming in; and as with Adam and Eve, things went wrong very early on, because man had a choice and didn't always make the perfect choice, God's choice; he made a wrong choice. So at some point, if we're presented with God's claims, with Christ's claims, and we reject them, and we go on rejecting them, then I think that what God says is – you're out.

Why Do People Believe?

Now at last we can begin to see the answer to the question I asked at the very beginning of these programmes. What is it about religions which makes their followers so angry and passionate and divided from each other? And what is it that makes them say they would rather die than give up their faith? Each one of these programmes has been a part of the answer. Religions matter because they do give a strong sense of identity. They do help people to make what seems to them to be a genuine connection with God. They do give structure and stability to the family. They do supply hope and courage in the face of adversity and grief.

And of course there's a whole heap of reasons not touched on in the programmes which analyse religions from the outside, and tell us why believers are passionate and unyielding. We can say, for example, with Freud, that religion is an obsessional neurosis – a symptom of mental dis-ease; or we can say, with Marx, that religion is a way of perpetuating class division, exploitation and alienation; or we can say, with both, that religion is the absurd illusion of the immature, who cannot face the fact that death is complete oblivion and who therefore construct a paradise *after* death as a substitute for growing up *before* death. Or we can see that many animals mark out and defend a territory, and we can see much in religious behaviour (and warfare) which bears more than a trace of that inheritance. Or we can observe that religions are elaborate cultural cocoons in which the programmes of the genes to replicate themselves are protected – so that religions, like other cultural systems, provide secure and stable contexts for the conception and nurture of children – and hence for the replication of *their* genes in due course.

All these are complicated issues and no doubt need much discussion. But looking back on the chapters of this book, I think we can safely say that every single one of these accounts is true – or to put it a bit more precisely, what they say can undoubtedly be illustrated and confirmed in these religions. But a lot more can be illustrated as well: there are *religious* reasons why people remain religious. What this book has shown is that the issues which religions raise are ultimate – they point to what we may *finally* – and enduringly – be able to become and to be. The religions may, all of them, be entirely wrong in what they claim to be the ultimate case; but clearly, there's a lot more on the table here than a choice between margarine and butter.

What makes the issue even more urgent is that the joys and the attainments to which religions point are already anticipated and realised in this life – maybe only as a momentary splendour; but maybe also as a steady change of fundamental character, with the words *about* a religion gradually coming to be spoken with increasing consistency and eloquence in the language of a human life. There may be many explanations of what is going on; but that *something* is going on is unmistakable.

And that really is the basic point, if we want to understand what religions do for people, and why they matter so much to those who believe. Religion raises such powerful emotions that discussion between non-believers and believers is usually trapped and disabled in what is known – a bit ponderously – as 'the fallacy of the falsely dichotomous question'. This is the fallacy which reduces complex problems to an either/or question: Concorde: technological marvel or white elephant? British Rail: burden or blessing? The fallacy lies in the fact that they may be *both* of these things at one and the same time – and more as well; or they may be neither.

So also with religion: it is not *simply* true or false, blessing or curse; nor is it the case that *either* the Freudian, *or* the Marxist, *or* the territorial, *or* the genetic, *or* the religious account of why people believe is correct: they may *all* be correct, at one and the same time; or some of them may be correct for some of the time – in particular instances. The point is that when we do anything – whether we go to the pub or don't go to the pub, say our prayers or don't say our prayers – the reasons are *always* many and complex. We may not know – consciously – all the reasons ourselves: some of them, anyway, go back to our earliest moments which we can't remember. But we should always recognise that there can be *many* reasons, many explanations combining together, for what we do; which is why G. K. Chesterton once defined charity as a reverent agnosticism about the complexity of the human soul.

So we cannot rule out the possibility that religious believers may indeed by obsessionally neurotic, class-consciously conservative, unwittingly working out the genetic programmes, *and also* making genuine discoveries in the religious ways of attending to themselves, to their neighbour, to the universe and to God. It's true that what they then say about those discoveries will be expressed in completely inadequate language, in forms which will have to be corrected and changed – reluctant though the adherents of a strong view of revelation may be to acknowledge it. But that is no different from the accounts which a physicist, say, or a cosmologist, makes of his or her own subject matter. Different subject matters evoke different languages. But we can never give a *complete* account in any language of anything of much importance. Here indeed we see through a glass darkly, but at least we begin to see; here we know only in part, but at least we are beginning to know; here we are only on the way, but at least we have begun the journey.

Issues of Truth Between Religions

But to say that, does *not* mean that anything that anybody says about their beliefs automatically becomes true – or even approximately true. There have been many examples in this book of serious issues between religions – or even within religions – in which the claims on each side are evidently incompatible. And that means that while the religions may all be wrong, they cannot possibly all be right – not in everything they say, because the contradictions are logically and factually incompatible. If one person tells us that the moon is square and another that the moon is a round balloon, they may both be wrong but they cannot both be right. Or can they?

There are two religious ways in which they *may* both be right. The first is by paradox and the second by poetry. Religions have frequently embraced paradox as a way of breaking through the restrictive shell of everyday appearance: 'Perceiving that the world is "dense",' observed Camus on the Myth of Sisyphus, 'sensing to what degree a stone is foreign and irreducible to us, with what intensity nature or a landscape can negate us . . ., that denseness and that strangeness of the world is the absurd.' More simply – and even more 'existentially' – the Zen Buddhist invites us to listen to the sound of one hand clapping. And Kierkegaard described the Christian claim that Deity participates in time as the Absolute Paradox.

So maybe we *can* imagine the moon as a balloon. Certainly we can in poetry, because that is exactly what e. e. cummings asked:

> who knows if the moon's
> a balloon, coming out of a keen city
> in the sky – filled with pretty people?
>   (. . . a keen
> city which nobody's ever visited, where
> always
>   it's
>   Spring) and everyone's
> in love and flowers pick themselves

Where else can flowers pick themselves (or for that matter, everyone be in love) except in poetry? And yet, for all that, when we have allowed the most outrageous voices of art and poetry to shake us awake – with a kind of contempt of the court of common-sense – common-sense does have *some* legitimate judgements to make. Religion is not entirely made up of paradox and poetry. *Some* of its claims are about what may in fact – in reality (whatever that is) – be the case. They are, to put it more technically, claims about putative matters of fact. And it is here that there are issues of truth *within* religions, issues of truth *about* religions, and issues of truth *between* religions.

What sort of issues? We've already had many examples of issues *within* religions – things that believers in each tradition argue about among themselves: the last part of Chapter 2 looked at some of those arguments, and many others have turned up on the way.

Issues of truth *about* religion have also come up along the way, particularly in the doubts which many believers have (just as much as unbelievers) about the validity of traditional items of belief. Many of these issues are raised by questions of coherence: a gap opens up between a traditional religious description and other ways of describing or accounting for the same thing; which then has priority? Or how can they be reconciled?

Many of such questions are by no means new – for example, is the earth flat and at the centre of the universe? Or, if we searched the universe thoroughly enough, would we find the heavens and the seven hells of the Buddhists, or the Garden and the Fire of the Muslims?

Religious fundamentalisms give absolute priority to religious answers, particularly if they are believed to be given by God in inerrant revelation (though there is an obvious additional issue of truth when claimed inerrant revelations contradict each other, as they do): scientism (the belief that true and valid accounts of anything must be derived from science or at least not be in contradiction) has little time for religion. Between those two extremes (both, incidentally, equally dangerous and narrow-minded) most of the rest of us live. And on that middle ground scientific (or other) accounts of the universe do raise questions for religions. But what appears to be the same question in content is not the same question to each religion. Thus I spent much time listening to people in all these religions talking about evolution: for Jews, Christians and Muslims it was *primarily* a question about the status of the accounts in Bible and Quran of creation and of Adam and Eve; but for Buddhists, there was an entirely different anxiety about how their account of a flow of continuous change even between species has any surviving, credible content.

Furthermore, religions have had *very* different histories in dealing with alternative or rival accounts of the same subject matter. Religions are extremely uneven in evaluating changes in the modern world, as they are also in sensitivity to criticism. But religious believers only create an enormous (and in fact unnecessary) schism between themselves and the rest of the human community when they give absolute and exclusive validity to their own tradition. In effect they are excommunicating reason; which may indeed be imperfect; but it is all we have as a means both of control and of community. François Jacob ended a recent book by saying: 'The Enlightenment and the nineteenth century had the folly to consider reason to be not only necessary but sufficient for the solution of all problems. Today it would be still more foolish to decide, as some would like, that because reason is not sufficient, it is not necessary either.'

So science may undoubtedly create problems of truth and coherence for religious believers. On the other hand, religious believers may create science. Historically, religions have been the impetus and the inspiration for many scientific revolutions; and in the present, many individuals find no conflict between research and religion. There is no automatic or inevitable warfare between science and religion. But there *is* warfare if either side refuses to listen to the questions of truth and judgement which the other poses. Both enterprises (of science and religion) are capable of finding a world and turning it into a devastation: they would be better employed together in recognising the devastation which exists already in this planet and turning it into a world.

So the questions of truth *about* religion are serious (and belief has much to learn from them). So too are the issues of truth *between* religions. Some of these have been occurring throughout the book: are we reborn through 84,000,000 births, or do we go from death to Judgement and/or God? If we *are* reborn, is there a self or soul (*atman*) being reborn, or is there no such reality, but only the process of unceasing change? Given that we have 'all sinned and come short of the glory of God', are we in need of radical redemption, or of education? Is there an existent reality correctly referred to as God, from whom the universe is derived as its creator, or is there not?

That last example shows that none of these issues is simple. It's easy to *over*simplify it and ask, Does God exist or not? and to reply, Most religions say yes, but Buddhism says no. But we've already seen that *in some sense* Buddhists themselves believe that they believe in God! And in practice, there's no doubt at all that the majority of Buddhists alive today do pray to theistic realities (gods) and do aim to get to heaven (not *nirvana*) after death. Mr Wickramaratne told me very firmly that Buddhism differs from all other religions in its refusal to believe in supernatural beings or in God: 'Whereas all other religions,' he said, 'cater for supernatural beings or God, Buddhism does not do that. Buddha has already established that there is no such being as a God, and that one has got to rely on oneself – self-reliance; and *you* are responsible for your actions.' But then I asked him how he explained the fact that Buddhists in, for example, Sri Lanka, do pray to gods. He replied: 'I think these are corruptions of

Buddhism over the centuries. Strictly, a Buddhist cannot believe in God, because Buddha has himself said that whatever other beings are there, they are second to humans; and humans are the highest form of life. So in Sri Lanka it's a contradiction, because you find in Buddhist temples Hindu gods, with a place kept for Hindu gods; and people will go to those gods and ask for help and so on. But I have never prayed to God as such. I have learnt Buddhism as not believing in a supernatural plane.'

But in that case, what is the status or reality of such figures as Mara or the *devas* who are clearly not on the same natural plane as ourselves? He said: '*Devas* are another form of life, but not necessarily superior to human beings. When we offer flowers to the *devas*, we pass on the merits so that from whatever state they are in they can get away from it and continue to the ultimate aim of the Buddhist in *nirvana*; so we can help them to achieve that. I know there are various forms of Buddhism in the world, and some give prominence to the next Buddha – the Coming Buddha – and they think that so-and-so is going to be the Buddha, and that takes various forms in Japan or in Tibet. But we in Sri Lanka have Theravada Buddhism which is the purified form of Buddhism, and we do not accept that theory at all.'

So here, on a most fundamental issue (whether there is a reality to whom it is legitimate and wise to pray), not only is there an issue *between* religions; there is a division in the very religion where the issue seems superficially to be most clear-cut. Clearly, while they may *all* be wrong about this, they cannot all be right. And that means that there *are* issues of truth (of what, for example, may or may not turn out to be the case beyond death – supposing that anything turns out to be the case), and therefore issues of choice, between religions.

And yet, and yet . . . even as one writes the words or reads them, a ghost of uneasiness stirs in the mind – or it does at least in Sikh and Hindu minds. Since all religions agree that when we try to talk about God, the only thing we can know for certain is that we cannot know what we are talking about (because God always lies beyond whatever language we use), might it not be the case that all religions offer provisional and approximate accounts of the same subject matter; and that consequently all religions are different paths leading to the same goal? That is exactly what Hindus and Sikhs were saying in Chapter 2 – and many others repeated the same point. Gurbachan Singh Sidhu, for example, summarised Sikhism as meaning that: 'Sikhism is a way of life considering all human beings as equal, and accepting the respect, the validity and the authenticity of all religions, and joining the people in the quest for God.'

In this respect, the point that was made repeatedly was that the unity of religions (and the judgement on human life) lies, not in the reconciliation of creeds, but in conduct: 'By their fruits shall ye know them.' And what undoubtedly reinforces that point is that when I asked people to summarise what their faith and belief really meant to them, most of them answered in that very practical way. Out of context, it's virtually impossible to know which religion these people are speaking from and describing:

> My main aim of this life is to lead a peaceful and helpful life, and to serve humanity in any way I can, and not to be a hindrance to anyone. That is the aim of my life, and I try my utmost to achieve this aim.
>
> Peace and harmony and tolerance and compassion and generosity: I think these are the things; and I think these are very, very important – and honesty: honesty for yourself and for others, without any discrimination, without colour or creed. And compassion has to extend not only to human beings, but beyond all human beings to all creatures.
>
> I wouldn't have said this a few years ago, but I think I'll say it now, that if you reduce the whole of it, as they say, to a few words, it's, Love thy neighbour as thyself. That incorporates and takes in the real ethic.
>
> I would say that the real characteristics are accepting things, and giving, caring, loving, about everyone, not just about your own family: I think it must include everyone that you come in contact with, that you must care – always to care, that's the important thing.
>
> Without my religion, my belief, my faith, I wouldn't be a human being at all: I would be just as useless as a weed in a garden. It's my belief that keeps me up. I walk in the street sometimes, and many people look at me and say a lot of things which they shouldn't say, but I forget all about it, because my religion says, Tolerance, patience, obedience. I take every other fellow as a human being. So my religion is important to me. It is because of my religion that I survive.

Those summaries (of what faith really and essentially means to people in practice) were in fact of Hinduism, Buddhism, Judaism, Christianity and Islam, in that order. At that level, the test of truth is clearly not one of coherence or correspondence to what may be the case, but of consequence: not creeds but conduct. Does this mean that we can dispense with creeds? Does it mean that it really makes no difference which religion we belong to because they're all essentially leading in the same eventual direction – the view which is known as 'indifferentism'?

In fact not so, according to those I listened to – and for one reason more than any other: the kind of self-giving, self-losing life which those people were describing is not at all easy to live. We need help (or many of us need help) to make that basic 'gear-shift' which gets and keeps the wheels moving. In other words, religions offer *resources* for life, just as much as they describe what that life should be. And those resources give a *different character* to life, which works its way into the very texture of what is acceptable or unacceptable, of what has to be done and what can be ignored. Clothes are clothes; but top hats and tails exhibit a very different style of life from dhotis and saris.

So does it matter which religious clothes I wear so long as I wear something? The answer, according to all these religions, is that it may do. To give just one example: it is much easier for Christians to receive into their spiritual lives the techniques of Buddhist meditation than it is for Buddhists to receive Holy Communion – what would be the point for them in accepting the continuing union of Christ with his disciples, which anticipates the final 'Messianic feast' in heaven (since the 'heaven' to which many Buddhists are indeed aspiring is not the final state and falls far short of *nirvana*)?

A Sikh, Harbans Singh Sagoo, made this point very powerfully, when he argued that all religions *are* leading to the ultimate goal, but that they *cannot* do so unless they are lived with absolute faithfulness: 'It would be wrong for me,' he said, 'to profess and say that Sikhism is the only way to *moksha*. Even Guru Nanak in his teachings said to Hindus and Muslims, that if you are a Hindu, be a good Hindu; if you are a Muslim, be a good Muslim.' 'But,' I said, 'to be a good Christian means responding to the command of Christ to go into all the world and make disciples from all the nations. So a Christian, to follow your advice and be a good Christian, must try to convert and baptise you.' 'Certainly,' he replied. 'So far as that command is concerned, then of course it's up to the Christians to obey the command and do what their Guru, or their leader, wants them to do; because it is the obedience which will eventually bear fruit.'

What this means is that all these religions are clear that it is possible to be religiously right – to be, for example, redeemed and forgiven by God; obedient to his Torah; on the Middle Way and the Eightfold Path to Enlightenment; receptive of the grace of the Guru; and so on. But if it is possible to be religiously right, it must be equally possible to be religiously wrong. And Buddhists don't hesitate to draw that conclusion. Mr Wickramaratne made the point that Gautama (before he became the Buddha, the Enlightened One) searched diligently in the available religious practices of Hinduism as it then was, and tried many of them for himself, but found that they were *not* the Way:

> Some people say that Buddhism was an off-shoot of Hinduism, but in fact at the time of the Buddha himself there were two or three different schools – for example, there was one which practised self-mortification, and there was another which practised over-indulgence. Now the Buddha himself went through six years of self-mortification; he suffered for six years. And then previous to that he had been the son of a Prince and had lived a rich, comfortable life. So he's had the two extremes, and he says that both extremes are wrong, and that the only correct way is the Middle Way. So because he has gone through all the range of experience I can trust him myself.

But it's not only Buddhists who recognise that it's possible to be religiously wrong. The other religions recognise it as well – with some of them, as we've just seen, talking about it in even more dramatic terms of punishment and damnation. Which brings us round in full circle to the beginning of this chapter. For the issue here is not whether you can be religiously wrong: all these religions agree that you can be. The issue is, how *seriously* wrong can you be? And what counts as being right? In its way, it is the traditional question, What must I do to be saved – or to attain Enlightenment? And with it go two related questions: is there only *one* Way? Or do I need to be converted to one particular religion, or from one to another, to be saved?

Conversion

So the real issue here between religions is whether it is enough simply to be on the way or whether it does make some difference, which road, which religion we choose to follow. Do they all lead to the same goal? Or are some of them going in the wrong direction? After all, all roads don't lead to London simply because they are roads; some lead to more exotic destinations like Bridlington-on-Sea. So is it necessary to change direction, to change religions in order to reach the goal? Here the religions are very different. Religions with a strong sense of rebirth feel very little urgency to convert others. We're all going to be reborn so many millions of times that we're probably going to go through all the religions eventually. So it may in fact be much better to go on *now*, in this life, as a good Muslim or a good Christian than to change. That at least is what Dr Fernando, a Buddhist, believes:

> We don't think in terms of conversion at all, unless someone asks me why I am this and why I am that, or why I believe in this; then I will discuss; but again I would not discuss it with the idea of converting him, because the term Buddhism is a Western term. The Westerners are very good at putting people into water-tight compartments. A Christian could be a better Buddhist than a person who has been born a Buddhist and who doesn't observe any of the Five Precepts. I have known a lot of Christians who lead very, very good beneficial lives. Christ himself has taught some very sweet things; and there is a common denominator amongst these religions. That's why we don't believe in conversion. When he talks about 'as you sow, so shall you reap', that is the law of *karma*.

Sikhs also believe in rebirth and they too maintain that any religion can lead a sincere believer into God, even if Sikhism is the most direct way, as Gurbachan Singh Sidhu put it:

> We are warned about saying anything about any religion which would offend anyone. We would never, for example, say that the Muslims or Christians or the Hindus are all wrong, and that ours is the only way. What we are supposed to say, and we say it very frankly, is that all the different religions are raised to the same God, like the spokes of a wheel going to the centre. They are the ways. Well, some people would like one way or the others would like the other way. But as every religion claims that their way is the shortest, we also happen to claim that our way is the shortest, and perhaps the best.

In fact so strongly do Sikhs believe that there should be no compulsion that a Sikh is supposed to beg for the *amrit* Ceremony – for the Baptism, for the admission to the *Khalsa* (see p. 189). And in that respect Sikhs are like Jews. Non-Jews can be converted to Judaism, but there are tremendous tests of sincerity and understanding before that can happen:

> I think the view of Judaism is basically that if somebody wants to become Jewish, there's a hell of a lot of tests one is supposed to go through, and it's a very stringent thing one has to go through. You have to look at every case carefully and make sure that that person really is fit for the religion. Not 'fit' in the sense of whether they are superior or lesser beings, but simply because it's a very harsh and very demanding religion. It demands attention to many little details, which people who are totally alien to it would find very strange and perhaps very hard.

Of course one reason why non-Jews don't have to convert is because they are already in the Covenant, the first Covenant made with Noah. So there really isn't any urgent point in someone becoming Jewish if they're not born into it, as Stuart and Merrill Dresner told me. He said: 'No, I don't think there's any reason why you should become Jewish. I think the ethical practices are common to Christianity and Judaism, the Christian practice being derived from Judaism; and therefore there'd be no point really in you taking on the ritual aspects and the festivals which celebrate the folk history of the people which are not yours.'

But she added: 'Unless, I feel, that you have such a strong feeling and commitment towards Judaism based on your studying and your knowledge and your relationships to Jewish people, that you do want to undertake this and take it on for yourself. And then I feel that a convert ought to be encouraged, but with reservations as well, in the way in which they are encouraged at the moment.'

But for Islam and Christianity there is a greater urgency to share with others what God has done for us – in the Quran for Muslims, in Christ for Christians. In these religions, *we* are not searching for God, God is searching for *us*; and it is for us to respond to that initiative. For Muslims the issue *is* urgent, as a Muslim schoolboy told me about his friends at school: 'Obviously,' he said, 'I want them to be saved from the Fire. I don't like to think of my mates going to Hell.' So I asked him how he could help them. He replied: 'There's nothing I can do, because, I mean, they're not going to listen to me.' 'Do they never listen to you?' I asked. He answered, 'Well, not in the matter of religion. They sometimes create the discussion, but they won't, you know, change, it's a fact. In fact, I think Islam says they're blind.'

One Muslim recognised that the urgency to convert is nothing like as strong now in this country as it was in the early days of Islam:

> Theoretically we should try to convert others, but practically we are all so much worried about our own lives, so we don't think it's that much important: if they are going to hell let them find their own way out, you know: why should we bother, let us do something else. But the time when Muslims were really Muslims, that was their prime job, you see, even the Governments used to write letters to the other Governments, to the Kings and the other rulers, 'You should join our religion, and why are you choosing hell for yourself? We are telling you for your interest.' But today, you see, Muslims like me, we are so busy on our personal affairs, we are saying, if you are going to hell, go ahead.

But how, the other way round, do Christians think of Muslims? One Christian said: 'I don't think they are saved. If I knew more Muslims, I would have to read the Quran to know what they believed, to get across to them what I believed, to argue my point of view more strongly.' So I asked what she felt would be the outcome when the argument was finished and the Muslims still disagreed. After all, according to the Muslim interpretation of the Quran, not only did Jesus *not* die for our sins: he didn't even die. So I asked her, 'What's going to happen to them?' She replied: 'Well, if they're not saved, then when they die, I think if they're not saved, then they go to hell, whatever that might be: separation from God.'

But other Christians disagree:

'I don't believe that at all,' said one. 'I don't think God is the sort of person that would turn round – and you cry out for God's help on your death-bed, and that he would ignore you. No way. God is all merciful.' And his daughter added: 'I don't think God would look down on anybody who doesn't go to church, but believes in him, and say "Oh, that's an evil person" or "I don't think he's fit to join everybody else in heaven" or whatever.' And her sister said: 'I was at a peace vigil a few months back, and there was a Buddhist there. He spoke for about an hour and a half, and he never related to God, he related to Buddha. But I think this idea of there being someone who is more powerful than them – I think in any religion, it's not necessarily *the* God, *the* Christ, it's some One, and they just have different names for it. But it's a Being, or just something which is above them.'

And that note of hesitation about hellfire and damnation is exactly what I heard from virtually all the Christians I listened to. They really cannot imagine that God would treat his children worse than they would their own.

That at least is how Ray Turner put it. As a trade union official, he had talked about the building of God's kingdom on earth, and how eternal life fits into that picture for him. 'If I've done enough,' he said, 'to create God's kingdom on earth, I think that eternal life will be a closer, or a more physical, contact with God.' But then I asked him, 'What happens if you *haven't* done enough?' He replied:

> Well, I could give you a nice catechism answer, and say I'd go to hell, but perhaps I'm in that place already. No, I think that the relationship with God will be incomplete. I don't believe that he's going to chuck me out somewhere and say, 'You've had it'. I believe that it's up to me to open all the doors. And the more doors I can open, the closer I can get to him; the closer I get to the sun – but gradually – the more I'm able to bear its rays. By throwing off all these resistances during this life, in the efforts that I make to build a Kingdom, the more able I will be to get closer to him at the end. I don't know whether that's a good example, but that's the way I feel about it. All this business of hellfire, I'm sure it's the way that the people who wrote the Scriptures – it was the only way that they could find to describe what it's like not to know God.

Then I asked him whether there *are* people who end up separated for ever from God. He said:

> Well, there again, I can only give you what I think. The way that I believe that God is, in all his mercifulness, is the way that Christ told us he is. That kind of God that Christ told us about, I can't see it. No matter how bad somebody's been, to shut them out altogether, I can't believe it. I'm sure that's heresy, or whatever you like to call it, but I can only say what I feel. I know the way I would be to one of my kids: perhaps they would make you want to throw them out, but they're flesh and blood, and I'm sure that God's love for me is greater than my love for my kids. And it must be great if it's greater than that! It would take a hell of a lot for me to disregard one of my kids altogether.

Mrs Emmett, who's done so much to bring children into a family circle of love, feels exactly the same:

> I find it very difficult to believe that the two things, God and condemnation, can be compatible. I know that some people live wretched lives, and have wretched endings and everything – people who have gone to the electric chair, people who've been hanged. But I just don't think that there isn't any place for them. They may not have really come to recognise all that God means, and certainly they've cut themselves off from him perhaps. But I don't think he would go from them, not even right to the bitter end.

'So,' I asked her, 'you couldn't imagine anybody being damned by God?' She answered emphatically: 'No, never, ever, no, no.'

Even Muslims, who talked so strongly about punishment in hellfire, even they expressed a similar hesitation. I asked one Muslim what will happen to Hindus, who worship what Muslims take to be idols, on the Day of Judgement? He replied:

> Basically, they can't go to heaven. But some of them are good human beings, so they will be treated better than the others. Though they did not believe in God as we believe, still we believe that one of the virtues of God is to do justice. So justice means that they should be given reward of their greatness, of their honesty, of their character, though they did not believe in God. So they will be treated as a Muslim of similar character or similar ability or similar honesty, or whatever it is.

Another Muslim emphasised that whatever happens must be all right because it belongs to the will of God. He said: 'Whatever is the will of Allah, I'll be pleased to go wherever he wants me to be. If it is his will that I shall go to the Fire, then I shall enjoy the Fire. If it is his will that I should go to Janna, then I will enjoy the Janna – wherever is his pleasure.' So I asked him: 'Supposing you went to the fire, would it be for ever?' He replied: 'Not necessarily so. Punishment is only temporary, according to the preponderance of good over evil; and that's true for everybody, everyone.' But what about *shirk* – that offence which some Muslims had said (p. 280) is unforgivable? He said, 'It doesn't matter; whatever good you have done will be remembered. The fact is that Allah, praised be his name, is the one who forgives, and nobody could tell what he will do. If he feels to forgive you, he forgives you. He didn't create us to punish, he created us to love.'

So even within religions with the strongest sense of urgency, there was an absolute refusal to make God's judgements for him, to replace God as Judge. And that was true of all the religions. Everyone I talked to recognised the seriousness of the religious issues, that it *does* matter how we live and what we do, and that there *are* issues of salvation between the religions. But virtually everyone agreed that the only conversion worth worrying about is the conversion of manners, the conversion of *behaviour*; and that can't be achieved by argument anything like so much as it has to be attempted by example, as Peter Thompson told me – not, surprisingly, in Liverpool, but in Manchester:

> If you say to somebody, 'I think Everton's the greatest football team in the world', and they support Liverpool; well, they're just going to get their backs up and argue and argue. Whereas, if they see you supporting the Club, and going week in and week out, and always having that Club in mind, they'll wonder, well, what is this that he's doing, why is he doing this? you know? What is *he* experiencing that *I'm* not? It's the example that's more important, I find.

So where does that leave us at the end of these programmes? It leaves us with a paradox. Religions are not going to disappear. They matter far too much to those who believe, because they release into their lives the inspiration of love and hope, of value and of judgement. And yet precisely because religions do matter so much, because they are more important to believers than anything else, they are going to go on fuelling the fires of passion and violence which divide us.

Meeting and listening to the people whose words made the programmes and created this book, it is obvious that in them there is a total rejection of any hatred of that sort. Indeed, as we've just seen, there is already going on a kind of practical exploration of how the different religions can live side by side, even while they recognise that they are separated from each other by real issues of truth. There is in fact a kind of practical and instinctive ecumenicism at work.

The ecumenical movement is usually confined to Christianity – to the attempt of different parts of the Christian Church to find a closer relation to each other. But the Greek word *oikumene* means 'the inhabited world', realising, as Epictetus put it a couple of thousand years ago, that we may indeed be citizens of one country or of one region, but that we are also citizens of one planet. It is on that basis that we need, deliberately and formally, to explore the conditions of our coexistence. No way does this imply that all religions are equally true. They may as a matter of fact all be equally false; they may, as someone wrote to me, all be licensed insanities. But as they exist, they are *not* the same; there are issues of truth *and* salvation between religions. As I put it earlier, they may all be wrong, but they cannot all be right. But the point of ecumenical exploration and dialogue is not to achieve some lowest common denominator of religious agreement: it is to isolate those highest uncommon factors of truth and vision which each religion has protected and preserved.

Just think for a moment of the Christian ecumenical quest: who would have thought, even 30 years ago, that Roman Catholics and Anglicans could have produced reports which clarified the genuine issues between them and yet pointed out the illusions and deceits and sheer blind wickedness of so many of what were taken to be the issues between them? ARCIC, the Anglican and Roman Catholic International Commission, had years of prayer and preparation behind it. But so too has the ecumenical issue between religions. For years there have been dialogues and organisations preparing the ground. Now is the time to move, to a serious and realistic exploration of where the issues between religions are genuinely and necessarily divisive, and where they are not – where indeed the religions reinforce each other by pointing to the real possibilities of human life. What is needed is something as formal and deliberate as the ARCIC exploration in Christianity, only this time between religions.

No way will it be arguing that all religions are the same, or that all religions are different roads leading to the same goal. Nothing seems less likely to be true than that, given what religions say about themselves. What we must establish are the conditions of coexistence while accepting the diversity – and indeed the seriousness – of the issues which divide us. Because they *are* serious: religions are immersed in virtually all the unremitting hatreds which disturb and could well destroy human life on this planet.

Yet politicians, economists, civil servants, industrialists, continue to treat religion as though it's a minor hobby – something people do during their time off. Nothing could be further from the truth. That's why we need very urgently to come to a much wiser understanding of what's really going on in religious life, and of how exactly religions both reinforce and yet also sometimes heal the many conflicts between us. What I think we need is something as formal and deliberate as the Brandt Report, which also explored the real nature of those other divisions, between the developed and the developing nations, which are an equal threat to our survival.

But will it happen? I doubt it. I've yet to meet a politician who takes the whole religious involvement in life and politics as seriously as it needs to be taken. Maybe that simply says I haven't met enough politicians. But I do wonder how many Members of Parliament actually listened to the programmes, even though it was their constituents talking about the things that matter to them more than anything else.

The time is extremely short. It is now certainly conceivable that we are in the last decades of human life as we know it on this planet. Religions won't be the only cause of the catastrophe if it happens. But if we want them to become a part of the resistance to it, then we must bring them into a more formal and deliberate connection with each other. Only then can we really begin to pray – and act – for the peace of Jerusalem; and of Belfast, and of Soweto, of Warsaw, of Assam, of El Salvador, of Cyprus, of Tehran and Baghdad. There have indeed been all too many evils and disasters in the past, and in the history, of religions. But the point of departure for all religions is not only to recognise those disasters, but to repent of them, and to turn back *in the power which religion also offers* to the renewal and the redemption of the earth. The realistic root of religion is repentance; and on that basis:

'Out of the spent and unconsidered earth,
The cities rise again.'

Participants

We interviewed, in all, just under one hundred and fifty people. A number of them asked that their names should not be mentioned in the programmes or in the book. To them, and to the others listed here, I offer my thanks – not least for their patience and their friendship in receiving me into their homes. The letters after their names indicate to which of the six religions they belong.

Mohammed Ali M
Nejma Ali M
Leila Ali M
Ranjit Arora S
Gurmukh Singh Bansal S
Solomon Benaim J
Annette Benaim J
Prem Kumar Bhakri H
Satyanand Bhakri H
Shaktidevi Bhakri H
Mrs Bhakri H
David Brandon B
John Callaghan C
Kushumika Chatterji H
Nora Chatterji H
Padma Chauhan H
Prabhadevi Chauhan H
Jaibharti Chauhan H
Gordhanbhai Chhaya H
Haribhai Chayya H
Lionel Cowan J
Ilse Cowan J
Kunvergi Dabasia H
Naran Dabasia H
Karsan Dabasia H
Amrik Singh Dhesi S
Bhupinder Kaur Dhesi S
Kamaldeep Dhesi S
Merrill Dresner J
Stuart Dresner J
Jean Emmett C
Nalaka Fernando B
Rohantha Panini Fernando B
Christopher Gajewski C
Raman Gokal H
Murari Lal Gupta H
Mamta Gupta H
Mohammed Hassan M
Amritpal Singh Hunjan S
Gurdial Singh Hunjan S
Inderpaul Kaur Hyare S
Parmjot Singh Hyare S
Rajinder Kaur Hyare S
Sarbjot Singh Hyare S
Surinder Singh Hyare S
Ann Iles C
Ray Iles C
Audrey Jacobs J
Leonard Jacobs J
Mr Kalia H
Mrs Kalia H
Ashraf Khan M
Barry Khan M
Mrs A Khan M
Douber Klein J
Sonia Klein J
Gurcharan Singh Kundi S
Lalubhai Ladd H
Ahmed Lakdawala M
Rafar Lakdwalla M
Mr and Mrs Levy J
Belmina Lynch C
Annetta Lynch C
Krishan Kumal Mittal H
Hajji Cassim Mohammad M
Jagat Singh Nagra S
Mandeep Singh Nagra S
Sundeep Singh Nagra S

Ugyan Norbu B
Abraham Oliver J
Dr V. J. Pancholi H
Nila Pancholi H
Asha Pancholi H
Pandit Chimanlal Pandya H
Babu Patel H
Gulabhai Patel H
Nairaj Patel H
Pranav Patel H
Vismita Patel H
Dave Phillips C
M. R. Poey B
Jamila Qureshi M
Abdul Rahman M
Jacqueline Rapson C
Harbans Singh Sagoo S
Jack Schild J
Gurbachan Singh Sidhu S
Chitra Pal Singh S
Balbir Sohal S
Michael Stevenson C
Peter Thompson C
Twewang Topgyal B
Ray Turner C
D. Wickramaratne B
Liz Williams C
Simon Williams C
Anis Zaidi M
Qaiser Zaidi M

Index